D0216727

SOVIET IMAGES
OF DISSIDENTS
AND NONCONFORMISTS

JC
599
.S58
P37
1986

SOVIET IMAGES
OF DISSIDENTS
AND NONCONFORMISTS

Walter Parchomenko

PRAEGER

PRAEGER SPECIAL STUDIES • PRAEGER SCIENTIFIC

New York • Westport, Connecticut • London

367965 Tennessee Tech. Library
Cookeville, Tenn.

Library of Congress Cataloging in Publication Data

Parchomenko, Walter.
    Soviet images of dissidents and nonconformists.

    "Praeger special studies. Praeger scientific."
    Bibliography: p.
    Includes index.
    1. Civil rights — Soviet Union. 2. Dissenters —
Soviet Union. 3. Soviet Union — Foreign relations —
1975-   . 4. Soviet Union — Politics and government —
1953-   . I. Title.
JC599.S58P37 1986   323.1'47   86-3178
ISBN 0-275-92021-6 (alk. paper)

Copyright © 1986 by Praeger Publishers

All rights reserved. No portion of this book may be
reproduced, by any process or technique, without the
express written consent of the publisher.

Library of Congress Catalog Card Number: 86-3178
ISBN: 0-275-92021-6

First published in 1986

Praeger Publishers, 521 Fifth Avenue, New York, NY 10175
A division of Greenwood Press, Inc.

Printed in the United States of America

The paper used in this book complies with the Permanent
Paper Standard issued by the National Information Standards
Organization (Z39.48-1984).

10 9 8 7 6 5 4 3 2 1

This book is dedicated to the emerging generation of Western students of Soviet dissent, in the hope that they will approach the study of Soviet official perceptions of dissidents, the nature of the conflict, and related issues with the same rigor and imagination that Western scholars have brought to their analyses of the behavior of dissidents and the tactics of Soviet authorities during the past two decades.

Preface

How Soviet authorities perceive contemporary dissidents and nonconformists is not simply a psychological problem, but one which shapes the political orientation and behavior of officials. This volume is not an exhaustive study of contemporary official images of dissidents, nonconformists, and their foreign supporters. Rather, it is intended as a preliminary effort to deal more rigorously with this important, but neglected, perceptual dimension of the dissent conflict. Working on this book, in fact, has convinced me that the subject is exceedingly broad, complex, and controversial, requiring several books to do it justice. It is my hope that the descriptive groundwork laid here, in the form of two intensive case studies and the tentative conceptual framework and method advanced, will leave students of Soviet dissent in a better position to undertake the research necessary for a fuller understanding of official perceptions of the dissent conflict.

This book is a slightly revised version of my doctoral dissertation "Soviet Official Images of Dissidents and Nonconformists" (Georgetown University, 1984). The cutoff date for new information appearing in the body and appendices of this book is summer 1984. The selected bibliography, however, has been updated considerably to include Western and Soviet titles published as late as summer 1985.

To avoid any confusion, several points should be emphasized from the outset. First, the two case studies that comprise the bulk of this volume are presented as illustrations and not proof of the basic hypothesis, which posits that official perception and policy during the Brezhnev era have been guided by stereotypic images of dissent and nonconformity and that these images have erased the important distinction between mild dissent and actual subversion for the authorities concerned. Empirical support for this book's theory about the influence of images on human perception and action can be found in the large number of systematic psychological and historical investigations underlying the conceptual framework, as well as from future efforts at image study. Here, it is appropriate to note that in an effort to extend this preliminary assessment of Soviet images of dissidents and nonconformists, I am presently preparing a second volume which will develop further this work's methodology and examine other key dimensions of Soviet dissent, such as workers' and nationalist dissent and disabled rights activism. Most importantly, the second volume will seek to identify any signs of change in official images of different types of dissidents, nonconformists, and their foreign supporters, attempting to identify the emphases of particular individuals and the perceptions of different institutions.

Secondly, it should be stressed that this volume focuses on *official images*, defined as the simplified models, or conceptions, of dissidents and nonconformists that are expressed in the government-controlled media, in the interaction of officials, and in *samizdat* trial transcripts. Whether these images are *real images* privately held by Soviet officials is, of course, an important and intriguing question. However, for various reasons, it cannot be answered for the foreseeable future, nor is it a crucial concern for this study. More relevant than the privately held images are the ones that are authoritatively expressed by Soviet officials. These images help shape part of the larger political process through which Soviet behavior toward dissidents and nonconformists is determined. Significantly, the fact that official images may not reflect what a Soviet official privately believes does not invalidate them as a measure of salient aspects of the official belief system. Even if they differ strikingly from images subjectively held, official images still represent a desire, whether voluntary or as a result of coercion, to maintain some degree of unity with prevailing images; therefore, they can permit detailed observations to be made on a few vital components of the official belief system—official images of internal and external adversaries and of the nature of the conflict—and on some important related issues.

Thirdly, the inclusion of Chapters 3 and 4 (entitled, respectively, "A Framework for Analysis" and "A Research Design") in the body of this volume rather than in appendices should be justified. As suggested earlier, Western study of Soviet perceptions of dissent and nonconformity remains in its infancy, and little dramatic progress is likely in the near future. Consequently, it is essential that some of the key conceptual and methodological problems surrounding the subject receive serious attention, rather than brief mention in an appendix.

Lastly, in any effort to advance our knowledge of a subject of importance, it is customary that the writer state clearly his biases. This writer has a "prodissident bias," a sympathy for individuals repressed by authorities for expressing their beliefs in a nonviolent fashion. I view the behavior of such men, women, and children as ethical, in accord with international standards of human rights, and, often, as courageous. In undertaking this work, I have made every effort to acknowledge the existence of this bias and to minimize its effect on my interpretation of Soviet official perceptions in order to profit from a conscious contrasting of different viewpoints regarding the nature of the Soviet dissent conflict and its key actors.

Acknowledgments

I am deeply grateful to Professors Jeremy Azrael, Walter Connor, and Angela Stent, whose many suggestions have been invaluable. If I have been unable to incorporate all of their ideas into this study, it is due largely to the preliminary nature of this inquiry and the far-ranging quality of some of their comments. Special thanks must also go to Hazel Sirett and Felix Fabian, who provided me with the continuing practical and moral support needed to complete this task, and to Dotty Breitbart of Praeger, Ken Hirschkop of Oxford University, and Cynthia Haller for their valuable editorial assistance. Finally, to the countless associates of the many research centers, universities, and libraries in Washington, New York, London, Amsterdam, and Munich—which I visited during successive stages of this book—many thanks for your expert advice and friendship.

Contents

Note on the Transliteration

The transliteration system used in this book is essentially the Popular English Transcription. In a few cases, however, the first names of prominent Soviet dissidents have been anglicized to conform to common English usage (for example, "Joseph" and not "Iosif" Brodsky).

1

Introduction

PURPOSE

This book has both a general and a specific purpose. The general one is to introduce the concept of the image to the study of Soviet official views of dissent and nonconformity. Currently, the effects of official images of dissidents and nonconformists on Soviet perception and behavior remain virtually unexamined.

The omission of official images from dissent study is both curious and significant. It is curious because in psychology, sociology, international relations, and other disciplines, images—defined loosely as the simplified mental models individuals hold of their environment—have long been considered important factors motivating behavior. Over the years, image study has proved to be a standard approach used to gain insights into historically rooted and deeply emotional conflicts.

The omission is significant because official images of dissidents and nonconformists are a salient fact of daily life in the Soviet Union. They pervade society and are important elements in the political socialization of Soviet citizens. Inculcated during early childhood, these images are incessantly reinforced by the official media and underlined in the interaction of officials. Significantly, official images of internal and external enemies have permeated Soviet society since the formative years of the Soviet state; and their roots are deeply embedded in Russian history.

The specific purpose of this book is to present data on Soviet official images of dissidents and nonconformists in order to better understand the conceptual barriers to any fundamental reform of Soviet orientation and policy toward dissidents. This work will seek to better explain why a post-Stalin leadership commonly defined by Western analysts as better educated and more sophisticated in its policy making than its predecessors continues to employ extreme coercion in dealing with even seemingly mild dissent. Underlying this question is the assumption that Soviet leaders, who undoubtedly are aware that extreme coercion breeds alienation and discontent, would like a more effective long-term policy, one that relies less on coercion and more on persuasion to gain the public's compliance.

The central hypothesis of the present work is that Soviet perceptions of, and policy toward, dissent and nonconformity during the Brezhnev era have been influenced by highly negative and stereotypic images of dissidents and foreigners rather than by accurate ones. Furthermore, the predominance of subversive and highly threatening general images of contemporary dissidents has blurred the distinction between mild nonconformity and radical dissent in the minds of the authorities and has, in effect, predisposed officials to view all dissent and nonconformity with an assumption of their inherent bad faith.

SPECIFIC OBJECTIVES

The specific objectives of this study are threefold: first, to describe the images of dissidents and nonconformists held by Soviet authorities based on official press statements, ideological pronouncements, and unofficial trial transcripts; second, to compare these images with those drawn from reliable Western and unofficial Soviet sources, particularly from the *samizdat* (self-published, uncensored) periodical *A Chronicle of Current Events*; and finally to suggest some hypotheses regarding the effects of official images on Soviet behavior.

This image study is designed to add two basic types of knowledge to the substantial findings of previous research on Soviet dissent. The first sheds light on the official belief system by investigating two of its vital components: the images Soviet officials hold of internal adversaries and official assumptions about the nature of this conflict.[1] The second analyzes the linkage between internal and external adversaries as perceived by Soviet authorities and assesses its impact on Soviet estimates of the internal threat posed by the dissidents and nonconformists.

DEFINITION OF KEY TERMS

The term *dissident* is used here to refer to an individual who, openly and outside channels approved by the Communist Party, disagrees with regime policies and seeks to expand the range of allowable freedoms. A nonconformist is distinguised from a dissident in that the former engages in a more passive and private deviation from official standards. A *nonconformist*—notable examples include unregistered religious believers and many modern Soviet artists—typically does not seek to influence policy by public criticism and, instead, pursues a lifestyle which often deviates radically from official norms, expectations, and requirements and includes unsanctioned group activity. It should be noted, however, that the distinction drawn between the terms dissident and nonconformist frequently disappears as the conflict with the authorities intensifies and as nonconformists, in reaction to increasing coercion, gradually organize and petition Soviet leaders and Western officials for assistance. It should be emphasized that both of these concepts are relative ones, in the sense that Soviet officials, both central and local, ultimately define what constitutes dissent and nonconformity. As indicated earlier, *official images* of dissidents and nonconformists are the simplified models, or conceptions, of dissidents and nonconformists that are expressed in the government-controlled media and in the interaction of officials. These images help shape part of the larger political process through which Soviet behavior toward dissidents and nonconformists is determined.

METHODOLOGY

The methodology of this book is traditional in that it avoids excessive quantification of data and uses the case study method to investigate official images and to illustrate the central hypothesis. By determining whether official images of a particular dissident or nonconformist are accurate, partially accurate, or false, a distinction is drawn between accurate and inaccurate images.

A major criterion in the selection of case studies has been diversity of image. The cases selected for study represent substantially different phenomena—important currents of dissent and nonconformity—and the official images presumably will reflect these differences. In addition to describing those general characteristics of official images common to the cases selected, this work makes a special effort to analyze their distinguishing features. Special emphasis also will be placed on official images that contradict and transcend those which are more typical.

Case study data on official images will be interpreted within an analytical framework that draws on theoretical and empirical research on the relationship between images, perception, and behavior and that is also sensitive to the early history of contemporary images of dissent and nonconformity. Such a formal framework is necessary because the effects of these images are not obvious, even to experts on the Soviet Union. Although the content of these images is self-evident, their actual effects are hidden and evasive and become clear only when they are viewed in their psychologically and culturally relevant context.

LIMITATIONS

Research on Soviet official images is limited by a number of serious conceptual and methodological problems. Attempts at conceptualizing and measuring these images in the context of Soviet dissent are in their infancy, and the task is no easy one. As a result, the framework for analysis that will be presented is far from definitive. It is intended only to orient in a general way the substantive discussions which will follow.

Research is limited further by the uneven, and at certain points fragmentary, nature of the data on official images of dissent and nonconformity. Despite this, the data are adequate for a preliminary assessment of this important but neglected dimension of dissent study. The data base available today is considerably larger and better than it was a decade ago and includes many more unofficial transcripts of the trials of dissidents and nonconformists. Moreover, if the experience of the recent past is any guide, new evidence will evolve to test this volume's judgments and to permit more systematic image study.

Lastly, a focus on official images should not be interpreted as a single-factor explanation of Soviet behavior toward internal adversaries. Instead, these images should be viewed as one important input into Soviet decision making and political style. Thus, when used with existing studies of Soviet dissent, which consider a variety of situational and personality variables, image study could offer a more complete understanding of the dissent conflict. It also may help us to better anticipate the future direction of official policy toward internal adversaries.

STRUCTURE

The structure of the book is as follows. Chapter 2 surveys the relevant Western literature on Soviet dissent to show which aspects of the problem have been treated and in which areas our knowledge is sketchy and inconsistent. Chapter 3 introduces the concept of the image to Western study of Soviet dissent and draws on the relevant literature to develop a framework which permits analysis of the relationship between images, perception, and behavior; essential historical background on contemporary official images is presented to make the framework culturally relevant. Chapter 4 presents a research design for the analysis of selected cases of dissent and nonconformity; it examines the principal methodological problems surrounding this image study and develops a research strategy to minimize them and permit case study analyses. Chapters 5 through 6 constitute the bulk of this image study and consist of two case studies, one of religious nonconformity and the other of intellectual dissent, selected to illustrate the major hypothesis. Chapter 7 concludes this preliminary assessment of official images of dissent and nonconformity. It summarizes the principal findings of preceding chapters and suggests some hypotheses regarding the implications of official images for Soviet behavior and the future course of the dissent conflict in particular.

NOTES

1.   Alexander George, "The 'Operational Code': A Neglected Approach to the Study of Political Leaders and Decision-Making," *International Studies Quarterly* 13 (June 1969):220. George identifies these two elements as particularly important and argues that knowledge of a political actor's belief system provides one of the most important inputs for behavioral analyses of political decision making and leadership style.

2

A Survey of the
Dissent-Related Literature

This chapter reviews the Western literature on Soviet dissent relevant to this study's problem. The problem, restated, is to better explain why a post-Stalin leadership, commonly defined by Western analysts as better educated and more sophisticated in its policy making than its predecessors, continues to employ extreme coercion in dealing with even mild dissent. The basic thesis of this chapter is that there is a significant need for Western scholars to spend more time investigating the standards by which Soviet officials perceive dissidents and assess their threat.

The purpose of this survey is threefold: to describe the explanations which have been offered for the above question; to review the extant treatment of Soviet official views and, in particular, official images of dissidents and nonconformists; and to highlight important contributions and deficiencies in the literature and assess its utility for the study of the dissent conflict.

Before turning to the writings on Soviet dissent, it is appropriate to consider briefly the more general scholarly studies on political and socioeconomic changes in the post-Stalin era. The rationale here is that to view contemporary Soviet dissent in proper perspective, it is necessary to consider it in the light of some broader changes in Soviet society.

SCHOLARLY STUDIES OF POST-STALIN CHANGE

Two types of studies are particularly relevant here: Western studies of Soviet political elites and the more broadly focused works on Soviet political and socioeconomic development.

Western analyses of Soviet political elites in the post-Stalin era vary considerably in foci and techniques of analysis. However, there is widespread agreement that the general trend is toward an increasingly complex, modern, and bureaucratic state which formulates policy rationally, on the basis of advice from experts and inputs from various interest groups.[1] William Welsh has surveyed this literature extensively, and his findings are of particular interest. According to Welsh, although the causes of this perceived trend toward a more bureaucratic state are not totally clear, the implications for political change are. He specifically cites three changes in the relationships between the political system and the elite: (1) a greater reliance on "rational-technical" criteria in the recruitment of elites; (2) a decreased role for ideological considerations in decision making; and (3) the emergence of a new kind of elite, a new "managerial class."[2]

Summarizing the thrust of an earlier volume of Communist elite studies, Jan Triska reaches a similar conclusion. He describes the changes in elite-political system relationships as follows:

The leaders [Soviet and East European] tend to perceive the command economy, command politics, coercive methods, and virulent ideological dogmatism of the past as dysfunctional for the present needs; the past personal leadership is slowly evolving to a more institutional and regularized leadership structure.[3]

What these elite studies are suggesting should be made clear. Together they point to the emergence of a more sophisticated and pragmatic elite, as well as to a more participatory decision-making process.

In addition to the authors of these elite studies, many other Western experts on Soviet politics have acknowledged that important, although somewhat ambiguous, changes are occurring in the post-Stalin political system. A few statements from the general studies of post-Stalin political change will illustrate this point:

Jerry Hough: ". . . since 1964 on all but the most central questions, party policy is less and less incorporated into clear-cut undebatable 'ideology' with a consequent widening of the areas open to public discussion."[4]

L.G. Churchward: "The general trend in Soviet politics since the fall of Khrushchev in October 1964 has been towards more regular, more rational but less spectacular policy-making, towards a modern bureaucracy."[5]

Rudolf Tőkés: "Capability for change without systemic crises . . . represents a new level of developmental maturity that the Soviet system has achieved after five decades of existence."[6]

Zbigniew Brzezinski: "The top leadership is doubtless better educated and trained than its predecessors and given its key role in running the system . . . this is presumably an improvement."[7]

Seweryn Bialer: [Since the fall of Khrushchev, the Soviet political] "elite as a whole became more secure in office. . . . The sober, more realistic, task-oriented and present-oriented style of leadership is much closer to the preferred style of almost all segments of the elite."[8]

Morton Schwartz: "The sentiments and the ideological beliefs of the past—the suspiciousness, secretiveness, xenophobia, self-doubt, fears, conceits, and messianic attitudes—are under pressure. They are being challenged by the new psychological environment in which the Soviet leadership finds itself."[9]

The list of similar viewpoints is quite lengthy and the recitation could continue, but the preceding should suffice. The point is that when the phenomenon of contemporary Soviet dissent and nonconformity is viewed against this background and against the fact of the increasing military power and external security of the Soviet Union, an interesting paradox emerges, namely, the "constant tendency [of Soviet leaders] to overreact and perceive even moderate public criticism channeled through other than officially approved avenues as a threat to the very survival of the system."[10] Stated differently, it is by no means clear why this more pragmatic post-Stalin leadership does not react more moderately toward mild dissent and nonconformity. It is possible to argue, as Dimitri Simes observes, that the dissidents do not pose a serious threat to the survival or even the stability of the Soviet system.[11] In the words of Simes: "The experience of the last decade [1968-78] shows that the government is not seriously threatened by the dissent that failed to attract any real domestic constituency except among alienated intellectuals and some minority groups."[12] And yet, Frederick Barghoorn, for example, notes that the period after 1969 has been marked by an increasing intolerance of open dissent, rather than the relaxation of political and ideological controls that many Western observers predicted would accompany detente.[13]

Why, then, are Soviet authorities so defensive about the subject; and why do they continue to employ extreme coercion in dealing with even seemingly mild dissent? Although some students of Soviet politics may be tempted to dismiss this question as inattentive to the very nature of authoritarian politics and Russian-Soviet history, this study proceeds in a different spirit. It acknowledges the important influence of historical legacy and political tradition, in particular, on the present, but argues that traditional Western explanations for the repressive behavior of Soviet authorities should not be applied automatically to explain more recent repression of mild dissent and nonconformity. Rather, such rationales should be justified and reconciled with the important changes in the post-Stalin era outlined earlier.   In summary, then, this book approaches the central question stated above in the following spirit:

> What is needed as we look at the future of the Soviet system—and at its recent past as well—is not certainty in our judgments, but openness in our approach. . . . What is needed is a willingness—indeed, a determination—to subject our assumptions to searching examination and to separate our distaste for the Soviet system from our descriptive analysis of it.[14]

The rest of this chapter reviews studies dealing extensively with Soviet dissent.

WESTERN STUDIES OF SOVIET DISSENT

Although the contemporary form of Soviet dissent is a relatively new phenomenon, originating in the mid-1960s, the relevant Western literature is vast and burgeoning. Since the 1966 political trial of the Soviet writers Andrei Sinyavsky and Yuly Daniel, several hundred books and thousands of articles have been written on various aspects of the topic. Given this situation, the survey which follows is selective and interpretive rather than comprehensive.

Two types of studies are reviewed here: studies for general readers or nonspecialists and scholarly studies written primarily for specialists in Soviet affairs. The former writings are included in this survey because many of them—particularly the earlier ones—provided scholars with some of the first information available about a relatively new phenomenon.[15] Consequently, these writings probably had an important early influence in shaping the judgments of scholars and Western observers in general.

STUDIES FOR GENERAL READERS

Western study of Soviet dissent is not a new field for descriptive-journalistic studies. Since the late 1960s the number and sophistication of such books and articles has grown significantly. Mostly journalistic in style, they are largely the writings of American and European press correspondents and free-lance writers on assignment in the Soviet Union. As such, they draw mainly upon previous research and personal experiences in Moscow and other accessible Soviet cities in order to provide descriptive accounts of contemporary dissent and Soviet life in general. Hence, the purpose of the writing is, for the most part, descriptive: to chronicle the behavior of dissidents and the authorities and not to analyze intensively the thought of these two principal actors in the conflict.

Descriptions and Explanations

The studies for nonspecialists typically pose the following very general types of questions. Who are the dissidents? What is the nature of the conflict between them and the authorities? What does repression of dissidents suggest about Soviet leaders, the nature of their policy, and the political evolution of the system? Why do the authorities respond to mild dissent with extreme coercion? How do officials and average citizens see the dissidents? What future direction will Soviet policy toward dissidents likely take?

With regard to definitions of dissidents, most of the studies under review here focus attention on prominent dissidents of the late 1960s, such as Yury Galanskov and Alexander Ginzburg, and on the hundreds of Soviet citizens who signed petitions in their defense.

All of these individuals are typically portrayed as loyal and non-violent citizens who lawfully protested against perceived injustices. For instance, Robert Kaiser, a *Washington Post* correspondent assigned to the Soviet Union from 1971 to 1974, suggests that many of these early dissidents simply protested the impropriety of persecuting writers.[16] Most of these studies tend to take an uncritical view of the characters and activities of prominent dissidents and their supporters. (An extreme case in point is Anatole Shub's book *An Empire Loses Hope*.)[17]

Journalists David Bonavia and George Feifer, drawing on first-hand experiences with Soviet dissidents, provide a more nuanced and critical picture of some of the early dissidents. In their separate writings, they challenge what they see as an excessively idealized Western image of Soviet dissidents and call for a more balanced and analytical approach to the subject. Feifer, in an article entitled, "No Protest: The Case of the Passive Minority," suggests that prevailing Western images of Soviet dissidents should be viewed skeptically and that the reliability of reports by dissidents should be verified and not simply accepted as accurate.[18] Bonavia provides support for Feifer's position. Drawing on his personal experience as a former Moscow correspondent for the London *Times*, Bonavia characterizes the behavior of one prominent early member of the dissident movement as immoral and provocative and provides details to substantiate his claims.[19]

The images of Soviet officials presented in these studies vary more in tone than in substance. Although few of the studies actually mention more than a few Soviet officials by name, the prevailing view is that all Soviet authorities are cynical, narrow-minded, anti-intellectual, insecure individuals. This is either a foregone conclusion or supported by scattered unnamed official and unofficial sources. Writing in the early 1970s, Shub, John Dornberg, and Abraham Rothberg all describe the post-Stalin political leadership as descendants or accomplices of Stalin. Predictably, much of Soviet political development after 1953 is Stalinized. Rothberg, for example, after a general analysis of the cases of dissidents such as Sinyavsky, Daniel, Brodsky, Solzhenitsyn, Amalrik, and Medvedev, characterizes Soviet political development after 1966 as neo-Stalinist.[20] Cornelia Gerstenmaier, a West German journalist, reaches a similar conclusion based on her interpretation of the cases of dissidents Ginzburg, Galanskov, and Dobrovolsky.[21] By contrast, Bonavia describes the leadership as caught between de- and re-Stalinization rather than as simply returning to Stalinism.[22]

More recent studies by Smith and Kaiser are exceptions. Both note important changes occurring in the composition and backgrounds of the post-Stalin political elite: they describe a trend toward a better educated, more pragmatic leadership. Yet each carefully qualifies this trend. Smith suggests that on the issue of dissent even the more sophisticated authorities seem threatened and insecure.[23] Better educated in the Soviet context, cautions Kaiser, generally means better technically educated.[24] Furthermore, he adds that the assumption that increased education may lead to more liberal values and a more liberal outlook among Soviet authorities may be inappropriate. In Kaiser's estimation, Soviet education "subtly imposes an ideological cast of mind" and not necessarily a more liberal outlook.[25] The result, as he sees it, is that Soviet authorities are "with few exceptions anti-intellectuals, hard-nosed bureaucrats and engineers from working-class families."[26] Smith provides some support for Kaiser's observations and also underlines the profound and pervasive cynicism of the authorities and the public as an important force in Soviet society.[27]

The prevailing view of Soviet policy toward dissidents during the Brezhnev era is that it is a major departure from Stalinist methods. Official repression, while still harsh, cynical, and counterproductive in many respects, is also typically described as selective, predictable, and avoidable. In describing the evolution of official policy toward dissidents since the 1966 trial of Sinyavsky and Daniel, Smith, for example, notes a general trend away from crude and counterproductive methods of gaining public compliance to authority and toward a more sophisticated and effective style of rule. However, qualifying this, he notes the persistence of overkill tactics in repressing a handful of dissidents who do not seem to pose any substantial threat to the stability or the security of the leadership.[28] Bonavia and Rothberg both advance the hypothesis that Soviet leaders could eliminate all manifestations of open dissent, but instead choose to permit a few dissidents to operate to ensure targets of surveillance. This hypothesis, while plausible, lacks any supporting evidence. The consensus in these studies is that, by the early 1970s, the authorities had adjusted their initially crude and counterproductive methods into more refined and effective methods of coercion. Most of the writers, nonetheless, seem to agree that, despite refinements, official policy remains unduly extreme, at least by Western standards.

On the crucial question of why this is so, only partial answers are offered. Generally, the reaction of authorities is described as the routine and reflexive response of a leadership intolerant of ideological diversity. Most of the studies, therefore, characterize the official response as normal if viewed in a Russian-Soviet historical context. The explanations provided for the persistence of the extreme control mentality of Soviet authorities are typically very general and include official insecurity, the authoritarian mind, Russian national character, official intolerance for heretics, habit, a desire to safeguard the power of the Communist Party, and the repressive nature of the Soviet system.

Dornberg, Gerstenmaier, and Rothberg each describe this extreme reaction as reflecting the insecurity of a dictatorship when confronted with any challenge to its illegitimate authority. Feifer supports this view, describing official repression of dissidents as the natural reaction of "a suspicious, jealous complex vis-à-vis the West."[29] Bonavia, on the other hand, sees Soviet authorities simply as striving to eliminate what they perceive as criminal behavior—defiance of police or party—in a Soviet context.[30]

The only studies that deal with the question of overkill tactics toward a small group of dissidents in any greater detail are those by Smith and Kaiser. Interestingly, both cite the theory of Mikhail Agursky, at the time a dissident scientist in Moscow. Agursky explains what he sees as the insecurity of the authorities and Soviet society in general in terms of the system's inherently low tolerance for unorthodox views.[31] In summary, most of the writers surveyed maintain, in varying terms, that Soviet officials are suppressing what they perceive to be a potentially serious challenge to the regime from its internal critics. Smith, in particular, stresses that most Westerners underestimate the seriousness of the challenge dissidents pose for the authorities: a result of both the force of their heretical views and the extreme jealousy with which the Party guards its monopoly of power.[32] Most of the writings underline the importance of Russian-Soviet historical experience for understanding the harsh official response toward dissidents.

No rigorous effort is made in these works to study official views of dissidents and nonconformists in order to better understand the nature of the conflict, as well as to anticipate its future direction.

Only Rothberg examines official views in detail. But his analysis of Soviet press criticism of dissidents is severely limited by the absence of any framework for classifying and interpreting his data. Rothberg's initial assumption that Soviet officials in the post-Stalin period are the "heirs of Stalin"—Stalin's insecure accomplices—renders his study of official perception of, and motivation toward, dissidents virtually a foregone conclusion.[33] The unstated assumption in most of these studies seems to be that official perception of, and motivation toward, dissidents is fixed by systemic needs and a Russian-Soviet authoritarian tradition, and therefore, is decided in advance.

As for the treatment of official images of dissidents, most of the studies provide only brief, passing reference to these images. Shub, for instance, claims that the official representation of dissidents is as "common criminals" and "psychopaths."[34] In line with this, Bonavia notes that officials view dissidents as criminals or schizophrenics.[35] Although most of the writers briefly mention official images, none probes the implications of these conceptions for understanding official perception of, and behavior toward, dissidents. A partial exception is Kaiser, who registers the importance of official images in the context of official propaganda, contending that "in every case the image [projected by the Soviet press and television] is more important than reality."[36] Yet he implies that official images and propaganda in general are unappealing to many Soviet citizens because they are unsophisticated and regarded as greatly distorted by the insecurity of Soviet leaders.[37] It should be noted that while most of the studies describe in varying terms and detail apathy, cynicism, suspicion, and anti-intellectualism as important forces pervading Soviet society, the effects of official images of dissidents within such an environment are not explored.

The images of dissidents held by average Soviet citizens are described as largely negative in the studies for nonspecialists. The prevailing impression is that most Soviet citizens probably view the dissidents as troublemakers. Writers frequently point to the fierce patriotism and the extreme cynicism of many Soviet citizens as providing strong support for the party line against dissidents. Rothberg and Smith, each drawing on empirical research as well as personal impressions, both estimate that the hostility of Soviet people toward dissidents appears to be as strong as the official press typically reports. Rothberg attributes this to widespread Russian chauvinism and the strong anti-intellectual biases of the public, both of which serve to isolate the masses from Soviet intellectuals and dissidents, in particular.[38] Smith highlights extreme cynicism as a pervasive societal force supporting official attacks on dissidents.[39] Kaiser also emphasizes the extreme isolation of Soviet citizens in the Brezhnev era not only from dissidents and intellectuals, but also from foreign influences; thus, most Soviet citizens probably support the party line against dissidents out of a deep patriotism rather than from any profound belief in Communism.[40]

Finally, the matter of future Soviet policy toward dissidents is a subject of speculation in most of the studies for general readers. All the forecasts are quite pessimistic. Typically, the writers simply project what they see as an insecure leadership trapped by historic influences, intolerant of public protest, and reacting in an instinctively repressive fashion. Feifer's position is representative. In his opinion, the future will witness only more dissent and consequent repression, Soviet propaganda continuing to manipulate and promote Soviet backwardness and the traditional anti-intellectual biases of Soviet citizens.[41] Smith and Kaiser view Western hopes for the evolution of a more liberal Soviet political system as unjustified. Kaiser supports this position by emphasizing that the expected norm in the Soviet Union is dictatorship.[42]

Contributions and Weaknesses

1. The dissent studies for nonspecialists provide only part of the solution to this work's central problem. They highlight the political and psychological setting of the conflict between dissidents and the authorities, describing conditions of apathy, cynicism, suspicion, and anti-intellectualism as important forces tacitly supporting official policy toward dissidents.

2. Most of these studies provide bits and pieces of evidence which suggest that the conflict is an emotionally charged one, which often evokes feelings of hatred and contempt not only from the authorities but from average Soviet citizens.

3. On questions of official perception of, and motivation toward, dissidents there is a marked tendency for the authors of these studies to overrationalize and overgeneralize. Explanations offered for the persistence of extreme coercion toward dissidents,

for example, often seem inspired less by evidence than by a desire to supply a rational explanation for this official reaction. Similarly, broad generalizations about political evolution ("re-Stalinization" and "neo-Stalinism") are often advanced and supported only by a lengthy series of impressions.

4. With few notable exceptions, the images of the authorities and dissidents found in these studies are black-and-white or one dimensional. Little effort is made by most writers to demonstrate the adequacy of their descriptions. Consequently, most of the explanations offered are superficial and amount to little more than a statement of the obvious: general references to the importance of history, culture, ideology, regime type. A serious question exists as to whether the very limited evidence adduced—often personal impressions—supports their images.

5. Despite important shortcomings—including occasional uncritical acceptance and injudicious use of source material—the studies for nonspecialists are an important source of information for study of the dissent conflict. When the limitations of these studies are properly acknowledged—when descriptions are verified, when description is separated from implicit prescriptive frameworks, when opinion and speculation are identified as such—these largely journalistic accounts can supplement and challenge existing sources of information on dissent-related issues.

SCHOLARLY STUDIES

Western scholars approach the study of Soviet dissent from varying perspectives and with different foci and objectives.[43] Still, most scholars direct their attention to one or a combination of the following research topics: the actions of dissidents, their relevant perceptions, and official policy toward dissidents (sometimes referred to as regime tactics for the suppression of open dissent). The result of these scholarly efforts over the past fifteen years is a vast and steadily growing body of literature. To evaluate each of these studies briefly and fairly (on its own terms) is neither possible nor warranted here. Works selected for review here are, for the most part, meant to be illustrative of those in which the authors have done serious and penetrating work to establish the facts of the dissent conflict. More precisely, this section, like the previous one, will survey writings relevant to this study's central problem in order to identify potential contributions and important weaknesses and raise some crucial questions regarding the nature of the literature.

The procedure is first to examine briefly and collectively the treatment of several points by a group of authors who interestingly discuss the questions raised in this volume.[44] Then, we will review individually and in greater detail the contributions of a handful of scholars whose writings are more directly relevant to the questions raised here.

Partial Insights

Most of the studies for specialists explain the extreme control mentality of the authorities toward open dissent briefly and in very general terms. Among the most commonly cited explanations are the authoritarian tradition of Russian-Soviet politics, the repressive nature of the Soviet system, the continuing influence of Soviet-Marxist ideology, the inherent inflexibility of the Soviet system, the enduring influence of Soviet political culture with its unique norms and practices, and the need to respond to attacks on the legitimacy of the regime and political system to safeguard the Communist Party's monopoly of power and control of information and to defend Soviet legal principles and the status quo in general. In short, all of these explanations emphasize, in varying terms, the need to consider the official orientation toward dissidents in terms of Russian-Soviet political and cultural traditions as well as in light of the contemporary norms and practices in Soviet society.

Gayle Hollander, in an article entitled "Political Communication and Soviet Dissent," draws on communications theory for insights into the persistence of harsh repression in the post-Khrushchev era. She defines the conflict fundamentally as one between official and unofficial communication networks. Based upon an historical survey of Soviet theory of political communication as well as policy, she concludes that the extreme control mentality evident in the Brezhnev era has deep and tenacious historical roots.[45] The threat posed by dissidents is one to the Party's monopoly over information. Walter Connor approaches the dissent conflict from a developmental perspective. In an article entitled "Differentiation, Integration and Political Dissent in the USSR," he defines open dissent as a relatively new phenomenon, a problem of Soviet modernity that presents officials with a complex problem of societal integration.[46] According to Connor, Soviet leaders maintain a "continuing commitment to the maintenance of a monolithic unity in Soviet society—in basic values, in belief systems"; consequently, any challenge from dissidents in the form of "diverse, idiosyncratic visions of reality" simply cannot be tolerated.[47] Erik Hoffmann supports this view. He asserts that Soviet authorities simply cannot tolerate the rejection of Marxist-Leninist ideology or any challenge to the basic norms and elements of the Soviet political system.[48]

Finally, in a theoretical essay on political regimes and tolerance of opposition, Robert Dahl briefly considers the question of extreme official coercion from the perspective of Soviet authorities. He characterizes the Soviet Union as a hegemonic political system and notes that official barriers to open dissent are quite high in such systems.[49] As a general explanation for the persistence of extreme coercion in hegemonic regimes, Dahl offers the notion of the self-fulfilling prophecy as a hypothesis:

> Since all opposition [included here is open dissent] is potentially dangerous, no distinction can be made between acceptable and unacceptable opposition, between loyal and disloyal opposition, between opposition that is protected and opposition that must be repressed. Yet if all oppositions are treated as dangerous and subject to repression, opposition that would be loyal if it were tolerated becomes disloyal because it is not tolerated. Since all opposition is likely to be disloyal, all opposition must be repressed . . . highly hegemonic regimes seem unable to wholly escape the force of this self-fulfilling prophecy, particularly if they are endowed with an official ideology that claims a kind of divine right to rule based upon exclusive possession of political truth and virtue.[50]

The images of the Soviet political elite and the authorities in general that emerge from these studies for specialists vary considerably. At one extreme, officials are described as despotic, extremist, and paranoid. Oleh Fedyshyn, for instance, based upon his very general historical survey of Russian and Soviet "autocratic reformers," discerns what he views to be a long-established and persistent pattern: "a repressive despotic Tsar, or a period of intensified repression, is followed by a 'despotic reformer,' or a period of at least partial easement of the usual suppression of civil and political rights."[51] In Fedyshyn's interpretation, then, Khrushchev was faced with the classic dilemma of enlightened despots: "how to enact necessary reforms without jeopardizing the despotic controls?"[52] In accord with this theory of "thaws and freezes" in Russian-Soviet policy toward critics of the regime, Fedyshyn views Khrushchev's successors as repressive, despotic rulers. More nuanced images of the Soviet political elite emerge in most of the other studies surveyed. Gayle Hollander, for example, describes the political elite in the Brezhnev era as more conservative and cautious than the Khrushchev leadership, but as still extremist in its orientation toward dissidents and nonconformists.[53] Robert Slusser, based on an intensive survey of *samizdat* documents, offers the impression that Soviet authorities are paranoid.[54]

More tentative and moderate images of Soviet officials appear in the writings of Theodore Friedgut and Walter Connor. Friedgut, in an article entitled "The Democratic Movement: Dimensions and Perspectives," undertakes a perceptual analysis of the views of forty Soviet emigres, all former members of the Soviet intelligentsia, and some former dissidents. From this vantage point, he constructs an image of Soviet leaders as isolated, unsophisticated, and ineffective pursuers of totalitarian goals, individuals who, in the opinion of most of those interviewed, "lack an intelligent understanding of their duties."[55] Walter Connor provides partial support for this interpretation. He sketches a "troubled elite," poorly informed and mediocre in style, and stresses important limitations on Western knowledge.[56] In Connor's words: "We know very little about them. . . . Who is in power, how knowledgeable are they, how successful are they, in responding to the problems they confront? Observers may well differ in their answers."[57]

At the other extreme is the image of Soviet authorities expressed by Rudolf Tőkés. In an article published in 1974 entitled "Dissent: the Politics for Change in the USSR," Tőkés defines Soviet leaders as "rational cost-benefit-conscious political actors," a definition derived essentially from the logic of his developmental model rather than from any empirical study of the political elite.[58] Furthermore, based on the logic of his "evolution-adaptation-model" of change, Tőkés describes Soviet domestic politics as marked by a "newly evolving relationship between rulers and ruled . . . in which both sides are groping for a new political equilibrium."[59] It should be noted that the latter image of Soviet officials is an uncommon one in the literature.

With few notable exceptions, Soviet official images of dissidents receive only scant attention in the dissent studies for specialists. This is not surprising. As mentioned earlier, most of these studies do not focus primarily on contemporary official perceptions of this conflict. The studies by Tőkés and Hoffmann are typical in this regard. They exclude study of what they refer to as official biases and prejudices from the scope of their inquiry. Instead, like most writers surveyed, they focus on the more observable and more easily researchable dimensions of the conflict.

Hollander, Friedgut, and Feldbrugge briefly discuss official views of dissidents and related issues without, however, probing the implications of contemporary official images of dissidents for understanding official policy and for anticipating the direction of the conflict. Nevertheless, some worthwhile points are made. Hollander's study of Soviet political communications is suggestive. Based on her historical survey of relevant Soviet writings, she suggests that the post-Khrushchev leadership is influenced strongly by its elitist consciousness, particularly with regard to the control of information, which she views to be a legacy of Leninist theory on public opinion.[60] Hollander also comments on official images of dissidents. Following a brief examination of official writings, she concludes:

> The few official reports of the trials of dissidents have consistently carried tendentious descriptions of the charges and abusive references to the defendants. In several cases the slanted coverage of such trials has backfired. . . . Beyond the misleading accounts of trials, regular propaganda campaigns have been waged against specific individuals.[61]

Hence, Hollander seems to view official images of dissidents essentially as crude political symbols, cynically, and occasionally ineffectively, manipulated by Soviet propagandists and other officials. Specifically, she mentions official images of dissidents as "social parasites, outcasts and people of different ideologies."[62] Hollander suggests the vulnerability of Soviet citizenry to these crude symbols, noting that the Soviet people have been fed "a one-dimensional view of reality" for a long time.[63] Ferdinand Feldbrugge, in his book *Samizdat and Political Dissent in the Soviet Union*, also briefly treats official images of dissidents. His impression is that official images serve to greatly oversimplify official perception of dissidents.

According to Feldbrugge, "most dissidents can be written off as non-entities by the regime (describing dissidents as parasites, spongers, drop-outs and marginal people is indeed a standard procedure in the official media)."[64] Theodore Friedgut's research is also relevant here. His interviews with Soviet emigres provide some support for the view that offical images are probably widely shared by officials and uninformed Soviet citizens. Significantly, Friedgut's interviews show that even former members of the Soviet intelligentsia who were sympathizers of dissidents found plausible much of the party line regarding the alleged activities of foreign emigre groups, the CIA, and anticommunists in general.[65] Friedgut's survey also revealed that "fear, prudence, patriotism, and a total lack of sympathy for emigre agencies such as the NTS" discouraged passive supporters of dissidents from active involvement because of the fear of possible espionage charges."[66]

More relevant to the central problem under investigation in this study are the efforts of a handful of Western scholars: Peter Reddaway, Frederick Barghoorn, Bohdan Bociurkiw, and Dimitri Simes. These now will be reviewed individually.

Peter Reddaway

Peter Reddaway, a British authority on various aspects of Soviet dissent, has contributed significantly during the past fifteen years toward advancing Western knowledge of the dissent conflict. He has done so principally by describing and analyzing the actions of dissidents and the authorities. In recent years he has devoted increasing attention to refining Western study of Soviet policy toward dissidents. The impressive result to date is a loose and tentative framework which allows for the consideration of the many factors—domestic and external—that shape official policy.

Although Reddaway's primary research purpose is not to rigorously analyze contemporary official views of dissidents, in several studies he does briefly examine official writings relevant to dissidents and official images in particular. For example, in his 1980 article entitled "Policy towards Dissent since Khrushchev," Reddaway at the outset draws attention to an important speech delivered by Brezhnev at the 16th Congress of Trade Unions of the USSR on

March 21, 1977 and reprinted in *Pravda* the next day. In a lengthy excerpt from that authoritative statement, Reddaway highlights Brezhnev's description of dissidents as "enemies of socialism," "traitors," "self-estranged" individuals, "mercenaries," active opponents of the Soviet system, and accomplices, if not "agents of foreign propaganda and intelligence services."[67] Reddaway judges the statement to be a fairly typical Politburo appraisal and, interestingly, observes that "while most official writings about dissent tend to be stridently defensive and vindictive, statements by Politburo members are usually (and *probably deceptively*) [emphasis mine] more measured."[68] Regarding the amount of attention paid by Soviet leaders to the subject of dissidents, Reddaway offers this admittedly impressionistic conclusion:

> Soviet leaders probably discuss it [their policy toward dissidents and nonconformists] in any detail or frankness only rarely, accustomed as they are to suppressing their awareness of such unpleasant matters in the back of their minds, and doubtless, most of the time, in their subconscious; but unspoken assumptions about it probably play a considerable role in the policy-formation process regarding many areas of policy. One such assumption is the basic axiom that dissent must unquestionably be suppressed, an axiom based on "traditional" practices dating from Lenin's time and reinforced by the fear that more liberal policies would make the USSR vulnerable to the sort of political process which developed in Hungary in 1956 and Czechoslovakia in 1968.[69]

Writing about five years earlier, Reddaway amplified on the extreme and traditional intolerance of Soviet leaders for open critics of the regime mentioned above: "The traditional Soviet tendency has been to see, or pretend to see, actual or potential opposition in almost all forms of persistent dissent."[70]

Reddaway's evaluation of the state of Western study of Soviet dissent is also of interest. Writing in 1980, he stressed the need for more rigorous study of Soviet official views of dissidents as a prerequisite to any systematic analysis of Soviet policy toward dissidents.[71] He called for "a close examination of the dauntingly voluminous official Soviet publications relating to dissent in newspapers, journals and books."[72]

Frederick Barghoorn

More detailed treatment of traditional and contemporary Soviet official views appears in the writings of Frederick Barghoorn, a veteran Kremlin-watcher. Perhaps Barghoorn's greatest contribution to the study of Soviet dissent has been his effort to illuminate the context of the dissent conflict. Beginning as early as 1950 with the publication of his classic study *The Soviet Image of the United States*, Barghoorn carefully scrutinized Soviet writings for clues into official perceptions of the Soviet Union's principal adversary, the United States, and, more broadly, into the political and psychological environment of Soviet officials.[73] An important contribution of this early work was that it shed light not only on the dynamics of Soviet-U.S. relations, but also on the Soviet Union's political culture, highlighting important forces in Soviet society such as mistrust, suspicion, and false perception of foreigners. On balance, Barghoorn's analysis suggested that the postwar leadership was insecure, extremely isolated, and poorly informed. Moreover, he underscored the traditional anxiety of Soviet officials about the dangers inherent in any contacts between the citizenry and foreigners.

Writing more than twenty-five years later in a book entitled *Detente and the Democratic Movement in the USSR*, Barghoorn elaborated on many of his earlier findings and, in particular, characterized members of the political elite under Brezhnev as profoundly suspicious and distrustful of not only foreigners, but of Soviet citizens as well.[74] Based on a close study of the authoritative writings of select party and police spokesmen, he concluded:

> . . . the party leadership does not trust its own rank and file, and it apparently feels particularly uneasy about the state of mind of Soviet intellectuals, especially if they are not CPSU members and hence are not subject to party discipline, and in particular about their potential susceptibility to "bourgeois" influence.[75]

In addition to mapping out the political and psychological context of the dissent conflict, Barghoorn, like Reddaway, has devoted considerable effort to refining Western understanding of the characteristics, origins, and significance of Soviet dissidents. He has also rigorously analyzed the regime's tactics to suppress dissidents, as well as the relationship between official policy toward dissidents and detente in U.S.-Soviet relations.

Beyond all of this, Barghoorn has managed to examine briefly the contemporary images Soviet officials hold of dissidents and their foreign supporters. Most notably in *Detente and the Democratic Movement in the USSR*, he draws attention to the early writings of Semyon Tsvigun, at the time a KGB chief and a leading Soviet authority on questions related to dissidents. Barghoorn highlights Tsvigun's portrayal of the USSR as a country besieged by a host of foreign enemies all seeking to subvert it ideologically—a situation necessitating, according to Tsvigun, heightened vigilance and control at home.[76]

Barghoorn's interpretation of official images, such as those expressed by Tsvigun, is significant. He describes them as "outbursts" which "seem almost ludicrous—so shrill is their language, so slender and unconvincing the evidence they present in support of their charges against the 'imperialists'"; yet, he concludes "they must nevertheless be taken seriously."[77] Barghoorn further speculates that it is very likely that many Soviet citizens find these official attacks and images convincing. In a 1975 article entitled "The Post-Khrushchev Campaign To Suppress Dissent," he asserts that official images of dissidents as "anti-Soviets" and "moral degenerates" probably seem plausible to the "woefully uninformed Soviet citizens."[78] A noteworthy conclusion regarding the influence of official images drawn by Barghoorn, based on his many years of analyzing Soviet official writings, is that the authorities probably consider what he views as the ritualized images or cliches that pervade Soviet society as "indispensable for the preservation of the dominant political culture and the system of rules associated with it."[79] It should be added that Barghoorn characterizes these official images or cliches as "ritualized doctrine" which is dull and irrelevant in contemporary Soviet society.[80]

It should be noted that Barghoorn explicitly confronts the issue of the persistence of the extreme control mentality of Soviet authorities toward dissidents. He approaches what he terms the paradox of "the increasing military power and external security of the USSR at the same time as [it demonstrates] a growing concern to prevent criticism that the leadership regards as subversive" with a general explanation: the "answer may lie in the enduring features of the dominant Soviet political culture."[81]

More relevant still to the general questions under examination here are several articles written by Bohdan Bociurkiw and Dimitri Simes, respectively.[82] In these writings, both authors focus attention on Soviet official attitudes toward the problem of dissidents and nonconformists and, more broadly, on the determinants of Soviet policy. Each seeks to improve our understanding of Soviet perception, motivation, and political calculation.

Bohdan Bociurkiw

Bohdan Bociurkiw, a noted authority on church-state relations in the USSR, has much to say on the matter of the Soviet leadership's extreme control mentality. He begins by placing the threat posed to the regime in historical perspective. Writing in 1970, he observes that the dissidents of the 1960s, although relatively small in number, presented the Soviet system with its most significant challenge in several decades.[83] In Bociurkiw's estimation, it was, above all, "a challenge to the legitimacy of the Brezhnev leadership and its claim to be the heir to a humanistic, internationally radical tradition."[84] In a later article entitled "The Shaping of Soviet Religious Policy," Bociurkiw examines the history and politics of church-state relations since the origins of the Soviet state. His analysis describes the traditional tendency of Soviet officials to perceive religious organizations—particularly unregistered groups—primarily as a security problem and the tendency of officials to link internal enemies with external enemies of the Soviet system.[85] Bociurkiw argues that religious groups may not pose a serious threat to the survival of the system, but they are nevertheless viewed as a risk, particularly with respect to their vulnerability to foreign subversion; for an extremely security-conscious leadership, this is an intolerable risk.[86] In Bociurkiw's words, the early and "continuous concern of the leadership about these 'islands' of ideological nonconformity and political subversion impelled it to surround religious organizations with a close network of covert police controls."[87]

An important conclusion emerging from Bociurkiw's historical review of Soviet religious policy is that the significance of ideological motives in shaping Soviet official perceptions of religious nonconformists and religious policy has been overestimated by Western and Soviet writers alike.[88] He offers a more complex interpretation of official perception and motivation. From his analysis of the behavior of Soviet officials and of their political culture, Bociurkiw infers that the Soviet political elite's views of religion are filtered through three prisms: historical memory, ideological legacy, and the authoritarian aspirations of Soviet rulers.[89]

Dimitri Simes

Dimitri Simes, a Soviet emigré whose research has focused on contemporary U.S.-Soviet relations and on aspects of Soviet foreign and domestic policy, has also directed his attention to the study of dissent and nonconformity in the Soviet Union. However, unlike most of the scholars surveyed, he has cast the subject in the broader context of U.S.-Soviet rivalry. Furthermore, he has stressed, as Bociurkiw does implicitly, the need to view dissidents and nonconformists as Soviet officials perceive them: from the perspective of officialdom's logic and reasoning and not merely through traditional Western concepts. Simes expresses this view in a 1978 article entitled "Human Rights and Detente."[90] The article is especially important because it briefly, but critically, assesses not only contemporary Soviet official views of dissidents, but also the actions and thoughts of dissidents and even their links with foreigners. Simes's analysis thereby highlights several dimensions of the conflict typically overlooked.

With regard to the traditional tendency of Soviet authorities to overreact and see even moderate dissent as a threat to the very survival of the system, Simes points to the Russian autocratic tradition and the prevailing political philosophy of Soviet rulers as an important part of the explanation. However, he cautiously adds that the reasons for contemporary official anxiety are by no means clear and are probably more complex than conventionally assumed by Western scholars.[91] Simes's analysis of contemporary official views of dissidents, and the dissent conflict in general, suggests that the foreign factor—in particular official perceptions of the intentions and actions of foreign supporters of dissidents—may be more important than typically assumed in shaping not merely regime tactics for the suppression of dissidents, but also elite perceptions of the nature of the conflict and the threat posed by dissidents.[92] According to Simes, a siege mentality, with paranoia in some members of the Politburo, continues to afflict the Soviet leadership. Consequently, those dissident challenges to the legitimacy of Soviet rule and to existing political controls (such as state censorship) that are supported by foreign governments and individuals are interpreted broadly. They are viewed as efforts by hostile foreigners to abolish political controls "without which the regime does not know how to preserve its political monopoly."[93] In short, the problem that the leadership faces, according to Simes, is that it does not know how to preserve its political monopoly without repressive controls.

Simes also takes a brief, but critical, look at official images—general and specific—of dissidents. Although he cautions that it is unclear whether Soviet leaders actually believe officially expressed conceptions of prominent dissidents as agents of hostile foreign interests or as a "Western fifth column" in the Soviet Union, his impression seems to be that they do.[94]

Also pertinent to this survey of the dissent-related literature are Sime's comments about Western scholarship on Soviet dissent. In the article mentioned earlier, Simes sharply criticizes Western writing on the subject. He describes most of the scholarly and popular writing on the subject as emotional rather than objective in content and concludes that very few serious analytical studies of Soviet dissent exist.[95] In Simes's estimation, "the study of dissent has become almost a total monopoly of scholars with a prodissident bias."[96] The result, as he sees it, is that such efforts have greatly oversimplified Western understanding of the conflict. They have promoted "black and white stereotypes of stupid, corrupt, and oppressive Soviet officials on the one hand, and heroic, selfless, and brilliant protestors on the other."[97] In summary, perhaps the greatest contribution of Sime's essay for this book is its stimulating and provocative nature. In addition to raising important questions about the objectivity of scholarly and general literature on Soviet dissent, it draws attention to frequently overlooked aspects of the dissent conflict. In particular, it suggests the need for a more rigorous consideration of official perceptions of dissidents and foreigners and other related issues.

Contributions and Weaknesses

1. Most of the scholarly studies surveyed offer only partial insights into the question of the persistence of extreme coercion

toward even seemingly mild dissent. They draw attention to the political and psychological environment of Soviet authorities. Typically, explanations are very general and emphasize factors such as political culture, Soviet ideology, regime, and system type. Unfortunately, most do not go on to investigate contemporary official perceptions relevant to the conflict.

2. A few writers do directly address this work's central question. They suggest the need for more rigorous attention to the role of foreigners in the dissent conflict, particularly as perceived by officials; the extreme security consciousness of Soviet officials; and, more broadly, the subject of exaggerated threat perception. Furthermore, they suggest the need to critically compare and contrast contemporary official views of dissidents on a case-by-case basis, with the best available evidence as to the dissidents' actual activities and thought, and note the availability of adequate data for such an effort.

3. Many of the scholarly studies of dissent, in varying terms and detail, seriously question Western speculation that a more moderate regime orientation toward dissidents might emerge following the influx of more professionals into the party-state apparatus. Reasons given include the intense concern of bureaucrats with job security and career development, as well as countervailing forces in Soviet society such as widespread apathy and cynicism.

4. Many Western scholars do seem to have a "prodissident bias," or a sympathy for the cause of Soviet dissidents, as Simes has observed. However, judging from this select survey of the scholarly literature, most scholars have managed to recognize this bias and to prevent it from seriously affecting their scholarship. Whether or not this bias has discouraged closer study of official perceptions and, in particular, images of dissidents, is a matter of speculation.

5. Most of the scholarly studies turn their essentially descriptive analyses of dissidents or official behavior into explanatory analyses, suggesting official motives, even anticipating the future direction of official policy, but, significantly, without giving detailed consideration to contemporary official perceptions and images.

SUBSTANTIVE GENERALIZATIONS

In addition to the contributions already discussed, it is possible to distill from the literature several substantive generalizations regarding the nature, origins, and characteristics of contemporary Soviet dissent and other subjects. Although only indirectly relevant to this chapter's purpose, these facts will serve as an essential background for the subsequent discussion of case-study findings.

Most of the scholarly, as well as nonscholarly, studies provide support for the following key points.

1. Open dissent in the USSR is a relatively new phenomenon, largely an unintended result of Khrushchev's de-Stalinization policies.

2. A major early motive for open dissent was ethical. Most of the early dissidents were loyal and patriotic citizens who spoke up simply to express concern and indignation over the arrests of nonconformist writers and what they perceived as the regime's abandonment of de-Stalinization—individuals who were hopeful that further progress could be made.

3. Initial protests typically took the form of persuasion and attempts to convince the leadership that a continuation of current practices would be counterproductive.

4. Many dissidents, who began as loyal petitioners for change, were progressively radicalized when the authorities proved unresponsive to their appeals and petitions or reacted with repression.

5. Foreign support has provided moral and material backing essential to the survival of the contemporary dissident movement.

6. During the course of their conflict with the state, many dissidents violated laws which they viewed as incompatible with the Soviet constitution. In addition, many violated important norms of the Soviet political culture.

7. There is a great deal of diversity in the ideas and activity of Soviet dissidents and nonconformists.

8. Although relatively insignificant in number, dissidents presented Soviet officials with the most serious domestic challenge in several decades.

9. Soviet policy toward dissidents and nonconformists probably has at least the tacit support of a population characterized frequently as inert, deeply apathetic, cynical, and fearful (of losing jobs and educational privileges and of legal sanctions for open dissent).

10. Soviet leaders traditionally have held rigid and negative attitudes toward the unauthorized dissemination of information that might embarrass the Soviet system to foreigners.

11. *Samizdat* communications used by dissidents directly challenge the party's monopoly on information and its interpretation of what is important and legitimate.

12. The conflict between authorities and dissidents is essentially domestic in nature: a fundamental challenge to the legitimacy of the Soviet leadership.

GENERAL CONCLUSIONS

The preponderance of previous scholarly and nonscholarly writing on contemporary Soviet dissent and nonconformity has focused on the behavior of dissidents and the authorities. More than fifteen years of often rigorous and imaginative research and analysis have significantly increased Western knowledge of Soviet dissidents and official policy. During the same period, Western study of *contemporary* Soviet official perceptions of dissidents, the nature of the dissent conflict, and related issues has advanced only marginally. Explanations for the persistence of the extreme control mentality of Soviet officials toward dissidents remain very general, impressionistic, and speculative. Despite the increasing availability of relevant data since the mid-1970s, the perceptual dimension of the conflict—in particular official perceptions—remains greatly underdeveloped. Potentially fruitful suggestions for advancing our knowledge have not been followed up.

The prevailing tendency is to accept conventional scholarly assumptions regarding official attitudes toward dissidents, rather than to comb contemporary official writings for evidence of any evolution in those attitudes. With few notable exceptions, contemporary official images of dissidents receive only scant attention in the scholarly literature. Frequently, they are not taken seriously by scholars, but ignored or dismissed as simply crude propaganda, misinformation, or blatant falsehood. Likewise, the important subject of exaggerated threat perception receives virtually no analytic attention in the available literature; particularly neglected are official perceptions of foreigners and their impact on official threat assessment. From the perspective of conflict study, the scholarly literature suffers a serious imbalance: scholars tend to focus on the perceptions and behavior of Soviet dissidents but not on the perceptions of Soviet officials nor rigorously on foreigners as actors in the conflict.

The impact of relevant social science theory and research in the areas of perception, motivation, and image study upon the study of the dissent conflict has been virtually negligible. No serious effort has been made to develop a useful methodology from this body of theory.

Traditional research on Soviet dissent should be complemented with rigorous analysis of official perceptions. This is a more fruitful line of inquiry than trying to infer Soviet perceptions and motivation solely on the basis of behavior. In other words, more scholarly effort should be spent studying the standards—the logic and reasoning—by which Soviet officials perceive dissent. Without rigorous study of contemporary official perceptions, and images in particular, Western explanations for the persistence of the extreme control mentality of Soviet leaders will be no more than partially informed guesswork. Moreover, in light of this serious deficiency in the literature, scholars should be critical of the claim that contemporary Soviet official views of dissidents have not changed from tsarist times.

NOTES

1. Two collections of elite studies which illustrate this point as well as the varying foci and techniques of analysis are: R. Barry Farrell, ed., *Political Leadership in Eastern Europe and the Soviet Union* (Chicago: Aldine Publishing Co., 1970), in particular Frederick C. Barghoorn, "Trends in Top Leadership in USSR," pp. 61-87, Frederick J. Fleron, Jr., "Representation of Career Types in Soviet Political Leadership," pp. 108-39, and Michael Gehlen, "The Soviet Apparatchiki," pp. 140-56; Carl Beck et al., *Comparative Communist Political Leadership* (New York: David McKay Co., 1973), see especially Frederick J. Fleron, Jr., "System Attributes and Career Attributes: The Soviet Leadership System 1952 to 1965," pp. 43-85, and Milton Lodge, "Attitudinal Cleavages within the Soviet Political Leadership," pp. 202-25.

2. William A. Welsh, "Introduction: The Comparative Study of Political Leaderships in Communist Systems," in Beck et al., p. 3.

3. Jan F. Triska, "Some Reflections in Conclusion," in Farrell, p. 339.

4. Jerry F. Hough, "The Soviet System: Petrification or Pluralism?" *Problems of Communism* 21 (March-April 1972): 31.

5. L.G. Churchward, *The Soviet Intelligentsia: An Essay on the Social Structure and Roles of Soviet Intellectuals during the 1960s* (Boston: Routledge & Kegan Paul, 1973), p. 149.

6. Rudolf L. Tőkés, "Introduction," in *Soviet Politics and Society in the 1970s*, ed. Henry W. Morton and Rudolf L. Tőkés (New York: Free Press, 1974), p. xxiv.

7. Zbigniew Brzezinski, "Soviet Politics: From the Future to the Past?" in *The Dynamics of Soviet Politics*, ed. Paul Cocks, Robert V. Daniels, and Nancy Whittier Heer (Cambridge: Harvard University Press, 1976), p. 348.

8. Seweryn Bialer, "The Soviet Political Elite and Internal Developments in the USSR," in *The Soviet Empire: Expansion and Detente*, ed. William E. Griffith (Lexington, Mass.: Lexington Books, 1976), p. 34.

9. Morton Schwartz, *Soviet Perceptions of the United States* (Berkeley: University of California Press, 1978), p. 203.

10. Dimitri K. Simes, "Human Rights and Detente," in *The Soviet Threat: Myths and Realities*, ed. Grayson Kirk and Nils H. Wessel (Montpelier, Vt.: Capital City Press, 1978), p. 141.

11. Ibid., p. 138.

12. Ibid., p. 131.

13. Frederick C. Barghoorn, *Detente and the Democratic Movement in the USSR* (New York: Free Press, 1976), pp. 1-6.

14. Hough, p. 45.

15. Selected for review from these writings are: Anatole Shub, *An Empire Loses Hope: The Return of Stalin's Ghost* (New York: W.W. Norton & Co., 1970); John Dornberg, *The New Tsars: Russia under Stalin's Heirs* (New York: Doubleday & Co., 1972); Abraham Rothberg, *The Heirs of Stalin: Dissidence and the Soviet Regime 1953-1970* (Ithaca, N.Y.: Cornell University Press, 1972); Cornelia Gerstenmaier, *The Voices of the Silent*, trans. Susan Hecker (New York: Hart Publishing Co., 1972); David Bonavia, *Fat Sasha and the Urban Guerrilla: Protest and Conformism in the Soviet Union* (New York: Atheneum, 1973); George Feifer, "No Protest: The Case of the Passive Minority," in *Dissent in the USSR: Politics, Ideology, and People*, ed. Rudolf L. Tőkés (Baltimore: Johns Hopkins University Press, 1975), pp. 418-37; An Observer [George Feifer], *Message from Moscow*, 2nd ed. (New York: Vintage Books, 1971); Hedrick Smith, *The Russians* (New York: Quadrangle, 1976); Robert G. Kaiser, *Russia: The People and the Power* (New York: Pocket Books, 1976). Not included in this review, but also noteworthy, are two more recent books: David K. Shipler, *Russia: Broken Idols, Solemn Dreams* (New York: New York Times Book Co., 1983); and Kevin Klose, *Russia and the Russians: Inside the Closed Society* (New York: W.W. Norton & Co., 1984).

16. Kaiser, p. 441.

17. Shub, *passim*, pp. 23-66, refers to prominent dissidents such as Daniel, Litvinov, Grigorenko, Amalrik, Sinyavsky, Galanskov, and Ginzburg not only as "saints," "finest brave people," "loyal critics," but also as "young rebels," "democrats," "new revolutionaries," "nonpolitical," "Soviet resistance," "liberal evolutionists," "dissidents," and as members of an "activist civil liberties movement."

18. Feifer, "No Protest," pp. 427-31.

19. Bonavia, pp. 25-37. The reference is to Pyotr Yakir; to provide Yakir anonymity, Bonavia refers to him as Pavel throughout the book.

20. Rothberg, p. 251.

21. Gerstenmaier, p. 157.

22. Bonavia, p. 88.

23. Smith, p. 457.
24. Kaiser, p. 224.
25. Ibid.
26. Ibid., p. 390.
27. Smith, p. 453.
28. Ibid., p. 253.
29. Feifer, *Message from Moscow*, p. 243.
30. Bonavia, p. 60.
31. Smith, p. 243, Kaiser, p. 188.
32. Smith, p. 442.
33. Rothberg.
34. Shub, p. 55.
35. Bonavia, p. 34.
36. Kaiser, p. 258.
37. Ibid., p. 257.
38. Rothberg, p. 375.
39. Smith, pp. 453-54.
40. Kaiser, p. 486.
41. Feifer, p. 317.
42. Kaiser, p. 490.
43.   No effort will be made in this section to enumerate and assess the utility of the many taxonomies developed by scholars to classify types of Soviet dissent. For a brief listing of types and a discussion of what one student of Soviet dissent terms "the considerable semantic confusion surrounding the subject," interested readers should see Rudolf L. Tőkés, "Introduction/Varieties of Soviet Dissent: An Overview," in *Dissent in the USSR: Politics, Ideology, and People*, ed. R.L. Tőkés (Baltimore: Johns Hopkins University Press, 1974), pp. 12-16.
44.   Selected to be reviewed collectively are: Erik P. Hoffmann, "Political Opposition in the Soviet Union," in *Political Opposition and Dissent*, ed. Barbara N. McLennan (New York: Dunellen Publishing Co., 1973), pp. 329-79; Robert A. Dahl, "Introduction," in *Regimes and Oppositions*, ed. Robert A. Dahl (New Haven: Yale University Press, 1973), pp. 1-25; Ferdinand J.M. Feldbrugge, *Samizdat and Political Dissent in the Soviet Union* (Leyden: A.W. Sijthoff, 1975); Oleh S. Fedyshyn, "Khrushchev's Liberalization and the Rise of Dissent in the USSR," ed. Ihor Kamenetsky (Littleton, Colo.: Libraries Unlimited, 1977), pp. 67-76; also in *Nationalism and Human Rights*: Peter Vanneman, "The Russian Civil Liberties Ferment since the Death of Stalin," pp. 55-66; Rudolf L. Tőkés, "Dissent: The Politics for Change in the USSR," in *Soviet Politics and Society in the 1970s*, pp. 3-59; and Tőkés, "Introduction," in *Dissent in the USSR*, pp. 1-31. The following articles also appear in *Dissent in the USSR*: Walter D. Connor, "Differentiation, Integration, and Political Dissent in the USSR," pp. 139-57; Theodore Friedgut, "The Democratic Movement: Dimensions and Perspectives," pp. 116-36; Gayle Durham Hollander, "Political Communication and Dissent in the Soviet Union," pp. 233-75; and Robert M. Slusser, "History and the Democratic Opposition," pp. 329-53.
45.   Hollander, p. 274.

46. Connor, pp. 139-42, 152.
47. Ibid., p. 148.
48. Hoffmann, p. 340.
49. Dahl, p. 8.
50. Ibid., p. 13.
51. Fedyshyn, p. 67.
52. Ibid., p. 69.
53. Hollander, pp. 272-75.
54. Slusser, pp. 351-53.
55. Friedgut, p. 119.
56. Connor, p. 147.
57. Ibid.
58. Tőkés, "The Politics for Change in the USSR," p. 45.
59. Morton and Tőkés, "Introduction," p. 45.
60. Hollander, p. 273.
61. Ibid., pp. 271-72.
62. Ibid., p. 272, ff. 85.
63. Ibid., p. 249.
64. Feldbrugge, p. 217.
65. Friedgut, p. 130.
66. Ibid.
67. Leonid Brezhnev, *Pravda*, March, 22, 1977, as cited by Peter Reddaway, "Policy towards Dissent since Khrushchev," in *Authority, Power and Policy in the USSR*, 2nd ed., ed. T.H. Rigby, Archie Brown, and Peter Reddaway (London: Macmillan Press, 1983), p. 159. It is important to note that Brezhnev's statement regarding legitimate and illegitimate criticism of Soviet policy and the system followed an unprecedented and highly publicized statement in which a U.S. president (Carter) strongly criticized the Soviet record on human rights and openly supported the struggle of several prominent, repressed Soviet dissidents. More detail on this subject follows in Chapter 6, a case study of Yury Orlov.
68. Ibid., p. 159.
69. Ibid., p. 180.
70. Peter Reddaway, "The Development of Dissent and Opposition," in *The Soviet Union since the Fall of Khruschev*, ed. Archie Brown and Michael Kaser (New York: Free Press, 1975), p. 124.
71. Reddaway, "Policy towards Dissent since Khrushchev," p. 184.
72. Ibid., p. 184.
73. Frederick C. Barghoorn, *The Soviet Image of the United States: A Study in Distortion* (New York: Harcourt, Brace, 1950).
74. Barghoorn, *Detente and the Democratic Movement in the USSR*, see especially pp. 130-46 for Barghoorn's discussion entitled "Ideological Subversion and Dissent."
75. Ibid., p. 135. A similar conclusion was drawn in a study of Soviet official views on issues related to dissidents and nonconformists during the Khrushchev era; see Jeremy Azrael, "Is Coercion Withering Away?" *Problems of Communism* 11 (November-December 1962):9-10.

76. Ibid., pp. 136-38.

77. Ibid., p. 137.

78. Frederick C. Barghoorn, "The Post-Khrushchev Campaign To Suppress Dissent," in *Dissent in the USSR: Politics, Ideology, and People*, ed. Tőkés, p. 71.

79. Ibid., p. 89.

80. Ibid.

81. Ibid.

82. Particularly relevant here are: Bohdan R. Bociurkiw, "Political Dissent in the Soviet Union," *Studies in Comparative Communism* 3 (April 1970): 74-105; Bohdan R. Bociurkiw, "The Shaping of Soviet Religious Policy," *Problems of Communism* 22 (May-June 1973):37-51; and Simes, pp. 135-47.

83. Bociurkiw, "Political Dissent in the Soviet Union," p. 104.

84. Ibid.

85. Bociurkiw, "The Shaping of Soviet Religious Policy," p. 43.

86. Ibid.

87. Ibid., p. 39.

88. Ibid., p. 38.

89. Ibid., p. 39. More precisely, historical memory, as defined by Bociurkiw, refers to the image Soviet officials hold of institutional religion—and, in particular, the Russian Orthodox Church—as an instrument of the real or imagined internal and external enemies of the Soviet system (p. 38).

90. Simes, pp. 138-40.

91. Ibid., pp. 136-37.

92. Ibid., p. 143.

93. Ibid., p. 140.

94. Ibid.

95. Ibid., p. 138.

96. Ibid., p. 135.

97. Ibid. p. 138.

3

A Framework for Analysis

The previous chapter found that the study of Soviet official images of dissidents and nonconformists is underdeveloped, that its theoretical content is inadequate, and that the analysis generally lacks rigor. The purpose of this chapter is to make a modest effort at redressing this situation. More specifically, it will construct a framework which seeks to facilitate the description and interpretation of how Soviet officials see dissidents and nonconformists, as well as setting forth the context of the conflict.

The justification for a formal framework of analysis needs to be made explicit. Students of Soviet dissent generally have assumed that the meaning of official images of dissidents and nonconformists is readily apparent and that, therefore, these images do not require close study. However, this is not the case. Although the propaganda and, in general, the political functions of these images are fairly obvious, their implications for official perception and action are less so. The thesis of this chapter is that official images of dissidents and nonconformists cannot be understood properly apart from a psychologically and culturally relevant context of analysis. Until the general utility of the concept of the image for explaining regularities in perception and action is clarified and grasped by students of Soviet dissent, official images will continue to be misinterpreted and an important dimension of this domestic conflict will remain over-looked.

In developing the proposed framework, several tasks are funda-mental: first, to establish the general relevance of the concept of the image for the study of perception and dissent study; second, to state the salient principles, concepts, and relationships underlying this framework; finally, to make the framework culturally specific and to provide essential background for subsequent case studies, a brief sketch of the history of official conceptions of internal adversaries and external enemies will supplement the theoretical discussion.

Before undertaking these tasks, a few disclaimers are in order. First, the provisional nature of the framework should be emphasized: it is intended only to orient discussion and suggest some general hypotheses. The framework's value should be judged by its ability to permit a more rigorous conceptualization of the factors affecting Soviet perception of dissent and nonconformity and to generate new data relevant to the analysis of Soviet perception of internal adversaries. Second, because the topic of Soviet images of dissidents and nonconformists is related to some of the traditional questions studied by students of psychology, sociology, and international politics, there is an abundance of theory and empirical research that is at least indirectly pertinent to the general questions raised in this image study. To survey the nature and substantive conclusions of this vast and growing body of literature in any detail would be impractical and far beyond the scope of this book. Instead, this chapter draws on the most relevant works for its key principles, concepts, and relationships. However, inasmuch as the general utility of the image approach to conflict study is not appreciated by students of Soviet dissent, a brief overview is appropriate. Two major currents of writing are relevant. The first of these and the more general is theory and research in psychology, international politics, and various other disciplines that take up the problem of the image. The second and older current is the literature on stereo-typing in psychology, sociology, and political science.

THE EMERGENCE OF IMAGE STUDY[1]

Although the use of the concept of the image as an organizing device to explain man-environment relationships may be traced back to Plato, image study fully emerged within the social sciences only during the 1950s.[2] During that decade, noted scholars such as Kenneth Boulding and Herbert Simon argued cogently that the mental image, defined as a person's simplified model of his environment, is a key variable affecting all human behavior.[3] They and other scholars argued that the explanation of a vast range of phenomena could be enhanced significantly by a consideration of the process through which man sees his environment.

The result of these pioneering and truly multidisciplinary efforts was no less than an "image revolution." Despite the often considerable methodological and data problems, interest in the image as an organizing concept for explaining regularities in human behavior has grown steadily, thus providing telling evidence of the approach's broad utility and considerable promise. Since the 1950s, scholars from a variety of disciplines, including geography and the field of criminology, have turned to image study in their search for a theory to better explain man-environment relationships.[4] This has led to a refocusing of interests, both in terms of the questions asked and the methods devised. It has opened a new range of questions on how people interpret and make sense of their environment and on how they organize and store information about environmental situations. In terms of methods devised, image study has provided a more empirical approach to the study of learned behavior—an approach which focuses on articulated content.

THE STEREOTYPING LITERATURE

An important precursor of the image revolution in the social sciences, and a closely related current of continuing research, is the considerable theoretical and empirical work on stereotypes, defined here simply as rigid images unresponsive to corrective evidence. This vast body of writing may be traced back to Walter Lippmann's influential book *Public Opinion*, published in 1922.[5] In that study, Lippmann introduced the concept of stereotypes and ably demonstrated its usefulness as an organizing device for discussions of the dynamics of human perception and action. Specifically, he noted the cultural roots of stereotypes and emphasized their resistance to change. Since 1922, much meaningful research into stereotypes has been undertaken. As a result, a great deal has been learned about the ways in which stereotypes are learned, their relationship to attitudes, and their importance as determinants of behavior. Writing nearly a half century after the publication of Lippmann's landmark study, John Brigham, an American psychologist, summarized the broad utility and considerable potential of the stereotype concept for research into, and analysis of, group conflict. After a comprehensive survey of the relevant literature, Brigham noted that stereotype is "one of the terms most frequently employed in research and theorizing concerning ethnic attitudes, prejudice, and intergroup perception and conflict"; in addition, he pointed out the enduring appeal of the concept, despite important methodological and data problems.[6]

IMPLICATIONS OF IMAGE STUDY AND STEREOTYPING LITERATURE FOR CONFLICT STUDY

The implications of these two closely related currents of scholarly literature for conflict study have been significant. By focusing more rigorously on man-environment relationships, image study, including stereotyping research, has provided a more humanistically oriented alternative to mechanistic approaches to conflict study, which too frequently ignore perception and emotion, seeing them as subjective and inaccessible to observation and, consequently, too complex and problematic to research. Rather than merely assume the social and psychological determinants of behavior, practitioners of image study have investigated the influence of images on perception and action. They have studied the formation, maintenance, and transformation of images of environmental situations in order to better understand the origins and dynamics of historically rooted and deeply emotional conflicts. From this more empirical understanding of how information is processed and knowledge is acquired, a more solid basis has been provided for assessing the prospects for conflict promotion and resolution.

IMAGE STUDY AND SOVIET STUDIES

What has been the impact of the so-called image revolution and related developments in the social sciences on Western analysis of

Soviet behavior? Generally speaking, the impact has been very limited. Discouraged by the failure of the psycho-cultural theories of the early 1950s to provide general explanations or keys to Soviet behavior, the reactions of many students of Soviet affairs to any news of psychologically oriented political theories range from deep skepticism to veiled hostility.[7] Despite this general state of affairs, the more general empirical work in psychology and the behavioral revolution in political science have had an important and enduring influence on at least one aspect of Soviet studies, the study of Soviet foreign policy. During the late 1960s and the early 1970s, students of Soviet affairs, many with interdisciplinary research interests and backgrounds, called on their colleagues to use the insights of general theory and empirical research on perception, motivation, and action to develop more sophisticated conceptualizations of the social and psychological determinants of Soviet behavior.[8]

Such a concern has not been evident in the field of dissent study, where there has been a conspicuous failure to account for the influence official images exert on official perception and action. Traditional research and analysis on contemporary Soviet dissent rarely have discussed this vital relationship; when they have done so, it has been in isolation from the general theory and research in psychology and international politics. Most writers, in fact, have viewed the relationship between these images and official action as a problem peculiar to Soviet studies. As a result, these images generally have been neglected or misunderstood. Typically, they have been viewed simply as crude propaganda symbols cleverly manipulated by the authorities to justify extreme coercion and authoritarian rule. The fact that these official images serve important political functions is undeniable and has been the subject of considerable discussion. However, little attention has been focused on the effects of these images on official perception and action. Most Western students of Soviet dissent have relied on the concept of ideology, although not exclusively, to explain Soviet views of, and actions toward, dissidents and nonconformists. It should be stated that the concept of ideology, defined commonly as Marxist-Leninist doctrine-on-paper or as a system of primary political beliefs, is important and indispensable for general discussion of Soviet perception and motivation. Unfortunately, the concept of ideology, as it is commonly used, too frequently simplifies and confuses the relationship between perception, belief system, and action and therefore is of limited use in explaining why Soviet authorities behave as they do.[9]

The omission of image study from analyses of Soviet perceptions of dissidents and nonconformists is both significant and curious. It is significant because psychological theory and research predicts that the images decision makers hold of phenomena are important motivating factors and not simply rationalizations of behavior. The omission is curious because the contemporary conflict between Soviet authorities and their internal adversaries, a historically rooted and emotionally charged group conflict involving ethnic tensions, discrimination, prejudice, and chauvinism, has much in common with other conflicts where image study has proven a useful approach generating new data and different kinds of explanations. By employing the image concept as an organizing device, this study seeks to move discussion of Soviet perception of dissidents and nonconformists beyond the current level of generality to an investigation of the dynamics and mechanisms of the official belief system.

KEY PRINCIPLES[10]

The principles which follow are derived from the substantive conclusions of the literature on the concept of the image. It should be emphasized that they are based solely on the results of psychological and historical research and not on an analysis of the conflict between Soviet authorities and their internal adversaries. Although many of these principles or generalizations may seem obvious, it is appropriate that they be stated explicitly, as they underpin the conceptual framework and the analysis which follow. In addition, they have not been integrated adequately into analyses of Soviet perception of dissent and nonconformity. These principles may be usefully considered under three headings: perception, images, and stereotypes.[11]

Perception

1. Perception, defined as the process by which persons see the world around them, is active rather than passive: each person

constructs his version of reality based on information provided by the senses.

2. How this sensory information is processed is strongly influenced by an individual's education, experience, cultural values, and role requirement, as well as the limitations of cognitive processes and the nature of the information received.

3. Perception is always selective and thus a distortion of the actual state of a person's physical and social environment.

4. Conflicts involving many interests, factors (historical, political, economic, or social), and value positions are likely to be perceived differently.

5. The perception of any act is determined both by the individual's perception of the act itself and by his perception of the context in which it occurs.

6. A person's decisions and behavior are determined largely by the way he perceives a particular issue or situation; thus, in choosing courses of action, persons respond more to their perceptions of reality than to the actual state of their environment.

7. Insecurities, fears, and anxieties tend to impair accurate perception and threat assessment.

Images

1. Every experience takes place within a vast background of cultural images; culture is a composite of images.

2. Images are learned and stable conceptions or mental models of environmental situations, which serve designative, appraisive, and prescriptive functions; they both summarize an individual's environmental knowledge and evaluations and predispose his behavior.[12]

3. Every decision maker possesses a set of images which filter perceptions of phenomena; these images condition perceptions, define environmental situations, and orient decision making.

4. An image is a mixture of fact and value, a product of the past, present, and future; values are its backbone and each of its components is emotion-laden.[13]

5. New information is assimilated to accord with existing images; hence, images change only slowly and often are maintained despite contradictory information.

6. A person's images of self and society and the tenacity with which they are held are often strongly influenced by the need to conform to the images of others, especially fellow group members.

7. Unexamined images become rigid stereotypes.

Stereotypes

1. Stereotypes, defined as rigid images or inadequate generalizations unresponsive to corrective evidence, are derived from the common habit of quick generalization from inadequate information.

2. Stereotypes enter into nearly all human thinking in one way or another and are applied to many persons with whom there is no daily, close contact.

3. Stereotypes are a distortion which may reflect what one group wants to believe about another group in order to justify its own traditional and privileged position in society.

4. Dependence on stereotypes prevents the development of the habit of constantly reexamining one's generalizations.

5. Stereotypes, although essentially distorting and misleading, generally contain some element of truth; consequently, they carry a measure of conviction because there is something definitely recognizable in them. They should not be considered as lying in the sense of deliberate falsehood.

6. Stereotypes acquired during childhood often are so deeply ingrained that most individuals are not conscious of how or when they were first learned.

7. A high degree of group cohesion and insulation obstructs critical thought and promotes stereotypic thinking.[14]

8. Even well-educated, sensitive individuals are not immune to stereotypic views and prejudices, although they are less susceptible.

CONCEPTS AND RELATIONSHIPS

A Systems Model

At this preliminary stage, a systems model will be employed to facilitate the discussion of some factors and relationships which typically are neglected or confused in dissent study.[15] Central to this model is the view that Soviet policy toward dissidents and nonconformists may be usefully considered as a system, or more precisely as a subsystem of the domestic policy system. Like all systems of action, it consists of an environment or setting, a group of actors, structures through which decision makers initiate decisions and respond to challenges, processes which sustain or alter the flow of demands, and products of the system as a whole.[16]

Within this system, two dimensions can be distinguished: the operational and the psychological parts of the decision-making environment. Most research and analysis on contemporary Soviet dissent has focused on the operational parts of the environment. These are the concrete and observable factors in the dissent conflict and include the activities of dissidents and nonconformists and Soviet policy toward them. Much less scholarly attention, however, has been paid to the psychological dimension of the conflict, that is, the worldview of Soviet officials and, in particular, their perceptions and beliefs regarding dissidents and nonconformists. This dimension is particularly important in dissent study because decision makers act according to their images of the operational environment, and these images may or may not correspond to the actual state of the environment.

Operational Environment

The operational environment is the setting for the day-to-day conflict between Soviet authorities and their internal adversaries. Within this physical and social environment, three major sets of actors may be highlighted: dissidents and nonconformists, the authorities, and foreigners. For the purposes of this book, the category *dissidents and nonconformists* will include intellectual dissidents and religious nonconformists. In future research, it may be expanded to include national, workers', disabled persons', and other types of dissent. *Authorities* will denote central and local officials as well as vigilante groups which actively support the implementation of official policy. Finally, *foreigners* will refer to non-Soviet officials, journalists, and private citizens (including tourists) living in or outside of the USSR who have either direct or indirect contact with dissidents or nonconformists, or who actively support their struggle without any contact. Also included in this group are

Soviet emigrés (individuals and groups) and those working at radio stations broadcasting to the USSR.

Communication

Objects and events within the operational environment provide the raw data for any dissent study and are of obvious importance. However, in the study of Soviet perception of internal adversaries, the operational environment has a limited and specific significance which needs to be defined. Although activity within this setting exists independently of its perception by Soviet authorities, it can influence central decision makers only to the extent that information about this environment is communicated to them.[17]

Information about aspects of the operational environment, for example, the intentions and activities of dissidents and their interaction with foreigners, may be transmitted to the decision-making elite in a variety of ways. In addition to the official media and to confidential sources, information may be obtained and transmitted from direct observation of the operational environment and from the monitoring of *samizdat* publications and the Western official and unofficial media. The impact of information gathered in such a fashion on collectors, local analysts, and local and central decision makers is, ultimately, a function of the degree to which the structure of a political system and, in particular, the official belief system are "open" or "closed."[18] Psychological theory predicts that in closed systems, such as in the Soviet Union, there is a greater likelihood that new information which contradicts fundamental and officially held views will be ignored or distorted, instead of being transmitted to the decision-making elite.[19] Consequently, in the analysis of any policy issue and in conflict study in particular, it is necessary to consider the communication network within the political system, specifically, "to assess the adequacy, accuracy, degree of completeness, and objectivity of the flow of information about the operational environment" to the decision-making elite.[20]

Psychological Environment

The crucial dimension of this analytic framework is the psychological environment of Soviet authorities and of the central decision makers in particular.[21] Psychological environment may be defined generally as "the sum total of all the perceptual and conceptual data which at any given moment are operative in directing the behavior of an individual or of a group."[22] It is in this setting that the information collected about activity within the operational environment is classified, categorized, differentiated, assigned meaning, and stored in the form of mental models. Alexander George has described the psychological environment "as a prism that influences the political actor's perceptions and diagnoses of the flow of political events, his definitions and estimates of particular situations" and that provides "norms, standards, and guidelines that influence the actor's choice of strategy and tactics, his structuring and weighing of alternative courses of action."[23]

Within this prism, images held by the elite are the key variables for explaining regularities in perception and for understanding and anticipating any fundamental shift in the Soviet official orientation toward dissidents and nonconformists. Every decision maker's psychological environment or prism is composed of a set of images of the past, present, and future that order for him what would otherwise be an unmanageable amount of information.[24] Particularly important in a political actor's belief system, they provide the crucial link between the operational environment and an individual's definition of environmental situations. Kenneth Boulding has summarized the vital intervening role of the image between incoming and outgoing information as follows: "The outgoing messages are the result of the image, not the result of the incoming messages. The incoming messages only modify the outgoing messages as they succeed in modifying the image."[25]

Although the specific sources of images are many and diverse, three attitudinal factors, positioned within a belief system, deserve special attention: (1) historical legacy (for example, historical experience; the conscious or unconscious fears, insecurities, and anxieties of individuals and groups; their action tendencies, and so on, (2) ideology (in the sense of doctrinal propositions and stereotypes), and (3) the personality predispositions of the decision-making elite.[26] These factors are active in a close and dynamic relationship with prevailing elite images; each exerts a potentially significant influence on the formation of new images, but no factor unilaterally determines an image. The resulting image thus is always a sum of the dynamic interaction of history, ideology, and personality;

images are modified to take account of historical experiences, the idiosyncrasies of key personalities, and changes in ideology.

While it is useful to distinguish the actual images from this closely related cluster of attitudinal factors in order to illustrate the complexity of a decision maker's psychological environment, it should be made clear that such a distinction becomes artificial in light of the frequently reciprocal and reinforcing relationship between these factors. The relationship between images held by the elite and Soviet ideology illustrates this point. Generally speaking, there are many issues where elite images and the principles of official doctrine overlap and are mutually reinforcing. In such cases, doctrinal propositions perform an important cognitive function by entering into basic thought processes and by becoming part of a mental image. However, where such overlapping and reinforcement is lacking, the doctrine will likely remain an abstract set of principles inactive within the belief system and having no formative influence on new images.[27] Thus, to describe a decision maker's belief system and its component images simply as an ideological prism is to greatly exaggerate the influence of ideology on image formation and to grossly oversimplify the complexity of human perception and motivation. A person's belief system fundamentally is a cultural prism, composed of a set of cultural images. The crucial fact for this framework is that these images are always a mixture of fact and value and a product of the past, present, and future.

Finally, despite the vital role of these images in shaping decision makers' orientations to specific issues, the influence of elite images, and the belief system in general, on behavior is limited and should be recognized as such. According to Alexander George, "A belief system influences but does not unilaterally determine, decision-making: it is an important, but not the only, variable that shapes decision-making behavior."[28]

HISTORICAL OVERVIEW

History in psychological terms, is the memory of nations. It is the repository not only of objective events, but also of illusions and misunderstandings that filter down to our lives.[29]

In order to understand the content and appeal of contemporary Soviet images of internal adversaries, it is necessary to appreciate the images' historical antecedents and development. Contemporary images of dissidents and nonconformists, after all, are not born overnight; nor are they formed simply in reaction to the activities of a particular dissident. They are predisposed by earlier official conceptions of internal as well as external adversaries. As Kenneth Boulding has noted: "The image is built up as a result of all past experience of the possessor. Part of the image is the history of the image itself."[30]

Historical Legacy

Soviet perception of internal adversaries, and threat perception in general, has been significantly influenced by historical memory.[31] Particularly important in this regard is the legend of the Soviet Union and historic Russia as a state under constant siege: the story of a proud people struggling valiantly against dangerous and often vastly stronger external and internal enemies. This widely shared and officially encouraged legend or myth is an essential part of Soviet culture and may be viewed broadly as an official image of the Soviet Union's past, present, and future. As such, it conditions official perceptions of opponents and constitutes the essential background for any effort to understand Soviet perception of internal adversaries.

Soviet images of internal and external adversaries, both past and present, are vital elements of this legend or broader image and are influenced by a legacy of insecurity, inferiority, and fear that has confronted officials since the formative years of the Soviet state.[32] This is a tradition rooted firmly in memories of historic Russia, in the Mongol invasions of the thirteenth century and the three-hundred-year Tatar occupation, the wars with Poland and Sweden, the Napoleonic invasion, and the Russo-Japanese war. It is a memory reinforced by the turbulent years of the Russian revolution, the Civil War and the Allied intervention, and the Nazi assault, a period when Soviet rulers operated from a perception of encirclement, diplomatic isolation, and substantial inferiority.

Despite the Soviet Union's subsequent rise to superpower status and the regime's ability to rely on a highly integrated military and industrial structure, this legacy of insecurity and deep-seated suspicion persists. It has been reinforced by many factors: the armed resistance of nationalist groups in the Soviet Union following World War II, the Cold War, a deep fear of a reunited Germany, the continuing Sino-Soviet dispute and the normalization of diplomatic relations between China and the United States, the Polish crisis and Western support for East European dissidents, the growth of organized dissent and nonconformity in the Soviet Union, and the intense ideological campaign started under President Carter and continued in a different form under President Reagan. This official insecurity and the Soviet drive for territorial, military, political, and economic security reflect traditional fears of encirclement, foreign interference, and invasion, as well as the problems of an overextended economy and an official mistrust of the Soviet people. In sum, it reflects the Soviet Union's peculiar conception of security. For the historical and psychological reasons noted, Soviet leaders are unwilling to settle for anything less than reliable protection against all foreign and domestic challenges. Within this broader context, the history of Soviet official images of internal adversaries will now be sketched.

History of Contemporary Images

The roots of contemporary official images of dissidents and nonconformists run deeper than the Marxist-Leninist notion that all opposition to the state is potentially threatening and dangerous. An official aversion to any challenge to authority can be found in pre-revolutionary Russia, particularly during the nineteenth century.[33] During that period, no legal means existed for alienated intellectuals and nationalist groups to peacefully protest against perceived injustice. Outwardly monolithic, but internally rigid, narrow-minded, and at times paranoid, tsarist regimes made little distinction between peaceful protest and violent revolutionary activity: both were brutally repressed. This view was reflected in an essentially undifferentiated image of all protestors, who were viewed as "Dostoevskian" or half-mad or described as heretics and subversives.[34]

The Soviet official image of political opposition and deviation developed during the formative years of the Soviet state. Amidst the turbulence of the postrevolutionary years—wars, revolutions, famines, revolts, and an occupation—Lenin set precedents that legitimated the suppression of political opposition and deviation and quickly transformed the Communist regime into a one-party dictatorship. Faced with raging factionalism and domestic violence, Lenin eventually came to view all opposition as counterrevolutionary and as an intolerable threat to the stability and integrity of the system. The Tenth Party Congress in 1921, and Lenin's famous resolution "On Party Unity" in particular, were crucial in formulating this official conception and in providing a doctrinal basis for Stalin's reign of terror.[35] As for external adversaries, a similarly rigid and hostile conception of external opponents, reinforced by the Allied intervention, increasingly prevailed in Soviet society. The Bolsheviks perceived their capitalist opponent as "thoroughly hostile at bottom, whatever facade he might display, and possessed of great shrewdness and determination to annihilate his class opponent."[36]

Under Stalin, Lenin's conceptions were carried to their extreme conclusion. Stalin expanded the "enemy" concept to include any regime critic, real or imagined. By automatically fixing the intent of any critic as hostile, the concept of the enemy, as formulated by Stalin, provided a convenient labeling device which eliminated the possibility of a dialogue or an ideological fight. In addition to Lenin's influence, this image was shaped significantly by Stalin's own personality—his paranoiac suspicion, fear of rivals, and insistence on single-handedly wielding all power. Such an environment nurtured an official image of all regime critics as traitors and enemies of the Soviet people. This internal enemy was supplemented by a similarly hostile image of external opponents. Stalin's fears of encirclement led to Soviet exaggeration of external threats and provided him with a permanent justification for repressive political and economic policies.[37]

Under Khrushchev, the problem of intellectual deviation resurfaced, following a policy of concessions and a relaxation of tensions at home and abroad. Significantly, the concept of the enemy was redefined and applied more selectively. Nevertheless, it survived. Indeed, with the revival of religious activity and the emergence of intellectual dissent, official images of dissidents and nonconformists as enemies of the state, traitors, and anti-Soviet persons again became common.

CHAPTER SUMMARY

This chapter has examined some variables which psychological theory, in particular, suggests are relevant in the relationship between perception, belief systems, and action, but which have been absent from previous discussions of Soviet perception of dissidents and nonconformists. It has supplemented this theoretical discussion with an historical overview of Soviet conceptions of internal and external adversaries in an effort to provide an essential background for the analysis of contemporary images and to demonstrate how certain historical events, personality factors, and doctrinal propositions have interacted to form and develop official images of opponents.

The next chapter describes this work's research design. Among the topics discussed are data reliability and validity, operational definitions, the case-study approach, measures of official images, and research questions.

NOTES

1. The discussion which follows on the emergence of image study within the social sciences draws heavily on the useful summary of the subject in Douglas Pocock and Ray Hudson, *Images of the Urban Environment* (New York: Columbia University Press, 1978), pp. 3-9.

2. Reference is made here to Plato's "Allegory of the Cave," found in the seventh book of his *Republic*, as cited by John G. Stoessinger, *Nations in Darkness* (New York: Random House, 1971), p. 3.

3. Kenneth E. Boulding, *The Image* (Ann Arbor: University of Michigan Press, 1956); and Herbert A. Simon, *Models of Man: Social and Rational* (New York: Wiley, 1957). For an updated review of relevant research, see Herbert A. Simon, "The Behavioral and Social Sciences," *Science*, July 4, 1980, pp. 72-78.

4. Two works which perceptively discuss and illustrate image research in geography and criminology are Pocock and Hudson; and Richard L. Henshel and Robert A. Silverman, ed., *Perception in Criminology* (New York: Columbia University Press, 1975). In the latter, see, especially, Ch. 3, "Deviance, Deterence, and Knowledge of Sanctions," and Ch. 8, "Perceptions of Punishment: Current Research."

5. Walter Lippmann, *Public Opinion* (New York: Harcourt, Brace, 1922).

6. John C. Brigham, "Ethnic Stereotypes," *Psychological Bulletin* 76 (1971):15. Simple recitation of the substantive results of the research on stereotyping can serve little purpose here. In addition to Brigham's comprehensive review of the literature, interested readers are directed to the works cited in his extensive bibliography.

7. For a summary of these psycho-cultural theories, see John S. Reshetar, Jr., *The Soviet Polity* (New York: Dodd, Mead, 1974), pp. 48-55. For a searing critique of perceptual approaches to the study of Soviet behavior, see Walter Laqueur, "What We Know about the Soviet Union," *Commentary*, February 1983, p. 13. A classic rejoinder to many of the standard criticisms of psychologically oriented approaches to Soviet studies may be found in Alexander George, "The Operational Code: A Neglected Approach to the Study of Political Leaders and Decision-Making," *International Studies Quarterly* 13 (June 1969):190-222.

8. See, especially, Jan Triska and David Finley, *Soviet Foreign Policy* (Toronto: Collier-Macmillan, 1968); and Erik Hoffmann and Frederic J. Fleron, Jr., eds., *The Conduct of Soviet Foreign Policy* (New York: Aldine-Atherton, 1971). More recent contributions usefully employing image as an organizing concept in the context of Soviet foreign policy are few. Notable are Franklyn Griffiths, "Ideological Development and Foreign Policy," in Seweryn Bialer, ed., *The Domestic Context of Soviet Foreign Policy* (Boulder, Colo.: Westview Press, 1981), pp. 19-48; and Karen Dawisha, "The Soviet Union and Czechoslovakia, 1968," in *Studies in Crisis Behavior*, ed. Michael Brecher (New Brunswick: Transaction Books, 1978), pp. 143-71. Griffiths examines Soviet ideological development and foreign policy in terms of four official images: the Communist Party's self-image, its image of its adversaries, the international situation, and its foreign policy. Karen Dawisha, on the other hand, focuses on Soviet official images relating to the 1968 invasion of Czechoslovakia; the general purpose of her case study is to illuminate crisis-decision-making by examining the interaction between decision makers' images and various external and internal influences.

9. For a valuable discussion of the importance and shortcomings of the concept of ideology as applied to analyses of Soviet motivation and political behavior, see Rita Kelly and Frederic Fleron, Jr., "Motivation, Methodology, and Communist Ideology," in *The Behavioral Revolution and Communist Studies*, ed. Roger Kanet (New York: Free Press, 1971), pp. 53-57. For a more general review of the concept's utility, see Lorand Szalay, Rita Kelly, and Won Moon, "Ideology: Its Meaning and Measurement," *Comparative Political Studies* 5 (July 1972):151-73.

10. The conceptual framework which follows synthesizes and adapts to the context of dissent study much of the important theoretical work found in Ole Holsti, "Cognitive Dynamics and Images of the Enemy," in *Image and Reality in World Politics*, ed. John Farrell and Asa Smith (New York: Columbia University Press, 1967), pp. 16-39; Michael Brecher, Blema Steinberg, and Janice Stein, "A Framework for Research on Foreign Policy Behavior," *Journal of Conflict Resolution* 13 (1969):75-101; and John Brigham, pp. 15-38.

11. Most of these principles are axioms of psychology and sociology; many are discussed at length in Boulding.

12. Pocock and Hudson, p. 3.

13. Boulding, pp. 6-18.

14. For a discussion of this point and other research on group dynamics and decision making, see Irving Janis, *Victims of Groupthink* (Boston: Houghton Mifflin Co., 1972); see, also, Irving Janis and Leon Mann, *Decision Making* (New York: Free Press, 1977).

15. The model which follows is a simplification and adaptation to the context of dissent study of the systems model developed by Brecher et al., for the study of foreign policy decision making. The components of the reconstructed model are illustrated in Appendix A in this study.

16. Brecher et al., p. 79.

17. Ibid., p. 79.

18. Milton Rokeach, *The Open and Closed Mind* (New York: Basic Books, 1960), p. 50.

19. Leon Festinger, *A Theory of Cognitive Dissonance* (Stanford: Stanford University Press, 1957). For an insightful discussion of Festinger's theory in the context of international politics, see Robert Jervis, *Perception and Misperception in International Politics* (Princeton: Princeton University Press, 1976), pp. 382-406.

20. Brecher et al., p. 85.

21. The concept of psychological environment will be used synonymously with a decision maker's belief system, psychological framework, and psychological prism; this is in accord with contemporary usage in psychology. Psychological environment, however, will not be used interchangeably with the concept of ideology. The latter, even when defined broadly, denotes much less than the total belief system; more discussion of this point will follow.

22. Philip Harriman, *Handbook of Psychological Terms* (Totowa, N.J.: Littlefield, Adams, 1968), p. 154.

23. George, p. 191.

24. Holsti, p. 18.

25. Boulding, p. 28.

26. Brecher et al., p. 80.

27. This practice has been termed the "selective acceptance of doctrine" by Darrell Hammer, *USSR: The Politics of Oligarchy* (Hinsdale, Ill.: Dryden Press, 1974), p. 98.

28. George, p. 191.

29. Stoessinger, p. 9.

30. Boulding, p. 6.

31. For an insightful discussion of historical memory in the Soviet context, see Boris Shragin, *The Challenge of the Spirit* (New York: Alfred Knopf, 1978), pp. 14-42.

32. See Vladimir Solovyov and Elena Klepikova, "Inside the Kremlin," *Partisan Review* 48 (1981):203-16.

33. This orientation could be traced back farther, but this will not be undertaken here. Interested readers should see Paul Avrich, *Russian Rebels, 1600-1800* (New York: W.W. Norton & Co., 1972).

34. Marshall S. Shatz, *Soviet Dissent in Historical Perspective* (Cambridge: Cambridge University Press, 1980), pp. 12-63. A more detailed discussion of tsarist images of Russian intellectuals follows in Ch. 6, the case of Yury Orlov.

35. For one of the best analyses of this period, see Leonard Schapiro, *The Origins of Communist Autocracy: Political Opposition in the Soviet State, First Phase, 1917-1922* (Cambridge: Harvard University Press, 1955).

36. George, p. 202.

37. R. Barry Farrell, "The Open-Closed Polity Dichotomy," in *Approaches to Comparative and International Politics* ed. R.B. Barrell, (Evanston, Northwestern University Press, 1966), p. 185.

4

A Research Design

Inaccessibility of data is a frustrating problem, but it is a pragmatic, technical problem. It is not a legitimate excuse for lowering standards for evaluation of empirical research. Further, absence of available data on relevant variables does not make those variables any less relevant; it merely means that we ought to be more cautious in our conclusions.[1]

Research into Soviet perception of internal adversaries encounters a number of formidable problems. The general purpose of this chapter is to examine the principal data and methodological problems encountered in such research and to design a strategy to minimize them. The discussion will be organized around four major topics: relevant data, available data, method of analysis, and procedure.

RELEVANT DATA

The study of a political actor's images of internal adversaries and of his assumptions about the nature of the dissent conflict involves difficult problems of data collection. This is because an actor's psychological environment—and, specifically, his sensory, cognitive, and evaluative processes—is internal and cannot be observed directly. It must be inferred, from some aspect of observable behavior such as overt verbal behavior.

In the case of the Soviet Union, such research is made more difficult by official secrecy and by the state's manipulation of the mass media. Data important for an image study, such as the records of official debates, open-ended interviews with authoritative officials, and political memoirs, are virtually unavailable to Western researchers, and there is little likelihood of any fundamental change in this situation in the forseeable future. Unfortunately, without such types of data, it is almost impossible to draw firm conclusions about Soviet perceptions of, and motivation toward, dissidents and nonconformists. Given this situation, it is important to ask: Does it really make sense to study official images of dissidents and nonconformists?

AVAILABLE DATA

The difficulty of obtaining reliable and valid measures of Soviet official images of internal adversaries should not be underestimated. Little research has been done in this area, and the available data are extremely patchy and uneven. Such a situation makes the investigation of Soviet perception frustrating and the conclusions one can draw necessarily tenuous. It does not, however, make the study of official images any less urgent.

Despite these limitations, a sufficient amount of reliable data is available to present a reasonably accurate picture of both Soviet perceptions of dissidents and nonconformists and their actual activities and to allow us to draw some tentative conclusions about Soviet perceptions of internal threat. In fact, since the political trials of prominent dissidents during the 1960s, the volume of *samizdat* reaching the West has grown steadily, reflecting not only the development of new types of contemporary dissent and nonconformity, but also improvements in *samizdat* channels (foreign visitors, journalists, emigré groups) for sending information and documents abroad.[2] The data base now includes several virtually verbatim *samizdat* transcripts of the closed political trials of various dissidents and nonconformists, as well as a significant increase in official commentary—both specific and general—on specific cases and on related issues.

Items of Available Data

The primary data for this volume are derived from two sources: (1) *samizdat* documents, periodicals, and books, and (2) Soviet official commentary (newspapers, journals, and books). This documentation will be supplemented by information gleaned from secondary sources such as Western newspapers, journals, and books. Particularly important primary sources of data for this image study are the *samizdat* transcripts of the political trials of Soviet dissidents and nonconformists. Unlike official commentary on a particular case of dissent or nonconformity, these are highly confidential records of official proceedings which have been compiled by other dissidents or sympathizers at great personal risk. Despite official statements to the contrary, political trials in the Soviet Union are closed trials. Only representatives of the security organs, their invited guests, and the immediate relatives of the accused, as a rule, are permitted in the courtroom. In addition, every effort is made by the authorities to prevent members of this carefully screened audience from recording any of the proceedings. Despite these constraints, the proceedings of many political trials have been secretly recorded. Since the mid-1960s, numerous detailed trial transcripts have been recorded unofficially and transmitted subsequently to the West through *samizdat* channels. These documents have been supplemented by hundreds of considerably shorter and only partial transcripts or summaries of other political trials.[3] Collectively, these transcripts and related *samizdat* documents provide a rare glimpse of official images in action and an important check on the images projected in the official media. It is within the carefully concealed environment of the courtroom that Soviet officials express official conceptions of internal adversaries, sometimes spontaneously and emotionally, but always officially, authoritatively, and with important consequences for the defendant. For analytical purposes, then, this environment may be viewed as a microcosm of the official belief system as it pertains to internal adversaries. Close study of the images expressed officially in this context can provide an important basis for reconstructing salient aspects of the official belief system and will permit at least a rough analysis of the relation of these official images to those Soviet officials who express them, that is, an estimate of the extent to which they are internalized and habitual.

Of all the available Soviet official commentary on cases and issues related to dissent and nonconformity, three items of data are particularly valuable: official commentary in the press on a particular case of dissent or nonconformity, vigilance campaigns in the mass media which focus primarily on general issues closely related to group dissent or nonconformity, and pronouncements made by key Soviet officials during ideological conferences and party congresses; the latter are particularly valuable reflections of official assumptions about the nature of the conflict.[4]

To discover the images used in these official sources, the general strategy will be to identify several authoritative spokesmen in areas such as state security and propaganda and to examine their public pronouncements and writings in publications intended primarily for domestic consumption. The views of such spokesmen, along with those of other authoritative officials, may prove extremely useful as indicators of official images of internal adversaries and official assumptions about the nature of dissent conflict.

Finally, a note on the volume of official commentary available is appropriate. Since the mid-1970s, there has been a significant increase in official commentary on cases and issues related to dissent and nonconformity, and this trend is continuing.[5] This is at least partly a result of the growth of contemporary dissent and non-conformity, the Helsinki process, and heightened Western official and unofficial support for Soviet human rights.

Reliability of Available Data

The *samizdat* documents and periodicals chosen for this work, without exception, have been judged authentic, reliable, and highly accurate sources of data. This is the collective opinion of numerous unofficial Soviet and Western experts on dissent. In the Soviet Union, the verification process begins with the compilers of *samizdat* periodicals and documents. These individuals, many of them working anonymously, carefully check the authenticity and factual accuracy of every piece of information on Soviet violations of human rights that reaches them. After an initial screening of new reports, any inconsistency or gap in reporting is noted and investigated further. Often this requires travel by a representative of a particular *samizdat* periodical to remote locations in the Soviet Union in order to interview the individuals cited in a particular document and obtain the necessary information. When new information has been satisfactorily verified, it is then published in the appropriate *samizdat* periodical; and only then is it transmitted both to key Soviet leaders and persons abroad.[6]

The verification process, however, does not end here. After a *samizdat* document or periodical arrives in the West, the verification process is repeated. This amounts to a thorough double and triple checking of every *samizdat* document by an extensive and closely linked network of Soviet affairs specialists at the Research Department of Radio Liberty in Munich, at Keston College and Amnesty International in Britain, at the U.S. Congressional Commission on Security and Cooperation in Europe in Washington, D.C., and at numerous other Western research institutes and universities.

The result of this painstaking process of data verification is a collection of unofficial periodicals whose reliability has, in many cases, been proven by more than a decade of continuous and highly accurate reporting.[7] Within this vast body of uncensored writing, two periodicals stand out and deserve special attention as sources for this study and for the study of official Soviet perception of internal adversaries in general: the *Chronicle of Current Events* (hereafter, CCE) and *The Chronicle of the Lithuanian Catholic Church* (hereafter, *CLCC*).

The *CCE* was started in 1968; and with the exception of an eighteen-month period of suppression (1973-74), it remains the most authoritative unofficial journal of the Soviet underground.[8] Edited anonymously in Moscow, the *CCE* draws together information on specific human rights issues not only from its own network of sources, but also from all the other major groups campaigning within the Soviet Union. The result is a time-saving catalogue of the voluminous writings of the Soviet underground and a factual record of the continuing conflict between the authorities and dissidents. Each issue contains detailed information on political trials, interrogations, the persecution of ethnic minorities and religious groups, and other *samizdat* publications.

Narrower in focus, but equally reliable as a source of information, is the *CLCC*. It was started in 1972, and its editors have closely modeled it after the *CCE*. In addition to collecting information from its own sources on the situation of religion and nationalism in Soviet Lithuania, the *CLCC* provides another important service. It reviews, critically evaluates, and catalogues information from the more than half-dozen other major Lithuanian unofficial periodicals.[9]

Among the other underground periodicals screened regularly and cited as authentic and reliable sources by the editors of the *CCE* and the *CLCC*, the following specialized *samizdat* publications are important sources of image data for this work and/or future research: *Documents from the Helsinki Groups* (a numbered series of documents issued by the Helsinki Groups in Moscow, Lithuania, and the Ukraine), the *Newsletters of the Christian Committee for the Defense of Believers' Rights*, the *Newsletters of Soviet Adventists*, and the *Bulletin of the Action Group To Defend the Rights of the Disabled in the Soviet Union*.[10] What makes these *samizdat* periodicals impressive and valuable as data sources for the study of official images of internal adversaries is that they are primarily chronicles of factual reportage. Although some of them do contain theoretical articles and editorial comments, these are clearly identified and kept separate from protest documents and other purely factual reporting. Underlying this policy is a firm and explicitly stated determination on the part of the compilers and contributors of the unofficial periodicals to counter official allegations of "slander" with accurate and verifiable information on Soviet violations of human rights. It should be stressed that the compilers of these other *samizdat* periodicals follow a careful procedure of data verification which closely resembles the high standards set by the editors of the *CCE* and the *CLCC*. When a piece of information has not been verified thoroughly in the Soviet Union, this is acknowledged openly; and when mistakes in reporting occur, these are retrospectively drawn to the attention of the readers. Information verified in the Soviet Union and then transmitted abroad is rechecked in a manner strikingly similar to that described for the *CCE* and the *CLCC*. The results of this painstaking process of data verification in the USSR and the West are *samizdat* periodicals of high quality which enjoy considerable prestige among human rights activists in the Soviet Union, as well as among Western experts on Soviet dissent and nonconformity.

Limitations of Available Data

Despite their unique value as a data source, *samizdat* transcripts do have several unavoidable limitations. First, although an increasing number of lengthy and almost verbatim accounts of the political trials of different types of dissidents and nonconformists have become available since the mid-1960s, the vast majority of these trial data, culled from several hundred trials, are incomplete and sometimes fragmentary. In many cases, no more is available than brief summaries of trial proceedings which have been reconstructed from memory by sympathetic observers after leaving the courtroom. Such reporting, while valuable for its description of key developments at a particular trial and for insights into Soviet law, is too sketchy and indirect for the close study of official images of internal adversaries and for a reconstruction of salient aspects of the official belief system.

Second, with the rare exception of a secretly taped trial, some distortion is inevitable even in virtually verbatim, handwritten transcripts. In cases where shortened transcripts are compiled after the proceedings from the notes and memories of one or more observers at a trial, the degree of distortion naturally will be greater. Such limitations are unavoidable and necessarily will continue as long as Soviet authorities strictly prohibit witnesses from recording political trials. It should be emphasized that *samizdat* reporters are acutely aware of this distortion and seek to minimize it. Most of the lengthy transcripts circulating in *samizdat* explicitly state the constraints under which a particular document was compiled and indicate what has been omitted.

Third, in the case of at least one type of dissent, disabled rights activism, trial data are not available because the authorities thus far have deliberately avoided the embarrassing spectacle a trial action could create. Instead, disabled rights activists and their sympathizers have been beaten, harassed, interrogated, expelled from the Soviet Union, and, on several occasions, confined to psychiatric hospitals for their outspokenness. A similar, though less significant, constraint exists with respect to data available on individuals who have organized unofficially to protest the denial of workers' rights. Nevertheless, even in such cases imaginative and pragmatic approaches to data collection can yield results. In the case of disabled rights activists and workers' protest, alternative strategies can be developed to exploit available image data. More stress, for example, can be placed on other types of data such as official interrogations and official press reporting on a particular case, as well as on more general official pronouncements and writings.

In any discussion of the limitations of available data for a study, the crucial question should be: are the available data so inadequate as to make an empirical approach impossible? In this case, the answer is a qualified no. A survey of the relevant *samizdat* documents and Soviet official commentary indicates that the available data are inadequate for a systematic analysis of official images of a large number of cases of different types of dissent and nonconformity. However, the data are sufficient for the examination of the central hypothesis and for detailed observations on aspects of selected cases. Furthermore, if the recent past is any guide, more data will be found to test this volume's tentative conclusions and to make possible a more systematic analysis of official images of internal adversaries in the near future. In sum, the significance of the new range of empirical questions posed by image study about official perception and motivation and the inadequacy of the Western literature on this important dimension of the dissent conflict justify a preliminary study of official images.

METHOD OF ANALYSIS

The methodology for this study avoids excessive quantification of data and complex behavioral jargon. Instead, a case study approach is used to examine instances where official images of internal adversaries had concrete and specific effects on official perception and action. Two case studies, one involving intellectual dissent and another involving religious nonconformity, are presented as illustrations of the basic hypothesis that official perception and policy have been guided by stereotypic images of dissent and nonconformity and that these images have erased the important distinction between mild dissent and actual subversion for the authorities concerned.

Case Study Approach

At this early stage in the study of Soviet official images of internal adversaries, the case study approach seems the most sensitive technique available to investigate the influence of official images in specific situations. Nevertheless, even when carried out with thoroughness and objectivity, case studies have important limitations. Unlike comparative studies or the sampling of many cases through some form of survey research, a case study deals, of course, with a single case or event. The conclusions drawn from the close study of a single Soviet dissident or nonconformist may not be generalizable to all dissidents and nonconformists, although, at the same time, such conclusions need not be relevant only to the case at hand. Even if it is not possible to generalize widely on the basis of a few case studies, they do make it possible to test the central hypothesis and to generate several new empirical hypotheses. Accordingly, the case studies which will follow should be regarded as expository rather than as substantiating evidence at even the lowest level. Empirical support for this work's theory about the influences of images on human perception and action can be found in the large number of systematic psychological and historical investigations underlying the conceptual framework, as well as from efforts at image study which follow.

Procedure

The procedure is to examine a few case studies in order to describe official images of internal adversaries and to assess their degree of correspondence with accurate images. The key to this research design is the relationship between the psychological and operational environments described earlier. This relationship provides a technique for assessing the accuracy of official perceptions of dissidents and nonconformists. Precise measurement of the gap between accurate and inaccurate perception is a very difficult task, and at this preliminary stage of image study only qualitative statements will be offered. More precisely, the procedure is to describe the images of dissidents and nonconformists held by Soviet officials based on unofficial transcripts of political trials, other related *samizdat* documents, and the images expressed in the official media and in major ideological pronouncements and writings; to compare these images with those selected from reliable unofficial Soviet and Western sources; and, finally, to draw some tentative conclusions regarding the sources of these images and their consequences for official orientation and action. Underlying this kind of inquiry is the realization that description of official images and assessment of their degree of correspondence with accurate images provide an empirical basis which is essential if inquiry into Soviet perception of, and motivation toward, internal adversaries is to move closer to levels of explanation and prediction.

Measurement of Principal Concepts

Next we will briefly provide an operational definition of the Soviet political elite and then turn to the problem of operationalizing official and accurate images of internal adversaries. This will be followed by a brief discussion of the validity of the proposed methods.

Soviet Political Elite

In identifying authoritative officials on issues related to dissent and nonconformity, a broad definition of the Soviet political elite seems in order, one which includes central and local officials, such as the security police, judges, and other members of the official legal system. Such a definition is justified because the conflict between Soviet authorities and dissidents is fundamentally a local, low-urgency (in contrast with the many more pressing foreign and domestic problems), domestic conflict, which apparently attracts the attention of key leaders and other central officials only rarely and under exceptional circumstances (such as when a particular dissident enjoys considerable prominence among influential and outspoken groups in the Soviet Union and abroad, or when influential foreign officials and emigré groups campaign actively on the individual's behalf).

Generally speaking, although top Party and government officials constitute the central decision-making elite and provide the local authorities with policy guidance in the form of major ideological statements, it is the local officials (especially the KGB) who shape and articulate official images and who are held responsible for identifying and dealing with dissidents and nonconformists. Whether or not key Soviet leaders accurately perceive dissidents and nonconformists or see only shadowy and exaggerated figures depends heavily not only on their interest in this low-urgency subject, but, more importantly, on the reporting of local officials. These are the individuals who collect and interpret information about issues related to dissent and nonconformity and decide which information to suppress and which to transmit to central officials. From this point of view, local officials are political actors who exert an important influence on the direction of the dissent conflict. Hence, to underestimate their role in this conflict and to overemphasize the interest and participation of central leaders is to misjudge the influence local officials exert on Soviet estimations of threat from internal adversaries.

Charting Official Images

Official conceptions of an individual's character, activity, and intentions will be assessed in select cases of dissent and nonconformity in order to provide a valid measure of official images. This analysis of the content of official images will be supplemented by a more general, but closely related, examination of official assumptions about the nature of the conflict between the authorities and a particular dissident or nonconformist.[11]

Charting Accurate Images

Accurate images, for analytical purposes, will refer to images that closely approximate a dissident's or a nonconformist's actual character, activity, and intentions. In addition, unofficial assumptions—those of selected dissidents and nonconformists—about the nature of the conflict will be examined to provide a counterpoint to the analysis of official assumptions.

The exact sources of accurate images naturally will vary from case to case depending on the available data. But in each instance, accurate images will be derived from reliable unofficial Soviet reporting which has been verified by at least two of the agencies in the West described; that is, the Research Department of Radio Liberty, Keston College, Amnesty International, the U.S. Congressional Commission on Security and Cooperation in Europe, and other research institutes and universities.

Samizdat transcripts will provide an important starting point for building accurate images of dissidents and nonconformists. Particularly useful for such a reconstruction are a defendant's opening and closing remarks during a trial. When checked against factual reporting from other reliable Western and unofficial Soviet sources, these descriptions of an individual's activities can serve as an important source of information on actual activity within the operational environment.

Validity of Methods

The crucial question to pose at this point is whether the proposed methods actually measure the image as it has been specified theoretically. As stated earlier, official images of internal adversaries may or may not correspond closely to the privately held images of officials. But the fact that official images may not reflect what some officials privately believe does not invalidate them as a measure of salient aspects of the official belief system. Even if official images differ strikingly from images subjectively held, they are still representative of a desire, whether voluntary or as a result of coercion, to maintain some degree of unity with prevailing official images.[12] These are the images that form part of the larger political process, and a tendency in the formation and implementation of Soviet policy toward dissidents and nonconformists finds partial expression in such images.[13]

Case Selection

To bring data to bear on the general research questions advanced earlier, case materials have been gathered on Vladimir Shelkov, religious nonconformist, and Dr. Yury Orlov, intellectual dissident.

Case selection was guided by the following major criteria. Individuals were chosen to represent a major dimension of dissent or nonconformity, and a special effort was made to select cases typical of the different groups. A second criterion was loyalty. In each of the cases selected, the subject chosen was essentially a system-supporting, reform-seeking citizen at the time of his initial appeal to or clash with the authorities; in other words, the individual approached the authorities in good faith and, at least initially, was hopeful that reform of some perceived injustice was possible. Neither of the individuals selected either explicitly or implicitly advocated the overthrow of the system at any time.[14] Third, the regime's reaction to each of the individuals chosen, it will be argued, constituted an overreaction. Fourth, the availability of adequate data— sufficiently detailed transcripts and official media commentary— was a crucial criterion in determining who ultimately would be selected to represent a particular type of dissent or nonconformity and which types would be represented. In situations where adequate data existed on several representatives of a particular type of dissent or nonconformity, a less-publicized and more typical case was selected.[15]

Finally, a note on bias in case selection is in order. Although every effort has been made to minimize bias in the selection of the case studies, it should be emphasized that there is no way to eliminate unconscious bias when selecting and summarizing case materials. Accordingly, it is suggested that the case studies which follow be regarded as part of the exposition of this volume's theory, rather than as substantiating evidence at even the lowest level. As research on official images of internal adversaries progresses and as more data develop, more systematic analysis will be possible and will make the empirical base for this work broader.

CHAPTER SUMMARY

Unlike the previous chapter, which was concerned with conceptual problems surrounding image study, this chapter has focused on some major problems of data and methods in the context of Soviet dissent. Despite important limitations in both of these areas, adequate data and methods were found to justify a preliminary assessment of an important, but neglected, dimension in the study of Soviet dissent and nonconformity.

The next chapter will focus on the case of Vladimir Shelkov and the issue of religious nonconformity in order to demonstrate the influence of official images on official perception and action.

NOTES

1. Kelly and Fleron, pp. 55-56.

2. Since the trials of Soviet writers such as Joseph Brodsky (1964) and Andrei Sinyavsky and Yuly Daniel (1966), the incidence of political trials of various types of dissidents and nonconformists has grown significantly. The development continues to be reflected heavily in *samizdat* reporting despite police campaigns against the compilers of these reports.

3. For a lengthy list of political trials in the USSR since the early 1960s, on which at least partial *samizdat* reporting is available, see Appendix B.

4. For a useful and concise guide to the use of Soviet newspapers and periodicals as sources of primary data for the study of Soviet affairs, see Mark W. Hopkins, *Mass Media in the Soviet Union* (New York: Pegasus, 1970), pp. 365-68.

5. In addition to the rise in press commentary, there has been a conspicuous increase in journal articles and books by key Soviet officials, such as Y. Andropov, L. Brezhnev, and K. Chernenko.

6. Any persistent inconsistencies are duly noted and typically reconsidered as more detailed reporting emerges. In the *Chronicle of Current Events*, for example, such information appears in the journal's endnotes and in an appendix entitled, "Addenda and Corrigenda." The discussion of reliability of sources which follows exceeds this study's immediate purposes. It is intended to provide support for suggestions which follow in Ch. 8's section on future research.

7. A summary of *samizdat* periodicals appearing in the West since the early 1960s may be found in Appendix C.

8. Issue No. 63 reached the West during summer 1983, despite an intensive and accelerating official campaign against dissent and nonconformity.

9. For useful background information on *CLCC* and Lithuania's other *samizdat* publications, see Marite Sapiets, "Lithuania's Unofficial Press," *Index on Censorship* 9 (1980):35-38.

10. The *Documents from the Helsinki Groups* have been assembled, translated, and published in several updated versions by the U.S. Helsinki Commission in Washington. Less relevant for this volume, but essential as sources of image data for any case study of an unregistered Baptist in the USSR, are the following *samizdat* periodicals: the *Bulletin of the Council of Relatives of Evangelical Christian Baptist Prisoners* and *The Fraternal Leaflet*. For useful background on the above religious periodicals and, in general, on Christian *samizdat* in the USSR, see Philip Walters, "Christian Samizdat," *Index on Censorship* 9 (August 1980):46-50.

11. These essential measures of the image concept and the official belief system as it pertains to internal adversaries are a synthesis of categories and suggestions found in Stoessinger, pp. 3-6; and George, p. 220.

12. On this point, see the discussion on overt verbal behavior and private attitude (manifest and latent content of messages) in the context of the content analysis of elite statements in P. Terrence Hoppmann, "The Effects of International Conflict and Detente on Cohesion in the Communist System," in Kanet, p. 323.

13. I have borrowed here and adapted the general distinction between "transactional" and "subjective" perceptions made by Franklyn J. Griffiths, "Images, Politics, and Learning in Soviet Behavior toward the United States," (Ph.D. dissertation, Columbia University, 1972), p. 2. In attempting to apply Griffith's useful distinction to the context of Soviet dissent, I have found it necessary to formulate it somewhat differently.

14. It should be noted here that, during the recent history of contemporary Soviet dissent and nonconformity, a small number of dissidents have made extreme demands on the regime, including calls for the secession of various republics from the Soviet Union and even the forceful overthrow of the regime. On this point see, for example, the historical overview of extreme dissent in Soviet Lithuania in Thomas Remeikis, *Opposition to Soviet Rule in Lithuania* (Chicago: Institute of Lithuanian Studies Press, 1980), pp. 19-38.

15. For example, although very good data exist on the political trials of Joseph Brodsky and of Andrei Sinyavsky and Yuly Daniel, these trials have received considerable attention in the scholarly and general literature; therefore, the much less-studied and more recent trial of Yury Orlov has been selected to illustrate intellectual dissent in the USSR.

5

Vladimir Shelkov:
"Religious Extremist and Fanatic"

PURPOSE

The general purpose of this and the following case study is to investigate in detail the influence official images of religious nonconformists and dissidents exert on official perception and action and thereby to test our central hypothesis about Soviet policy toward dissidents and religious nonconformists in the post-Khrushchev period. Particular attention is paid to the way in which hostile images ultimately lead to a blurring of the boundaries between mild dissent and genuine subversion in the minds of the authorities.

RESEARCH QUESTIONS

The common objectives of the following case studies may be cast in the form of research questions, which are intended to organize and guide the data selection and analysis. Are official images of the subject accurate, partially accurate, or false? If false, are the images emotionally charged and stereotypic? Does the predominance of a particular stereotype of a dissident or non-conformist in official pronouncements and informal party opinion serve to reduce or eliminate the significance of certain mitigating facts about an individual or group while letting pass, or even exaggerating the significance of, incriminating information? Are official perceptions of low hostility self-liquidating and perceptions of high hostility self-fulfilling? In each case studied, do the authorities exaggerate—mildly or grossly—an otherwise modest challenge to the regime and, subsequently, effect a self-fulfilling prophecy? In other words, do they, through the use of extreme and occasionally erratic repression, progressively alienate and politicize individuals who, at least initially, are system-supporting and reform-seeking Soviet citizens? Do the authorities drive them to seek out of desperation the support of prominent Soviet human rights activists and Western officials and public opinion? More broadly, do dominant official images prejudice or culturally condition officials to view any dissent or nonconformity as subversive; that is, are the authorities capable of accurately distinguishing between mild nonconformity and radical dissent or do they tend to blur crucial differences? Finally, has a trend toward more perceptive official conceptions of dissidents and nonconformists begun to emerge in recent years, not only in Soviet academic journals, but in the official media and in unofficial *samizdat* transcripts of political trials? If so, how prevalent and authoritative are these images, and have they influenced official action?

The following discussion of the case of Vladimir Shelkov—as well as the case of Yury Orlov—will be organized in five sections: essential background, presentation of the main hypothesis, description of the structure and content of official images, analysis of any discrepancy between official and accurate images, and conclusions. The essential background section is intended to provide accurate images of a particular dissident or nonconformist; in addition, it seeks to demonstrate how previous experience and present knowledge of both parties in the conflict influence their current mutual perceptions and actions. In the Shelkov case, background information on a nonconformist movement—Soviet Adventism—precedes a factual review of the individual's biography.

ESSENTIAL BACKGROUND

Russian History of Soviet Adventism

It is impossible to understand the nature of the conflict between Vladimir Shelkov and the authorities without at least a brief overview of the Russian roots of Soviet Adventism and of the early history of the struggle between Soviet authorities and the Adventists.[1]

The Church of the Seventh-Day Adventists was first formed in 1844 in the United States. In 1866, it was introduced to Russia by a German who was attracted to it in the United States.[2] For the next thirty years, Soviet Adventism remained a tiny movement of less than 7,000 members. Despite its insignificant size and non-violent religious activity, this Christian sect of Western origin was severely persecuted by tsarist rulers who were intolerant of all non-Orthodox religions. For example, many Adventist leaders and their followers who were initially concentrated in the Ukraine, the Baltic provinces, and the Caucasus were deported to Siberia. Ironically, this policy, which was intended to isolate Adventist believers and eventually suppress the movement, instead sowed the seeds for the future growth of Adventism in the USSR.[3]

Teachings of Soviet Adventism

The orientation of Soviet Adventists, both registered and unregistered, toward Soviet authority has always been complex and contradictory. Although the teachings of Seventh-Day Adventists contain millennial hopes and predict an eventual overthrow of the existing world order, they also encourage members to accept their political rulers and to work for the improvement of their social environment.[4] In accord with these beliefs, Soviet Adventist leaders have adopted a worldly and highly realistic orientation which encourages members to enter the mainstream of society, to be progressive and humanitarian, to accept state power as God-given, in short, to live the Ten Commandments. Unfortunately, in the case of the True and Free Adventists and other unregistered Christian sects, their interpretation of faithfulness to several of these Commandments has brought them into conflict with Soviet authorities.

Soviet History of Adventists

After the Russian Revolution, the situation for Soviet Adventists changed dramatically. The tumultuous events surrounding the Revolution led to a more relaxed attitude toward non-Orthodox sects and Adventists in particular. During the next decade, authorities persecuted the Orthodox Church and other symbols of the old regime, while Adventists experienced an interval of relative freedom. However, much of this same period was marked by an increasingly heated debate in Adventist communities over the issue of loyalty to the new regime. In 1924, the debate came to a head. At the fifth All-Union Congress of Seventh-Day Adventists, the church was called on to make explicit its relationship with the new regime. A call for full support for the new government produced a schism between those who fully supported the Bolshevik government and a breakaway faction which refused state control of its activities. The central issues were freedom of conscience and separation of church and state. The defiant group, known as the Church of the Faithful and Free Seventh-Day Adventists of the True Remnant sect, in obedience to the fourth and sixth Commandments, refused combative military service and insisted on keeping Sabbath on Saturday. The latter, in practice, meant a refusal to work or attend school on Saturday, a typical work and school day in the USSR.

Such religious nonconformity prompted early Soviet rulers to pass legislation in 1929 requiring all religious groups to register with the state in order to function legally. The next fifteen years were a time of decline and obscurity for the True Remnant group and other groups as well. Unable to register without compromising their fundamental beliefs, the True Remnant sect was labeled an "anti-Soviet organization" and survived the 1930s and 1940s as an illegal organization subject to mass arrests.

Probably more than any single event, World War II served to exaggerate and reinforce this early image of the Adventists as fugitives, criminals, and anti-Soviets. Overtaken by the speed of the German advance, many Soviet Adventists found themselves behind enemy lines for much of the war. In the eyes of Soviet officials, this amounted to collaboration with the enemy, and Adventists were quickly labeled as "servants of fascism" and later simply as "fascists."[5]

Following the war, the authorities were busy rebuilding the economy, and, consequently, most Soviet Adventists enjoyed a decade relatively free of government interference in their affairs. Notably, this interval of freedom did not extend to leaders of the True Remnant sect: G. Ostwald and P.I. Manzhura, the first leaders of the illegal church, died in Stalin's camps in 1949. Nor was there any sustained improvement in the situation of Adventists following Stalin's death. Instead, the relaxation of antireligious propaganda and the decline in arrests for violations of the laws on religious cults lasted only until Khrushchev consolidated his power, at which time religious repression was stepped up quickly. From 1959 to 1964, unregistered and even officially registered Adventist congregations became a major target in Khrushchev's full-scale campaign against organized religion; many congregations, out of desperation, began to function underground, and there was a religious revival. In 1965, this policy led to another break in the official Adventist movement, with many congregations leaving the official church to merge with the True and Free sect.

After Khrushchev's ouster, religious believers enjoyed a brief respite from the extreme persecution, which lasted until Brezhnev had consolidated his power. Thereafter, extreme, but selective, repression was applied to religious nonconformists in an effort to suppress a vigorous religious revival evident particularly among various Christian sects of Western origin in the Soviet Union. In 1977 and 1978, as part of this policy, the KGB launched a violent country-wide campaign against Adventist communities that led to the arrest of numerous key leaders of the unregistered church.

Profile of Vladimir Shelkov[6]

Vladimir Andreyevich Shelkov was born in 1895 in the village of Bolshaya Viska in the southern Ukraine. Little information is available about his youth and formal education. According to his daughter Dina, his parents were Baptists in tsarist Russia at a time when non-Orthodox believers lived as second-class citizens and were persecuted harshly for their religious activity and even exiled to Siberia.[7] Still, his parents were proud of their faith and made sure that their son received a religious upbringing. Thus, even as a child in the rural Ukraine, Shelkov probably developed a deep religiosity and a strong feeling for nature.

Conversion to Soviet Adventism

Inspired by the apocalyptic prophecies and other writings of Ellen White—the founder of Seventh-Day Adventism—important changes took place in Shelkov's inner life. In 1923, at the age of twenty-eight, he left his Baptist faith behind to become a Bible worker in the Seventh-Day Adventist Church. This occurred during a period when the Orthodox Church was persecuted severely, but other Christian churches which tried to adjust to the new regime went relatively unmolested. Meanwhile, Shelkov's commitment to Adventism continued to grow, and in 1927 he was ordained a pastor.

Beyond this point, the life of Vladimir Shelkov may be described as one of continual persecution by the authorities, punctuated by only short intervals of relative freedom.

A major turning point for Soviet Adventism, and Shelkov in particular, was the fifth All-Union Congress of Seventh-Day Adventists held in 1924, at which Shelkov joined that group of Adventists which refused to accept state control of their religious activities. The dissenting faction subsequently broke away from the original group and formed the True and Free Adventist Church under the leadership of G. Ostvald and P.I. Manzhura. The regime reacted to this and similar tendencies among other religious groups with legal measures. In 1929, officials passed the Laws on Religious Associations (or Cults), which required all religious groups to register with the state, and, in effect, to be approved by the secret police. The Reformist Adventists opposed this legislation and strongly campaigned against state registration between 1929 and 1931. Shelkov was active in this campaign among the Adventists of Tyumen in the Ural mountains.

Soviet authorities responded to such illegal activity with their own campaign. In 1930, for example, Vladimir Shelkov was harassed and fined by local authorities for holding unregistered Adventist services and for proselytizing. Shortly thereafter, in 1931, he was arrested for the first time. Shelkov was charged with anti-Soviet agitation, but received no trial, at least none in the conventional sense of the word. Instead, his guilt and the length of his sentence were determined in a secret session by one of Stalin's notorious *troikas*—three-man tribunals composed of members of the secret police. This body sentenced Shelkov to three years' exile with forced labor in the Urals.

In 1934 Shelkov left his place of confinement a marked man. To Soviet authorities who subsequently would have contact with him, he was a convicted criminal, a leader of an anti-Soviet group. With this stigma attached to him, Shelkov spent the next decade hiding to avoid persecution and almost certain rearrest. During this period, Shelkov reportedly changed his place of residence twelve times; in official eyes he was a fugitive, not having registered with the police as all Soviet citizens are obliged to do within three days of their arrival in a new city. It should be noted that this illegal activity occurred at a time when Stalin was at the height of his power and even members of legally registered churches feared for their own safety.

Shortly after 1936, a major event occurred in the life of Shelkov. He was elected deputy chairman of the All-Union Church of True and Free Seventh-Day Adventists. Although in hiding to avoid persecution and rearrest, he continued his religious activity. In particular, he struggled against state registration of congregations and supported the pacifism of young Adventists and the efforts of parents to raise their children in the Adventist faith.

World War II exacerbated the conflict between the Reformist Adventists and the authorities. The German advance into the Soviet Union resulted in the occupation of territories inhabited by numerous Adventist communities. Prior to this, the church's German origins and the ethnic connection of many of its members with Germany, including Ostwald, had already cast suspicion on the loyalty of Soviet Adventists. The war reinforced official suspicions about the "German or foreign connection" and, no doubt, adversely affected official assessments of the character and intentions of a sect which continued to violate the Law on Religious Associations.

After the war was over, the Soviet army recaptured Pyatigorsk, and Shelkov and other Adventists were arrested. Shelkov eventually was convicted of "anti-Soviet agitation," "inciting dissatisfaction with the system," and "having links with German Adventist centers sympathetic to Fascist Germany."[8] In 1946 Shelkov was sentenced to death by firing squad for his allegedly treacherous activity. However, after he had spent fifty-five days on death row, an appeal was heard and his sentence was commuted to ten years' strict regime labor camp.

It should be noted that at the time of his second arrest, Shelkov was viewed officially not only as a traitor to the Motherland—a Nazi collaborator—but also as a repeat offender, a previously convicted criminal whose unrelenting religious activities had earned him the contempt of local authorities charged with eliminating security risks. These activities among the True and Free Adventists included efforts to establish a wide network of unregistered Adventist congregations all over the Soviet Union and the publication and distribution of a number of religious works.

Shelkov served his sentence in Karaganda, the largest camp complex of the Stalinist era. Significantly, even in one of the most severe labor camps in the Soviet Union and after spending fifty-five days on death row, Shelkov resumed his missionary activities, trying to convert fellow prisoners to the beliefs of Seventh-Day Adventists. While he was still in confinement and not scheduled for release until 1955, another important event occurred. In 1949, Manzhura, the chairman of the True and Free Church, died in a labor camp, and Shelkov was appointed his successor.

In 1954, Shelkov was released from Karaganda six months early, due to a serious illness. Undeterred by his sickness or long confinement, he immediately resumed his previous religious activities and new responsibilities as the church's chairman. During the next three years (1954-57), he settled in Dzhambul, in Kazakhstan, and from there gradually began to consolidate the network of True and Free Adventist congregations that were beginning to revive as religious prisoners were released from the camps following Stalin's death.

Despite failing health and the constant threat of rearrest, Shelkov continued his campaign for the church's independence and, in particular, his opposition to the 1929 Laws on Religious Cults. For this and related activity, Shelkov was arrested for the third time in 1957 for anti-Soviet agitation. Viewed officially, once again, as a recidivist, he was sentenced to ten years in the strict regime labor camps of eastern Siberia, in Vikharevka, Chuna, and Novo-Chunka. Ironically, it was during this period of forced isolation that Shelkov met and spoke extensively with many dissidents (for example, human rights campaigners who openly expressed their disagreement with Soviet policies), individuals who had been labeled as renegades or subversives by the authorities prior to their arrest. These early links, which Shelkov and his associates would later develop, were, thus, unwittingly forged by Soviet officials.

Samizdat Activity

Shelkov seems not only to have influenced imprisoned dissidents, but to have been influenced by them.[9] Determined to continue his struggle for religious freedom and acutely aware of the regime's determination to suppress unregistered believers, Shelkov discussed survival strategies with prominent dissidents. Subsequently, after his 1967 release from confinement, the activities of his sect followed a pattern strikingly similar to that of the human rights movement. His group first began to publish unofficial publications, unsanctioned religious works and other materials disapproved by the authorities; next, it petitioned Soviet officials regarding state-sponsored discrimination against Adventist believers; finally, when all else failed, it appealed abroad for support and publicity to President Carter, to influential West German Adventists, to the signatories of the Helsinki Accords meeting in Madrid in 1977, and to others.

After Shelkov's release from confinement in 1967, most of his energies were absorbed by *samizdat* activity. Under his chairmanship of the All-Union Council of the True and Free Adventist Church, *samizdat* activities were considerably expanded. In 1969, he founded the Adventist publishing house, the "True Witness." This unofficial—and, therefore, unlawful—press published copies of basic religious publications as well as timely and factual reports on official discrimination against Adventist believers by relying on a network of hidden storehouses and committed Adventist believers.

In 1969 the police apprehended Shelkov on a street in Samarkand, in the Uzbek SSR, where he was living with his family. They placed him in a preliminary detention cell; and for the next three days, the KGB carried out an intensive search of Shelkov's home. When the search yielded no incriminating evidence, Shelkov was released, but ordered not to leave Samarkand. At this point, Shelkov decided once again to go into hiding in order to avoid another camp sentence.

The following decade—Shelkov's last interval of freedom—was another period of intense repression of the Reformist Adventists.

As in the past, Shelkov moved from one "safe house" to another to elude KGB investigators and to avoid rearrest. Despite this underground existence, Shelkov managed to find time to refine his thinking and to write prolifically about the conflict between church and state in the USSR. During this period, Shelkov's works for the "True Witness" press included a history of the True and Free Adventists and eight volumes on *The Legal Struggle for Freedom of Conscience in the USSR*. In addition to the books and pamphlets he produced for the "True Witness" press, Shelkov also made tape recordings of talks and sermons, which were circulated among True and Free Adventist groups all over the Soviet Union. In all, 110 works were catalogued by the prosecution at his 1979 trial, thus making him a leading *samizdat* writer.

Strengthening Links with Dissidents and Foreigners

During this decade, Shelkov developed contacts he had made earlier in the camps with Soviet human rights activists. Instrumental in this effort was Rostislav Galetsky, one of Shelkov's closest assistants. As a church representative whose responsibility it was to tour Adventist communities throughout the USSR, Galetsky was in a unique position to hear and compile firsthand testimony on the religious persecution of unregistered Adventists. He documented numerous violations of religious rights, and in 1974 the first report on state-sponsored repression of Reformist Adventists reached the editors of *A Chronicle of Current Events*, the main unofficial journal of the Soviet human rights movement.

In 1976 even closer links were established with human rights activists Alexander Ginzburg, Yury Orlov, and other members of the Moscow Helsinki Group. A natural result of this relationship was that Shelkov became active in the defense of these individuals once they were arrested for documenting Soviet violations of human rights. In 1977 the desperation of Shelkov and his fellow believers reached its peak, and they appealed to foreigners for support and publicity in their struggle against KGB persecution.

In March 1978 Shelkov was arrested in Tashkent following a violent four-day search by the secret police, which left much of the home of his daughter demolished. The arrest—the fourth for Shelkov—marked the culmination of several years of intense investigation by the KGB. This All-Union search apparently was accelerated after leaders of the True and Free Church increased their contacts with Soviet dissidents and foreigners. In January 1979, ten months after his arrest, Shelkov was moved from pretrial detention and made to stand trial with four of his associates. In January 1980, at the age of eighty-four, the frail Adventist leader died in a Siberian labor camp near Tabaga.

Summary of Charges

The state's indictment of Vladimir Shelkov and his "accomplices" was the product of ten months' work by the KGB Investigation Department and was nearly one hundred pages long. It charged Shelkov with "disseminating knowingly false fabrications slandering the Soviet state and social system (Article 191-4 of the Uzbek SSR Criminal Code)" and with "encroaching on the personality and rights of citizens under the guise of carrying out religious rituals (Article 147-1 of the same code)."[10] The indictment emphasized that Shelkov was the leader of an illegal sect of Reformist Adventists, which split from the officially recognized Seventh-Day Adventist Church shortly after the Russian Revolution following a refusal to declare loyalty to the government. The bulk of the document was devoted to a listing of *samizdat* publications produced and disseminated by the "True Witness" Adventist press. The most slanderous, according to the indictment, were those addressed to prominent foreigners and "inviting interference in the internal affairs" of the country.

On January 15, 1979, the trial of Vladimir Shelkov and his codefendants began in Tashkent City Court. After several lengthy recesses, the court passed sentence on March 23, 1979. Shelkov was sentenced to five years' regimen in a labor camp.

THE HYPOTHESIS

The basic thesis of this chapter is twofold. First, throughout much of the history of the conflict between Soviet authorities and Reformist Adventists and during the 1979 trial of Shelkov in particular, Soviet officials greatly exaggerated the challenge or potential threat posed to the regime by this sect; this was due to the extreme and stereotypic conceptions prevalent in official pronouncements and informal Party opinion. This is not to say that without these distorted official images there would have been no conflict between True and Free Adventists and the authorities. The objective conditions of the conflict were real enough. Important reasons divided both sides, and valid reasons existed for Soviet concern and anxiety over any potential challenge to the Party's primacy from a competing ideology. Nevertheless, early Soviet rulers greatly miscalculated any challenge posed to the regime, as well as to the future construction of their society.

Second, in addition to conditioning official perceptions, the false images of Reformist Adventists held by the authorities had another concrete effect. They justified extreme and erratic repression. Furthermore, repeated often enough and with conviction, this pattern of repression eventually set in motion a self-fulfilling prophecy. By pursuing a policy of severe repression, the authorities slowly but steadily transformed Adventist believers, who were as loyal and hardworking as nonbelievers, into fugitives, convicted criminals, repeat offenders, and, in official eyes, slanderers of the Soviet state and supporters of renegade dissidents and Western enemies.

The remainder of this chapter will describe official images relevant to the 1979 trial of Vladimir Shelkov; analyze any discrepancy between these and accurate images; and, finally, draw some conclusions regarding the sources of dominant official images and their consequences for official perception and action.

OFFICIAL IMAGES

Historical Legacy

As stated in an earlier chapter, contemporary Soviet images of dissidents and nonconformists are not born overnight; nor are they formed simply in reaction to the activities of a particular individual or religious group. They are predisposed by earlier official conceptions of internal, as well as external, adversaries. In the case of the True and Free Adventists, contemporary official images of this sect have been conditioned by early Bolshevik images of organized religion; by official conceptions of the Reformist sect and its leaders formed during the late 1920s, the 1930s, and 1940s; by ideological legacy; and, of course, by the authoritarian aspirations of Soviet rulers.[11]

Particularly important is the historical memory that filters down to current Soviet officials from early Soviet history, especially memories of the hostility of organized religion to the new regime. Immediately after the Russian Revolution, the Bolshevik regime did, in fact, face a serious threat to its very existence and to its vision for a future society. The threat came from the Orthodox Church and took the form of open hostility from leading officials of a church with enormous political and economic power.[12] Years later, after the power of the Orthodox Church had seriously eroded and its leaders had become relatively docile, severe repression, nonetheless, continued—a testament to the power of historical memory.[13] This memory has been summarized as

> the memory of the Russian Orthodox Church's interdependence with Tsarist autocracy, its collaboration with the anti-Bolshevik forces during the 1917 Revolution and the Civil War, and its early opposition to the Soviet regime—a memory which has thus tended to identify institutional religions as an instrument of the internal and external enemies of the Soviet system.[14]

Not only in terms of historical legacy, but also through the prisms of the Marxist ideological legacy and the regime's authoritarian aspirations, Bolshevik rulers eventually came to view any institutionalized religion as

> a kind of commercialized vice, catering to the displaced needs of the ignorant and backward elements of society and diverting them from socially useful endeavors—a vice providing a livelihood to a parasitic stratum of the clergy which, despite its professions of loyalty, has always been inherently hostile to the communist worldview and determined, should a suitable occasion arise, to subvert the Soviet order.[15]

Decades later, in the 1960s, this general image was reinforced by images dominant in several official works on Soviet Adventism. In *The Adventists*, a book published in 1964, Alexander Belov, an authoritative Soviet spokesman on questions of atheism and religion, provides a useful survey of official images of Adventists prevailing nearly twenty years after World War II.[16] The general image which emerges from Belov's work is extremely negative. Adventists are portrayed as a reactionary and obscurantist sect of Western origin opposed to any cooperation between church and state, an association of charlatans and fascists whose behavior is corrupt, fanatical, and violent. New converts, according to Belov, are victimized constantly by pastors who demand large contributions from poor members in order to support their lavish life styles. Fanatical religious rites such as baptism in icy waters, excessive prayer, and fasting cause heart disease and death in young and old members; and Adventist parents savagely beat children who try to join state-sponsored youth organizations such as the Komsomol.[17] Furthermore, Belov singles out Shelkov and his Reformist sect as particularly dangerous criminals and as fascists. The latter charge is justified not only by the sect's pacifist stance, but also by the German background of some members and the contact of others with the Germans during World War II.

A strikingly different image of Soviet Adventists appeared just two years after the publication of Belov's book. In a short book entitled *The Seventh Day Adventists*, V.N. Lentin, a colleague of Belov's, depicts Soviet Adventists not as obscurants, but as the most progressive religious group in the Soviet Union. Unlike Belov, he sees most Adventists as loyal in their attitude to the state and asserts "there are no grounds for bringing political accusations against them."[18] According to Lentin, Adventists are honest people with a profound sense of duty to the social, physical, and spiritual needs of the community; they are loving, forgiving, meek, humble, and tolerant. Like Belov, Lentin devotes little specific attention to the True Remnant sect and Vladimir Shelkov. However, he does stress that delinquent or extremist pastors are uncommon.[19]

The surprisingly different images of Soviet Adventists which emerge in the books by Belov and Lentin appeared just two years apart; and, no doubt, this difference was made possible by the period of the drift and relaxation that accompanied Khrushchev's ouster. The divergent images of Belov and Lentin represent two contrasting orientations toward how best to deal with the problem of organized religion and Adventists in particular.[20] More relevent than a detailed analysis of these two conflicting approaches among

Soviet officials is the question of which tendency emerged as dominant.

The answer came in 1968 with the publication of another book by Belov, *Adventism*.[21] Appearing well after Khrushchev's ouster, the work provides a telling indication of the images prevailing among Soviet officials at the time. In the book, Belov renews his vigorous and extremely hostile attack against all Adventists and the Reformist sect in particular as criminals, fanatics, and fascists.[22] Noteworthy, also, is an article by Belov published in 1978—the year of Shelkov's final arrest—in *Nauka i religiya*, a journal which often sports lively debate over the future course of official antireligious policy.[23] Although Belov focuses chiefly on the origins and development of Adventism in the United States, he does address the issue of Soviet Adventism. He characterizes Adventists as cunning, deceitful, and antisocial and the True Remnant sect in particular as extremists: individuals performing charitable acts solely to develop a good reputation and persons who shirk their civic duties.[24]

To summarize the general image of Vladimir Shelkov and his sect dominant in the period preceding his final trial, it is useful, perhaps to note that it was fundamentally in tune with the conception of religious extremists expressed by Vladimir Kuroyedov, chairman of the Council of Religious Affairs (under the USSR Council of Ministers). Writing in 1976, Kuroyedov observed that the phenomenon of religious extremism is characteristic only of individuals or groups of religious activists, clergymen, and sectarian preachers who "try to circumvent the law and provoke in believers dissatisfaction with the Soviet state's policy toward religion—normally for self-seeking purposes and using religion only as a cover."[25]

Against this general background, attention will now shift to a description of official images—general and specific characteristics—directly relevant to the 1979 trial of Shelkov and his Adventist codefendants. However, first a note on the nature of political trials in the USSR is in order.

Although Article 155 of the Soviet constitution guarantees that judges and people's assessors will be independent—subject only to law—this pledge is not upheld in political trials. One writer has summarized the situation as follows:

> The Soviet court is officially regarded as a political and administrative instrument, and hence is more vulnerable to "nonjudicial" influences

than are the court systems in many other countries. This vulnerability is most pronounced when the court is called upon to deal with "political crimes"—criminal acts that involve the security of the Soviet state. In such cases, the antennae of the court officials are sensitively attuned to the party line, and no defendant who has been brought to trial under Article 70 has even been acquitted.[26]

Dina Kaminskaya, a former criminal attorney in the Soviet Union, reinforces and elaborates upon this characterization. According to Kaminskaya, Soviet judges, in pronouncing sentences in politically sensitive cases, are acutely aware that their actions are monitored carefully by the Central Committee of the Party and that final sentences are reported to appropriate Party officials; judges are subject to the influence of the USSR Ministry of Justice and the corresponding republic ministries which direct and inspect the work of "cadres of court organs"—this includes semiannual review of the sentences handed down by individual judges.[27] In addition, the court's independence in political trials is limited severely by several other considerations: all members of the judiciary are Party members and, hence, subject to its directives and responsible for faithfully implementing Party decisions—failure to do so carries the threat of expulsion; also, Party organs control the nomination of candidates, the recall of judges, and the renomination of judges who desire to remain in their posts for more than one five-year term.[28]

Political and Psychological
Atmosphere of Political Trials

All of these political considerations weigh heavily on court officials and visibly affect the psychological setting of such proceedings. Collectively, they breed an atmosphere of tension, of official suspicion, hostility, and acute concern that no unofficial—*samizdat*—record of the proceedings be leaked to the public or to foreigners. Consequently, special precautions are taken to select an audience for political trials that will not obstruct the work of the court. Without exception, the KGB carefully screens all prospective observers. Typically, they select "loyal" citizens—such as local party members, off-duty policemen, Komsomol members, and occasionally drunken factory workers—who then are admitted to the courtroom through a special entrance. Meanwhile, relatives and close friends of the defendant are kept waiting outside the public entrance. Eventually, only a few of the closest relatives are admitted, often after the proceedings are well underway. Outside the courtroom, friends maintain a vigil of support, despite police harassment and brutality.

Nor is such a setting peculiar to the trials of nonconformists and dissidents. Even criminal cases (criminal in the conventional sense of the word) with political overtones are set in a similar environment. Based on her role as a defense attorney in such a criminal case, Dina Kaminskaya observes that an atmosphere of "suspicion, covert observation and unconcealed malevolence" permeated the courtroom during the six weeks of the first of several trials.[29] Moreover, she notes that, as the trial progressed, she became painfully aware that she was faced with a judge who had decided on a verdict of guilty even before the start of the trial and who was now putting the decision steadily into effect.[30] Based on her experience in this case and observations of others, Kaminskaya concludes with the generalization that political trials conspicuously lack prosecutors who are totally honest and gifted with the rare ability to cast aside prejudices and to weigh the pros and cons of an argument objectively and dispassionately.

OFFICIAL IMAGES: THE "TRUE FACTS"[31]

The trial of Vladimir Shelkov and his four Adventist codefendants opened in Tashkent on January 15, 1979 and, after several lengthy recesses, closed on March 23, 1979. From the outset, the courtroom's atmosphere did not promote the sober analysis of evidence. As is customary in Soviet political trials (and in the continental European tradition), the judge did not act as a disinterested arbiter, but conducted an extensive examination of the defendants from the bench. Evident throughout the trial was the open presumption of guilt by the judge and prosecutor. Selected to preside over the hearings was Judge N.S. Artemov. He had a reputation of unconcealed hatred for religious nonconformists and dissidents, and this was reflected in 1979 when he sentenced Mustafa Dzhemilev, the Crimean Tatar activist, for his nonviolent defense of national rights. During the 1979 proceedings, Artemov made clear his intolerance and anger toward the defendants. He constantly interrupted Shelkov and on several occasions lost his temper and began to shout. He repeatedly ruled Shelkov's remarks irrelevant and warned him not to speak about his religious beliefs. The intensity of Artemov's emotions and contempt, in particular, were reflected in the following sample statements:

[Judge to Shelkov]: "We are trying a criminal case here, not a religious faith."[32]

[Judge, shouting
angrily to Shelkov]: "I do not need any help from you in knowing the law and the recorder knows what to write and what not to write. Who is in charge of this court anyway, you or I?"[33]

The prosecutor, V.I. Baimeyev, also vented his anger frequently and visibly at Shelkov and the other defendants.

The hostility of KGB officials sitting in the courtroom toward the Adventists was revealed spontaneously following a scathing attack on Shelkov delivered in a highly charged oratorical style by the prosecution's chief witness, V.V. Illarionov, the son of True and Free Adventists and an imprisoned criminal prior to this appearance at the trial.

[KGB to one another]: "You could really learn from him, I wish I could speak like him."[34]

In addition to such official remarks, Soviet legal procedure was violated during the early days of the trial by the court's refusal to allow close friends and relatives of the accused to attend the trial. Contrary to official claims that the trial was open, the time of the hearings was kept secret and relatives and friends of the defendants were not admitted freely. As is customary, admission was by special permission of the KGB. Eventually, the close relatives of the accused were admitted into the courtroom. Official anxiety was evident throughout the trial, but particularly visible at the end of the second day, when about eighty KGB officers surrounded the three Adventists who had observed the trial after they met with other Adventists outside the courtroom.

Shelkov was defended by V.G. Spodik. Although an officially appointed attorney, he provided an aggressive defense. He sharply criticized the manner in which the pretrial investigation was conducted and the court's treatment of Shelkov. The court also appointed two other lawyers to defend Shelkov's associates.

During the ten-month pretrial investigation, Shelkov denied state charges that the religious *samizdat* written by him was slanderous and libeled the social system.[35] More generally, he contended that there was nothing anti-Soviet about the True and Free Adventists. According to Shelkov, his literature was not directed against Soviet power and its fundamental laws, but against the dictatorship of militant state atheism and the antireligious laws which promoted the religious persecution of loyal Soviet citizens. He rejected the official allegation that Adventists refuse to work, study, or serve in the military. He said that they merely seek to observe the Sabbath and to serve the state in a nonmilitary capacity.

General Images

During the course of the 1979 trial, a number of general images of Shelkov and his sect emerged in statements made by the prosecutor, the judges, witnesses for the state, and members of the officially sanctioned audience and recorded in the unofficial transscripts. Viewed collectively, these statements provide a composite and authoritative picture of Vladimir Shelkov as a religious fanatic, an extremist, an evil genius, a nonbeliever (of religion), a politician, a pervert (who corrupted Soviet youth), a parasite, a thief, a frightful criminal, a usurper of the rights of other citizens, a reactionary, a fascist collaborator, and a supporter of Western enemies in the psychological war with the Soviet Union.

Shortly after the court sentenced Shelkov and the other Adventists, an eyewitness account of the trial appeared in *Izvestiya*.[36] Filed by two Soviet journalists, the item is unusually long and, in effect, provides an official, but greatly abridged, transcript of the proceedings. It is noteworthy for its descriptions of the accused and of the Reformist sect in general. Interestingly, these characterizations are strikingly similar to those in the unofficial transcript. The writers depict Shelkov as a religious fanatic, an inveterate criminal and thief, the son of a kulak (a rich and allegedly exploitive peasant), riff-raff, a reactionary, a servant of fascism and not God, and a henchman of Western psychological warfare centers.

A few weeks later, this article inspired another eyewitness account, this time in *Pravda Vostoka*, the Russian-language daily of Uzbekistan, entitled "A Fanatic in the Role of an 'Apostle.'"[37] Written by Vladimir Illarionov, the prosecution's chief witness in the 1979 trial, the article refers favorably to the *Izvestiya* account and then proceeds to describe Shelkov's emergence as a fanatic, an ambitious and unscrupulous leader, a Nazi collaborator, and an anti-Soviet slanderer. Illarionov stresses his previous personal contact with the sect and ridicules the notion that Shelkov was a "Christian" or a "fighter for human rights." Instead, he depicts him as a religious extremist with the potential to "destroy the lives of many thousands of simple, trusting people."[38]

In another press article, this one triggered by the arrest of two Seventh-Day Adventists who were distributing leaflets in defense of Shelkov in Ashkabad, a similar composite image of Shelkov and his sect surfaces.[39] The piece, called "Obscurants," appears in Ashkabad's Russian-language daily *Turkmenskaya Iskra*. In it, the author, Yu. Yulin, describes True and Free Adventists not only as obscurants, but also as anti-Soviet activists, renegades, political agitators, reactionaries, perverts, and uneducated and disloyal citizens. Yulin devotes much of the article to the demands of sect members for religious education of children. Shelkov and his associates are described as poorly educated persons who seek to pervert the minds of children with their brand of religious instruction and who try to dissuade young men from fulfilling their military duty to the Motherland. Such efforts, if tolerated, would, in the author's estimation, mean "raising the next generation in a spirit of fanaticism and obscurantism."[40]

Despite the death of Shelkov in a labor camp in January 1980, official press attacks against him did not cease.[41] Scattered attacks appeared in subsequent years and on July 1, 1983—more than three and one-half years after his death—a major attack, authored by N. Shalamova, appeared in *Pravda Vostoka*.[42] Shalamova fiercely attacks Shelkov and the other leaders of the Reformist sect, ridiculing the notion that they are "martyrs for the faith" and describing Shelkov as a forger, "a hater of humanity," a slanderer of the Soviet system and country, "a cunning pro-German agitator," and a collaborator with foreign intelligence services.[43] Much of the article is an effort to detail, and convince readers of, the subversive links between the True Adventists and the German occupying forces during World War II.

References to Shelkov and his sect in official journals are scant. E. Filimonov, in an article entitled "The Crisis of Faith and Religious Extremism," briefly mentions Shelkov and his sect.[44] He portrays them as "religious extremists" and slanderers who promote the myth of a "dictatorship of State atheism." According to Filimonov, this myth falsifies the true status of religious believers and ignores the crucial fact that the authorities are intolerant of only a small group of individuals who violate religious laws and incite others to do so.[45]

Character

The official images of the character or personality of Shelkov which emerged during the 1979 trial did not conform to the generally positive view of Adventists as loyal, hard-working, and progressive citizens found in Lentin's book. Rather, officials saw Shelkov's character more in the manner of Belov's writings: in official eyes, he was cunning, fanatical, and incurably anti-Soviet.

Throughout the trial, the prosecution stressed, and the entire court reinforced, Shelkov's deep hatred for anything Soviet. The following excerpt from *Izvestiya* accurately summarizes the official images of Shelkov's character dominant during the proceedings; it also reflects the deep contempt for the defendants evident in the courtroom:

> . . . Shelkov was the son of a kulak who had eight hired hands. An individual who imbibed hatred for everything Soviet virtually with his mother's milk. Under the cover of the reactionary splinter trend of Adventism he embarked on the path of fighting Soviet authority back in the thirties, urging believers not to recognize this authority but to oppose all its measures. To substantiate his anti-state "sermons" Shelkov referred to the religious teachings he "professed," seeking in religious books "explanations" and interpretations which suited him.
>
> Shelkov was exposed at that time and arrested. However, he had scarcely returned from prison when he created a new underground center for the Reformist sect.

The war against fascism began. Shelkov and his associates did not limit themselves to propagandistic activity urging others to refuse service in the Soviet military. Rather, on Soviet territory occupied by the Hitlerites, they became active collaborators with the fascists. That was how Shelkov behaved, living at the time in Pyatigorsk; Manzhura joined German–fascist–intelligence under the nickname "Old Man." Together, they subordinated all of the activity of the Reformist sect to the pernicious aims of the occupiers.[46]

Hence, unlike most religious believers in the USSR, portrayed by the press as "generally honest and conscientious citizens," Shelkov, according to the authorities, had a fundamentally deviant character.[47] He had the personality of a fanatic with delusions of being an apostle and a prophet. Moreover, as the prosecution's chief witness testified during the trial, Shelkov was driven in all his dealings by insatiable greed. According to *Isvestiya*:

Not suffering from excessive modesty, Shelkov declared himself to be a senior apostle, "God's deputy on earth." He was not short of funds since his entire flock paid him 10 or even 20 percent of their entire wages. The entire course of the legal investigation proved that these funds, allegedly earmarked for "aid to believers" and religious affairs, went to maintain Shelkov and others who did not work anywhere. It was this money which was used to print and distribute all sorts of riot-inciting literature. Shelkov exploited the religious feelings of believers, although he himself believed in nothing. He had one idol—money, profit, an incessant passion for wealth—and he did not stop at any criminal methods, even the most sordid, to acquire his wealth.[48]

In short, Shelkov's character placed him in the company of religious extremists—a group which includes "a considerable number of persons with a shady past, individuals dissatisfied with the Soviet way of life, currently in conflict with the organs of Soviet authority; persons concealing their antisocial views and sentiments under the cloak of religion."[49]

Nature of the Conflict

The conflict between Shelkov's sect and the authorities, judging from official statements relevant to the case as well as the unofficial transcript of the 1979 trial, had two fundamental dimensions: a domestic and a foreign one. From the viewpoint of the court, Shelkov and his associates had long been involved in ideological subversion at home under the cover of religion. They had broken religious laws and tried to discredit the new constitution (of 1977) in the eyes of religious believers by alleging that it did not guarantee religious rights. They meddled in politics and incited Soviet youth to avoid normal relations with the state. Put simply, Shelkov and the Reformist sect acted as a political and not a religious organization.

Soviet authorities categorically refused to accept the Adventist position that the conflict was a struggle for genuine separation of the church and state, for real guarantees of freedom of conscience, and for the equalization of believers' rights with those of non-believers. From the standpoint of the authorities, the essential character of the conflict could not be understood properly apart from the concept of religious extremism. As defined by one official Soviet writer, religious extremism refers to a deliberate violation of the law, an effort by some religious leaders to overcome the crisis of religion (the erosion of organized religion's influence in modern Soviet society) through extreme actions which, in an effort to increase group membership, result in violations of Soviet laws.[50] It is an interdenominational phenomenon, one imbued with Western individualistic, nationalistic, and anarchistic tendencies.[51] It is a phenomenon that is encouraged by Western enemies of the Soviet Union.[52]

Soviet officials found the foreign dimension of the conflict particularly objectionable. Not content to undermine the system from within, Shelkov and his followers, according to the authorities, collaborated with the West in its psychological war with the Soviet Union. *Izvestiya* explicitly noted: "There is no question of any faith here. There are sordid politics and murky intrigues everywhere. Shelkov and company were henchmen of the Western psychological warfare centers acting under the cover of a phony concern for faith and religion." In summary, the conflict between Shelkov and the authorities was portrayed officially as a struggle against religious subversion.

Activity

Although Shelkov and his codefendants insisted that their activity was purely religious and lawful, Soviet authorities interpreted their behavior quite differently. A summary of the objectionable activities appears in *Izvestiya*:

> Disobedience to the laws of the Soviet state, propaganda urging the refusal of universal military service, wresting Soviet citizens from participation in the country's socio-political and cultural life, educating children and young people in an anti-Soviet spirit, expanding the organization by recruiting new people. These actions are being carried out both by reading sermons at illegal assemblies and by preparing and distributing manuscripts and typewritten brochures. . . . Shelkov acquired fake documents in the name of Pyotr Andreyevich Pavlov. . . . The hiding places in the homes of Shelkov and his accomplices contained publications calling for the overthrow of the existing system and cooperation with "loyal friends" abroad.[53]

Writing in *Pravda Vostoka* more than three years later, Shalamova reinforces these official images of the Adventists' activities. She singles out pastors of the sect for their attempts to "blacken Soviet laws on religious cults" by indulging in anti-Soviet activity and by obstructing the construction of a socialist society.[54]

Shelkov's publishing operations particularly aroused official anger and concern. This is reflected in the nearly one-hundred-page indictment, much of which listed *samizdat* letters and publications produced by Shelkov and printed by the "True Witness" secret publishing house. The most objectionable publications are those addressed abroad and to foreigners in the Soviet Union. These are described as "inviting interference in the internal affairs of the Soviet Union"; and included here are Shelkov's letter to President Carter and his two letters to the West German Adventist K. Gutknecht, in which he appeals for support and publicity.

In addition to printing and disseminating publications viewed officially as slanderous, Shelkov—according to the authorities—did not hesitate to forge documents for fellow Adventists. "If someone did not have a secondary education, that was no problem," reported *Izvestiya*. "For a certain fee, Shelkov could not only raise their educational qualifications but also could issue a fake passport with an official stamp and register them illegally."[55]

However, Shelkov and his colleagues were not content with trying to subvert Soviet society from within. According to court officials and representatives of the press, they worked actively to undermine the system through collaboration with foreign enemies of the USSR: first with German occupying forces and more recently with Western special services. In the official story, Shelkov and other Reformist Adventists living under German occupation during World War II had conducted various collaborationist activities: they organized religious services, studied German, publicly confirmed atrocities committed by Stalin's secret police, and encouraged individuals not to bear arms in the military.[56] Furthermore, during the 1970s, they increased their contacts with Soviet dissidents and foreigners. Secretly, they sent abroad "filthy slanders and baseless attacks" on the Soviet system.[57] According to an official report:

> Shelkov's agents were in constant contact with several foreign journalists in Moscow. One Adventist named R. Galetsky was used for this purpose. He maintained close contacts with convicted anti-Soviets like Orlov . . . and all the "publications" from Shelkov's kitchen began to be passed on to him. He in turn gave them to certain Western journalists, in particular former *New York Times* correspondent Christopher Wren . . . [who] is closely linked to the CIA . . . [and] the BBC's Moscow correspondent Kevin Ruane.[58]

Intentions

What, in official eyes, motivated Shelkov and his followers to pursue such activities? Actually, as is customary in Soviet political trials, the court paid less attention to the motives of Shelkov and his codefendants than to the harmful consequences of their actions. Throughout his testimony during the 1979 trial, Shelkov attempted to demonstrate that there was nothing anti-Soviet about the True Adventists. Their aim, he argued, had been to act as a purely religious organization composed of peaceful Christians: to render to Caesar what was Caesar's while preserving for God what was God's.[59] As for the refusal of Reformist Adventists to bear arms in the military, the authorities were not convinced—before and during the trial—by Shelkov's explanation that Adventists avoided army service and forbade their children to attend school on Saturdays not because they were anti-Soviet, but because they were trying to obey the fourth and sixth Commandments. The authorities saw the refusal of Adventists to bear arms in recent times as a malicious refusal to carry out civil obligations and not as a matter of conscience. In official eyes, this stance reinforced the memory of an earlier betrayal of the Motherland: the remembrance of the speed with which Shelkov's sect and other religious organizations abandoned their loyalty to the Soviet state once they found themselves under German occupation.

According to the authorities, a similar motive was behind the increasing appeals of Shelkov and his sect to foreigners. During the trial, court officials scornfully dismissed assertions by Shelkov and his associates that their appeals to foreign leaders and dignitaries were religious and defensive in nature. Instead, authorities viewed them as political acts intended to invite foreign governments to interfere in the internal affairs of the Soviet Union.

In summary, it seems that the official images of the intentions of Shelkov and his codefendants corresponded closely to and reinforced official conceptions of religious extremists as individuals whose work is "intended to subvert the spiritual and social unity of Soviet people, to suggest to believers the idea of their inequality and thus to stimulate in them a negative attitude toward the organs of authority and toward Soviet laws."[60]

DISCREPANCIES BETWEEN OFFICIAL IMAGES AND TRUE IMAGES

Was the general image held by Soviet authorities of Vladimir Shelkov—as a religious extremist, fanatic, politician, inveterate criminal, anti-Soviet slanderer, traitor, fascist supporter, and henchman of Western enemies—accurate, partially accurate, or false? Before attempting to answer this larger question, we will compare official images of the character of Shelkov, the nature of the conflict, and the activity and intentions of Shelkov and his sect with reasonably accurate images and decide whether the official images are accurate, partially accurate, or false.

Character

Was Shelkov anti-Soviet to the core? Did he "imbibe hatred for everything Soviet," as the *Izvestiya* article asserted? Was he an incurable criminal, a traitor to the Motherland, a politician obsessed with power and wealth?

The official image of Shelkov's character did have a partial basis in fact, although on balance it was grossly exaggerated. As indicated earlier, Shelkov and his sect had indeed been in conflict with the state since the late 1920s, following the state's refusal to register the Reformist congregations because of their failure to meet certain provisions of the 1929 Law on Religious Cults. Moreover, Shelkov's determination to resist state interference in church and school affairs did lead to three convictions prior to this 1979 trial; and so he was a convicted criminal, a repeat offender.

Was Shelkov a politician cloaked in religion and obsessed with power and wealth? As a leader of the True and Free Adventists, he undoubtedly was concerned—and at times greatly preoccupied—with considerations of power and status in a church whose leadership was constantly under attack and imprisoned. However, there is no evidence to suggest that Shelkov was obsessed with personal power and status. His concern for wealth, for example, seems to have been limited to concern about raising contributions from members to finance the church's activities and the publication of religious materials.

Lastly, Shelkov had not been implacably hostile to the Soviet state since childhood. Particularly before the 1929 religious laws and after the signing of the Helsinki Accords (1975), he and his fellow Adventists were still hopeful that central officials would see them as loyal, hard-working, and hard-praying citizens who were not against Soviet power and who repeatedly expressed their respect for "Leninist laws" (in other words, 1929 religious laws of the Bolshevik regime). Noteworthy is the self-image of True and Free Adventists. Throughout the decades of religious persecution, they viewed themselves as loyal and true citizens of the Soviet Union who were worldly, rather than fanatical, in their teachings. Furthermore, Shelkov insisted in his writings and during the course of the trial that he was not against the Soviet political or economic system.[61]

Nature of the Conflict

Was the conflict between the Reformist Adventists and the authorities essentially a matter of ideological subversion at home (disruption of law and order) and support for Western enemies in their campaign against the Soviet Union? Or was it, as the Adventists maintained, a purely religious struggle for separation of state from church and state from school: a campaign for equal rights for discriminated and persecuted believers?

The official image of the nature of the conflict was partially accurate. What began in the 1920s simply as a struggle by True Adventists for observance of pre-1929 religious laws, which safeguarded the independence of church and state, overnight became a law-and-order issue. Marginally political at first, the conflict increasingly assumed a political dimension as True Adventist leaders, now subject to arrest under the 1929 law, went underground and lived illegally on false passports without residence permits.

During the height of Stalinism, mass imprisonment of Adventists established in official eyes the criminal nature of the conflict and at the same time obscured its religious roots. Subsequent connections between the True Adventists and foreigners during extremely sensitive episodes in Soviet history—World War II and after the Helsinki Accords—added a decidedly foreign dimension to the conflict and blackened official images of Shelkov and his sect yet further. Nevertheless, ideological subversion was never at the essence of the conflict. The teachings of Soviet Adventism would not permit it. Shelkov and his fellow leaders avoided contact with foreigners until rather recently in their history.[62] Significantly, they were driven to this course of action by extreme repression and a growing sense of desperation.

Activity

Was Shelkov involved in "hostile deeds" and "loathsome actions"? Did he "sow malice"? Did he repeatedly engage in criminal activity, including illegal assemblies and anti-state sermons? Did he and his associates print and distribute riot-inciting literature, educate children and young people in a nonconforming religious and therefore anti-Soviet spirit, produce publications which called for the overthrow of the existing systems, forge documents, create an illegal underground printing house, encourage youth to refuse to bear arms? Did they collaborate—even implicitly—with German occupation forces and appeal to foreign leaders and organizations for support and publicity in their conflict with the authorities?

Legal and constitutional issues aside, Soviet official images of the activities of Shelkov and his followers were partially accurate. Shelkov himself recognized that by violating the Law on Religious Cults—a law he considered unjust and a violation of Leninist principles—he was engaging, strictly speaking, in illegal and criminal activity. Moreover, from the viewpoint of officials charged with maintaining discipline in Soviet society, by calling for the repeal of this law he was agitating for the overthrow of a part of the existing system. In addition, Shelkov admitted during his 1979 trial that he was engaged in many of the activities which the state found "hostile" and "loathsome": illegal assemblies, sermons critical of the state, religious education of children and young people, and production of publications calling for repeal of certain laws. He also encouraged youths to refuse to bear arms and work on Saturday, and he did collaborate with dissidents who admittedly had contacts with foreign correpondents and emigré groups.

However, it should be stressed that although official images of the activity of Shelkov and his sect were partially accurate, they were greatly exaggerated. They failed to incorporate such important facts as the willingness of True and Free Adventists to perform alternative service—in place of combat—in order to demonstrate their loyalty to the state. Also, official images failed to register the crucial fact that True Adventists tried not to act "conspiratorially." They avoided contacts with dissidents and foreigners for a long time, and they appealed to them only out of a growing sense of desperation after pleas to local and central officials were met with indifference.

Finally, on the issue of active collaboration with the Germans during World War II, the official image of the Adventist activity greatly distorts the situation. Clearly, Shelkov and other Adventists did live under the German occupation forces during World War II; and after the severe persecution experienced under Stalin, it would be surprising indeed if many did not greet this change in their political status with hope. However, there is no evidence to suggest that they abandoned their loyalty to the Soviet Union and collaborated with the German intelligence services or the military. In fact, the pacifist and religious orientation of the True and Free Adventists would have placed them squarely in opposition to any active support for the German war effort.

Intentions

Were the actions of Shelkov and the Reformist sect intended to subvert the unity of the Soviet people and to stimulate a negative attitude in them toward authority?

Here the official image was false. Critical facts in the history of the conflict simply were not acknowledged by authorities pre-occupied with a search for facts to confirm the dominant official conceptions. It is quite clear that the congregations which joined the True Remnant sect in the 1920s intended only to act as representatives of a religious organization composed of peaceful Christians. But special legislation quickly transformed this sect into an illegal and criminal organization. Despite subsequent efforts by Shelkov's group to gain official recognition for their largely religious appeals, the local authorities responded repeatedly and instinctively to these good faith efforts with severe repression; when Shelkov and his associates eventually appealed to dissidents and foreigners, their intentions were labeled as political and hostile.

CONCLUSIONS

1. Most of the official images of Shelkov and the Reformist Adventists analyzed were misleading and outdated, but did have a basis in fact. For example, many of the allegations regarding the 1978 arrest of Shelkov and the others, which, at a glance, seemed totally fabricated and unbelievable, were found to be partly accurate and held with conviction (by, for example, Judge Artemov, Samuil Zivs).

2. Shelkov and his followers were loyal, but disobedient, Soviet citizens.

3. A review of the history of the conflict indicates that contemporary Soviet officials greatly exaggerated any challenge or potential threat posed to the regime by the True and Free Adventists and grossly magnified the sect's foreign connections. Under the influence of extremely negative stereotypes of the sect (born in the late 1920s, developed during the 1930s and 1940s, frozen immediately after World War II, and emerging fundamentally intact during the 1979 trial of Shelkov), officials misread any hint of Adventist criticism of Soviet laws or any contact with dissidents

or foreigners as additional evidence of the sect's long-standing hostility and fundamental disloyalty to the system.

4. Contrary to expectation, it was found that official stereotypes of religious extremists have not conditioned Soviet officials to view all religious nonconformists as extremists. Judging from the *samizdat* trial transcript and the relevant official press commentary, it seems the authorities do distinguish between nonconforming believers and their allegedly extremist leaders. They direct most of their hostility and criticism toward the latter in an apparent effort to drive a wedge between the two. In practice, however, this distinction is often blurred (see, for example, Appendix F on the severe repression of average True and Free Adventists).

5. Since 1966 (the appearance of Lentin's book) more sophisticated official conceptions of Soviet Adventists (and even criticism of the heavy-handedness of antireligious policy) have surfaced in Soviet scholarly writings. These considerably less hostile and more nuanced conceptions have not succeeded in replacing the stereotypes dominant in the official press and in informal party opinion. However, they do suggest a major policy debate over how best to combat the influence of organized religion.

NOTES

1. For a chronological history of Soviet Adventism, see Appendix D.

2. Much of the general background information which follows is taken from "The Struggle for the All-Union Church of Faithful and Free Seventh-Day Adventists for Freedom of Conscience in the USSR," by Vladimir Shelkov, as quoted in *CCE*, no. 48, pp. 117-18.

3. Between 1932 and 1945, membership in the Adventist Church reportedly doubled to about 14,000 persons. Estimates available for the 1960s and more recent times are extremely rough, unverifiable, and exclude unregistered congregations. Estimates for registered Soviet Adventists in the 1960s vary from 21,500 members, according to a Soviet source, to 40,000 according to a Western source; see, for example, Christel Lane, *Christian Religion in the Soviet Union* (London: George Allen & Unwin, 1978), pp. 167-68.

4. Lane, pp. 168-69.

5. For more details on the history of Soviet Adventism, see Michael Bourdeaux, "Adventists through the Eyes of Soviet Atheism," *Radio Liberty* 327/76, June 28, 1976, pp. 1-5; Trevor Beeson, *Discretion and Valor: Religious Conditions in Russia and Eastern Europe* (London: Collins, 1974), pp. 90-92; Lane, pp. 167-74. The latter also includes a description of the movement's organization and strength in contemporary Soviet society.

6. The following profile of Shelkov draws on basic facts found in *CCE*, no. 49, p. 57; *CCE*, no. 48, pp. 117-18; as well as in Ch. 4 of Marite Sapiets' book-length manuscript of Vladimir Shelkov and Soviet Adventism. For a chronological biography of Shelkov, see Appendix E. The author gratefully acknowledges the generosity of Marite Sapiets, a staff researcher at Keston College in London, in making available the manuscript and for detailed discussions on Soviet official attitudes toward Adventists and religious believers in general. The talks were held during the summer of 1983, while the writer was a visiting researcher at Keston College.

7. Dina Lepshina-Shelkova, "In Defense of Vladimir Shelkov," *Chronicle of Human Rights*, January-March 1979, p. 19.

8. Sapiets, p. 3.

9. Former Soviet dissidents such as A. Shifrin, A. Sinyavsky, and A. Ginzburg have testified, based on their camp experiences, that while in the camps Shelkov earned the respect not only of dissidents, but even of common criminals. See, for example, the testimony of Andrei Sinyavsky, *International Sakharov Hearings*, Third Session, September 29, 1979, Washington, D.C.

10. Keston College Summary of True and Free Adventist Documents Submitted to the Madrid Conference," *Keston College Archives*, p. 5.

11. Bociurkiw, "The Shaping of Soviet Religious Policy," pp. 38-39. According to Bociurkiw, the Soviet elite's perceptions of religion are shaped by these four factors. Ideological legacy, defined as "the vulgarized, militant version of Marxist atheism developed in the writings of Lenin and his followers," in Borciurkiw's estimation, has been overemphasized in Soviet and Western writings on Soviet perception of organized religion.

12. David E. Powell, *Antireligious Propaganda in the Soviet Union* (Cambridge, Mass.: M.I.T. Press, 1975), p. 7.

13. Here it should be recalled that Bolshevik hostility toward organized religion during this period was not indiscriminate. Between 1917 and 1927 non-Orthodox Christian sects enjoyed a considerable freedom. This early, discriminating approach supports the argument that although ideology (Marxism-Leninism with its militant atheism) served early Soviet rulers as an instrument for ordering and comprehending reality, it was not the key determinant of the state's attitude toward organized religions. More important, apparently, was the perceived threat from a group and the ability of officials to control congregations.

14. Bociurkiw, "The Shaping of Soviet Religious Policy," p. 38.

15. Ibid., p. 39-40.

16. Alexander Belov, *Adventisty* [The Adventists] (Moscow: Izdatelstvo "Nauka," 1964). For a critical review of this and subsequent books on the subject by Belov and V.N. Lentin, see Bourdeaux, pp. 1-5. Bourdeaux, a British authority on church-state relations in the USSR, describes Belov as an authoritative spokesman on atheism and religion and speculates that "Belov almost certainly wrote his book under [official] instructions," p. 3.

17. Belov, p. 131, as cited by Bourdeaux, p. 3.

18. V.N. Lentin, *Adventisty sedmogo dnya* [The Seventh Day Adventists] (Moscow: Izdatelstvo "Znaniye," 1966), p. 37. Despite this clearly more

tolerant and understanding attitude, Lentin carefully balances his remarks here and elsewhere in the text by adding and illustrating that political loyalty does not alter the unscientific character of Adventist ideas. He concludes his analysis by stressing that the struggle against religion should remain an ideological one: a battle against religious ideas and not religious people, p. 62.

19. Bourdeaux, p. 3.

20. For an insightful discussion of "fundamentalist" and "pragmatic" orientations in Soviet church policy, see Bociurkiw, "The Shaping of Soviet Religious Policy," pp. 41-42.

21. Belov, *Adventizm* [Adventism] (Moscow: Izdatelstvo Politicheskoy Literatury, 1968). A second edition was published in 1973.

22. Ibid., pp. 68-182.

23. Belov, "Captives of Unattainable Hopes," *Nauka i religiya*, March 1978, pp. 30-33. This issue is unusual because it carried four articles on Adventism. The other three articles, authored by S. Orlov, V. Franyuk, and D. Koretsky, respectively, depict Soviet Adventists as facing a deepening religious crisis; as individuals manipulated by foreign instigators who continually seek to incite them to subversion with talk of the Soviet Union's lack of freedom of conscience; and as loyal and hard-working individuals who are illogical and unscientific, pp. 33-38.

24. Belov, "Captives of Unattainable Hopes," pp. 31-33.

25. Vladimir A. Kuroyedov, *Sovetskoye gosudarstvo i tserkov* [The Soviet State and the Church] (Moscow: Izdatelstvo Politicheskoy Literatury, 1976), p. 59.

26. John E. Turner, "Artists in Adversity: The Sinyavsky-Daniel Case," in *Political Trials*, ed. Theodore L. Becker (New York: Bobbs Merrill Co., 1971), p. 119. More than a decade and several hundred political trials later, this generalization remains accurate.

27. Dina Kaminskaya, *Final Judgment: My Life as a Soviet Defense Attorney* (New York: Simon & Schuster, 1983), p. 100.

28. "Soviet Law and the Helsinki Monitors," Appendix to the *Hearings before the Commission on Security and Cooperation in Europe*, Ninety-Fifth Congress, second session on the Implementation of the Helsinki Accords, vol. 6, Soviet Law and the Helsinki Monitors, June 6, 1978, pp. 131-32.

29. Kaminskaya, p. 103. In the case in question, two boys were accused of the murder and brutal rape of a close female companion.

30. Ibid., p. 127.

31. Samuil Zivs, author of *Human Rights: Continuing the Discussion* (Moscow: Progress Publishers, 1980) and an authoritative spokesman for the Soviet leadership on questions of law and order and human rights, asserted that the "true facts" of the Shelkov case could be found by interested Western readers in official press accounts published after the trial by *Izvestiya* and *Pravda Vostoka*. He did so in reply to a paper on "Soviet and American Perspectives on Human Rights," delivered by Berman at the Congress of the International Political Science Association held in Moscow on August 16, 1979. An adaptation of the paper was reprinted in *Worldview*, November 1979, pp. 15-21.

32. Unofficial transcript of the trial of Vladimir Shelkov and his codefendants, contained in Keston College archives and submitted to the Madrid Review Conference, November 1980. The transcript, which numbers 134 pages, is one of the most detailed to reach the West (hereafter, cited as "Shelkov Transcript"), p. 11.

33. Ibid., p. 71.

34. Ibid., p. 95.

35. V. Shelkov, "Complaint to the Central Committee of the Uzbek SSR Communist Party," December 1978 contained in "Materials on the Persecution of Soviet Adventists Submitted by the True and Free Adventists to the Madrid Conference," *Keston College Archives*, November 1980, original document and summary contained in pp. 8-12 of a special report prepared by the Keston staff.

36. V. Kassis and M. Mikhaylov, "What Was Going on in the 'Apostle's' Bunker," *Izvestiya*, May 13, 1979, p. 5. The Soviet press—in the wake of the signing of the Helsinki Accords, President Carter's human rights campaigns, and other developments—has become more informative on political trials and law-and-order issues in general. Although the coverage is highly selective and intended to present the state's viewpoints and convince readers of its correctness, it is valuable for the purposes of this study.

37. Vladimir Illarionov, "A Fanatic in the Role of an 'Apostle,'" *Pravda Vostoka*, May 27, 1979, p. 5.

38. Ibid.

39. Yu. Yulin, "Obscurants," *Turkmenskaya Iskra*, November 1, 1979, p. 3.

40. Ibid.

41. Indirect attacks on the True Remnant group and other unregistered religious sects, which contain relevant general images of religious nonconformists, included: D. Yaroshevich, "Finding the Truth," *Molodyozh Moldavii*, May 14, 1983, p. 3; and Mikhail Derimov, "False Prophets," *Pravda Ukrainy* (a two-part article), January 31, 1981, p. 4, and February 2, 1982, p. 3.

42. N. Shalamova, "The Truth Unveiled," *Pravda Vostoka*, July 1, 1983, p. 2.

43. Ibid.

44. E. Filimonov, "The Crisis of Faith and Religious Extremism," *Nauka i religiya*, no. 2, 1980, p. 27.

45. Ibid., pp. 27-28.

46. Kassis and Mikhaylov, p. 5.

47. G. Luparev, "Religion and Recognition of the Law," *Kazakhstanskaya pravda*, April 3, 1980, p. 2 provides a good example of the positive official image of conforming religious believers promoted in the Soviet press.

48. Kassis and Mikhaylov, p. 5.

49. Filimonov, pp. 27-28.

50. Filimonov, pp. 26-28. It is noteworthy that Filimonov and a few other Soviet writers explicitly note that not all religious fanatics are extremists and that religious extremists should not be equated with religious sectarians. The latter, according to the author, generally are not extremists and are beginning

to understand that the activities of the extremists go beyond those related to religion and are placing them in conflict with the state. This is a much more discriminating view than typically found in the press and among local authorities.

51. Ibid., p. 27.

52. Ibid., p. 28. Filimonov, surprisingly, adds that religious extremism is also encouraged unwittingly by the overreaction of local authorities who try to struggle against religious ideology by administrative means. This view is not representative of relevant comments made in the press or during the trial. It seems to reflect the debate on antireligious policy and other policy questions frequently found in specialized Soviet journals.

53. Kassis and Mikhaylov, p. 5.

54. Shalamova, p. 2.

55. Kassis and Mikhaylov, p. 5.

56. Shalamova, p. 2.

57. Ibid.

58. Kassis and Mikhaylov, p. 5.

59. Shelkov transcript, pp. 69-71, 48-65.

60. Filimonov, p. 27.

61. Shelkov transcript, pp. 100-106.

62. With the unavoidable exception of those who lived under the German occupation.

6

Yury Orlov:
"Renegade"

ESSENTIAL BACKGROUND

Profile of Yury Orlov[1]

Yury Orlov was born in 1924 of working-class parents in the Smolensk *oblast* (region, an administrative division) of the Russian Republic. His early childhood was both peaceful and tragic. He spent much of it in the country with his grandmother and, consequently, seems largely to have escaped the unprecedented and violent economic transformation which disrupted much of Soviet society. However, these sheltered years were numbered. When Yury was nine years old, his father died of tuberculosis, and when he was eighteen, his stepfather was killed in the battle of Kharkov.

An important biographical event occurred in 1941. While working as a lathe operator in a Moscow factory, Orlov went from being a true believer in the system to being a skeptic. For the first time, he had doubts about the credibility of the regime. This intellectual awakening followed a talk at the factory between the seventeen-year-old Orlov and an older worker and family friend. In a private conversation the latter expressed the hope that Soviet cooperation with the Allies during World War II might lead to a democratization of Soviet society. Orlov was stunned by the remarks and left with a vexing question: was the pervasive and officially inculcated conception of the Soviet Union as the only genuine democracy possibly false?[2]

Several uneventful years passed before Orlov was drafted into the army in early 1944. He attended an officer training school and there became a candidate-member of the Communist Party. Subsequently, he served for about a month as a front-line officer at the 1st Ukrainian Front before the war ended.

From Skepticism to Private Criticism

After the war, Orlov completed his military service in the northern Caucasus region. There the twenty-year-old frequently participated in intensive group discussions with three or four of his fellow officers. Together with the others, Orlov privately criticized the "dictatorship of the bureaucracy" and urged a return to true Marxism, as embodied in the early philosophical writings of Marx.[3]

During this period of relative quiet and isolation, Orlov intensively studied the writings of Marx and Hegel. In an autobiographical sketch written several decades later, he recalls this period in his intellectual development:

> I had two thick exercise books filled with seditious extracts from Engels, etc. I burned them once, when I was summoned to the special department. It turned out, however, that this was a proposal to become a secret agent. For a long time I could not understand what was the actual reason for the summons, but when I understood I gave a categorical refusal. Persuasion continued for two days; at the end one quite high-ranking officer, to whom I had been conducted, asked me absolutely unexpectedly: "Why do you think that it is the same with us as with the Gestapo?" . . . Strange though it seems, I *did not know*, I did not guess, and no one told me what was the *actual* extent of the repressions in our country, and what their character was; I did not myself think of inquiring, perhaps out of fear, since it was dangerous even to ask a question. In our "circle," we did not even touch on this subject.[4]

Late in 1946, Orlov completed his active military service and enrolled as a physics major at Moscow State University. According to Orlov, any political doubts he previously held were suppressed entirely during this period of intensive study.[5] In 1952 he graduated with a degree in physics and as a full member of the Communist Party. He subsequently worked at the prestigious Institute of Theoretical and Experimental Physics in Moscow. During this time he published his first scientific article, delivered several scholarly papers, and completed his thesis.

The Road to Open Dissent

In 1956 Orlov's promising career took an abrupt and decidedly negative turn. At issue were remarks made by Orlov and some of his colleagues at a Party meeting of the Institute of Theoretical and Experimental Physics. Encouraged by the more permissive political climate following Stalin's death in 1953 and instilled with new hope following Khrushchev's de-Stalinization or "secret speech" to the 20th Party Congress in early 1956, a small group of young intellectuals made speeches which drew attention to the general loss of honesty and morality in the Party; and, as a sign of their constructive criticism, they proposed a program for democratic reforms in the Party. Orlov and his like-minded colleagues passed a resolution calling on all members of the Party's Central Committee to account for their activity under Stalin.

Word of this secret meeting at Orlov's institute quickly reached top Soviet leaders, and their response was swift. They dissolved the Party organization at the institute and canceled its resolution on official accountability. Shortly thereafter, *Pravda*, in a special article, roundly attacked Orlov and the other reformists; in addition, a secret letter reinforcing official displeasure was sent from the Central Committee to the institute's Party members.[6] In the end, Orlov was expelled from the Party and fired from his job. Furthermore, officials struck Orlov's name from his scholarly publications because it was viewed as a disgrace to Soviet science.

Blacklisted in Moscow, Orlov's career seemed finished until the influential Soviet nuclear physicist Kurchatov interceded on his behalf. Kurchatov reportedly told Khrushchev, who was furious with the insubordination of Orlov's Party committee, that if an exceptionally gifted young person such as Orlov was excluded from scientific research, he, too, would not pursue scientific research.[7]

Faced with such pressure from a leader of the scientific intelligentsia, Khrushchev compromised and agreed to permit Orlov to pursue his research, but only far away from Moscow. Without work for six months and with no prospects for employment in his profession, Orlov grudgingly accepted a semivoluntary exile in the Armenian Republic. He followed the suggestion of A.I. Alikhanyan—the brother of the director of his previous institute—and went to a similar research center in Erevan to help develop an electron ring accelerator.

Except for a few trips to Moscow, Orlov seems to have spent the next decade and a half close to the Turkish border, exceedingly isolated from the intellectual ferment which gripped many intellectuals in Moscow following the official attacks on Boris Pasternak, Joseph Brodsky, Sinyavsky, and Daniel; the subsequent political trials of their supporters; and the intellectuals' protest over the Warsaw Pact's intervention in Czechoslovakia in 1968. In fact, while Moscow dissidents were actively writing and circulating appeals protesting official acts of repression, Orlov was busy building a reputation as an outstanding scientist. During this period he published seminal work which attracted serious attention not only in Moscow, but also at Berkeley and at the European Center for Nuclear Research.[8] As a result of his distinguished research, he eventually was awarded a doctoral degree in physics and the title of professor, and in 1968 he was elected a corresponding member of the Academy of Science of the Armenian Republic. It should be noted that Orlov's accomplishments would not have been possible had Khrushchev not ordered Party *apparatchiks* (bureaucrats) in Armenia (on the fortieth anniversary of Soviet Armenia) to forget the past and rehabilitate persons such as Orlov in order to permit them to resume important work for the state. This meant that Orlov was granted not only permission to complete his doctorate, but also a secret clearance required to read classified reports. Without this, it would have been virtually impossible for Orlov to develop his earlier research, which was of a classified nature.[9]

In 1972, well after Khrushchev's fall, Orlov managed to gain the permission necessary to relocate to Moscow and to work at the Institute of Terrestrial Magnetism and Radiowave Propagation. Keenly aware, no doubt, of the likely outcome of any open criticism of the regime's active campaign against Soviet dissidents, Orlov avoided active involvement in the human rights movement. However, as the KGB campaign accelerated and as Andrei Sakharov increasingly became the target of official press attacks, Orlov found it impossible to remain silent. In late 1973 he made the leap from passive support of repressed dissidents to occasional open criticism. In an open and respectfully worded letter to Brezhnev, for example, he emphasized the need for democratic reforms and raised his voice in defense of Sakharov. The official reaction to his letter was predictable. In January 1974 Orlov was fired from his job and lost his secret clearances. The official pretext given was the need for a staff reduction. However, the actual reason was the letter to Brezhnev and the fact that Orlov was a co-founding member of the illegal Moscow chapter of Amnesty International.

From early 1974 until his arrest in February 1977, Orlov was not able to find work in his profession; even the president of the Armenian Academy of Sciences was not able to accept Orlov, in spite of his personal willingness to do so.[10] Orlov survived this period of personal and family hardship by tutoring high school students and probably through contributions from sympathetic former colleagues. In addition, he managed to continue his scientific research, even though he was greatly hindered without the special research facilities made available for those holding secret clearances. Despite this overburdened lifestyle, Orlov increasingly found time to participate in the Soviet human rights movement.

During the next three years Orlov's views changed drastically. Like many other Moscow intellectuals he grew steadily disenchanted with the regime after observing the unabating campaign of repression against the human rights activists in the Soviet Union and intellectuals in several East European countries. For Orlov this led naturally to a life of open dissent against the regime's violations of internationally accepted standards of human rights.

Despite repeated official warnings and increasing harassment, Orlov steadily stepped up his outspoken defense of political prisoners and related *samizdat* activities.[11] Between 1974 and his arrest in early 1977, Orlov signed the Moscow Appeal, which protested the arrest and expulsion of Alexander Solzhenitsyn from the USSR, and campaigned actively for the release of numerous political prisoners in the Soviet Union, including Sergei Kovalev, Mustafa Dzhemilev, Paruir Airikian, Andrei Tverdokhlebov, Vasyl Romanyuk, and Leonid Plyushch. Notably, these and other cases supported by Orlov encompassed a broad spectrum of issues, including psychiatric abuse of political prisoners, ethnic discrimination against the Soviet Union's Crimean Tatar minority and other nationalities, emigration, and religious rights.

In addition to signing appeals to Soviet and foreign officials, much of Orlov's time was spent preparing and circulating *samizdat* documents. Several types of *samizdat* writings can be identified. In 1974 and 1975, for example, Orlov directed his attention beyond Soviet borders, addressing the following documents to foreigners: a letter to Amnesty International in London requesting support for the recently convicted human rights activist Airikian; a letter to the International Committee for Human Rights requesting that a lawyer be appointed to help Leonid Plyushch's wife seek his release from a psychiatric hospital where he had been put because of his nonviolent human rights activity; an appeal to public opinion in Western countries arguing that the struggle for human rights in the Soviet Union is of vital interest for the West; an appeal to members of the U.S. Congress in defense of the rights of political prisoners in the USSR; a letter to the Rev. Michael Bourdeaux of Keston College (formerly called the Center for the Study of Religion under Communism), located near London, in defense of the imprisoned Ukrainian Orthodox priest Romanyuk. During the same period Orlov and other dissidents signed and addressed the following *samizdat* documents to Soviet officials: a statement to President Podgorny protesting recent KGB actions against human rights activists; a petition to the Presidium of the USSR Supreme Soviet calling for a general political amnesty; an open letter to KGB Chairman Andropov in defense of the Crimean Tatar rights activist Dzhemilev; and a statement to Soviet leaders in defense of Sakharov and nine other Moscow intellectuals on the occasion of Political Prisoners' Day. Finally, Orlov circulated personal writings in *samizdat* channels which discussed, primarily for a Soviet audience, his background and ideas. Two essays deserve special attention: Orlov's "Autobiographical Sketch" and an essay published in December 1975 entitled "Is Socialism without Totalitarianism Possible?" In the latter, he argues forcefully that such a development is possible given a fundamental decentralization of the economy and the introduction of a large measure of private political initiative.[12]

During this same period Orlov also focused his efforts on "prisoners of conscience" outside the Soviet Union. In his capacity as a cofounder of the Moscow chapter of Amnesty International, he campaigned actively for the release of political prisoners and torture victims in Spain, Sri Lanka, Yugoslavia, and Uruguay.[13] He also signed appeals for a general political amnesty.

Orlov's activity, however, did not stop with the pen. He was not only followed and harassed by the KGB, but he also followed and inevitably infuriated them. He did so in an effort to lend support to fellow dissidents who were under official attack. He rushed to the homes of Moscow dissidents during KGB searches to provide moral support; attempted repeatedly, though unsuccessfully, to attend the political trials of his associates; and visited Soviet psychiatrists to plead for the release of Plyushch. In addition, he conducted physics seminars in his home and attended some held elsewhere.[14] In retaliation for such unofficial activity, Orlov, on several occasions, was placed under house arrest, most notably during the 1972 visit of President Nixon to the Soviet Union.

The Helsinki Accords

In August 1975, an historic event occurred that would place the issue of Soviet treatment of dissidents squarely on the international agenda and eventually elevate Orlov next to Sakharov as an undisputed leader of the Soviet human rights movement: the Soviet Union signed the Helsinki Accord, the Final Act of the Conference on Security and Cooperation in Europe. Together with the United States and thirty-three other countries, the Soviet Union pledged, among other things, to protect human rights and fundamental freedoms. In return for this promise, the USSR received a document that affirmed its borders and legitimized the status quo in Europe. Soviet officials left Helsinki elated: they had witnessed the culmination of twenty years of Soviet diplomatic efforts. In exchange the West received a Soviet pledge to act in conformity with international commitments on human rights—Basket Three and Principle VII of the Final Act.

At the time the Helsinki Final Act was signed, most official and nongovernmental observers in the West attached little significance to the agreements. The Final Act's high-sounding principles were part of the unfolding relaxation or detente in Soviet-American relations. The West certainly entertained no hope of reversing Soviet territorial gains in World War II; and the Soviet Union, to the mind of most Western observers, would ratify the agreement and then simply ignore it.[15]

In the Soviet Union, however, a strikingly different view of the Final Act was held. For Orlov and other veteran dissidents, the Helsinki Accord brought new hope to a seemingly hopeless situation. Disillusioned with official reactions to the constructive criticism of members of the Soviet human rights movement and dissenting intellectuals and workers in Eastern Europe, Orlov and others clung to the Final Act as a vehicle to legitimize their campaign for Soviet adherence to international standards of human rights.

A few weeks after the Helsinki Accord was signed, Orlov and other Moscow dissidents were describing the Final Act as an unprecedented means to defend human rights and to revive their struggle and build Western support.

The U.S. Connection

It was during this period that Orlov and several other leading Moscow dissidents met with a delegation of eighteen members of the U.S. Congress who were visiting the Soviet Union. During the meeting, Orlov and his colleagues argued persuasively that the human rights provisions of the Final Act should be taken seriously and that implementation of the agreement should be monitored openly by the United States and the other signatory countries. Such a course, in the estimation of the dissidents, could put pressure on Soviet leaders and lead to a relaxation of KGB repression.[16]

Impressed by how seriously the dissidents viewed the provisions of the Final Act, the delegation, and in particular Congresswoman Millicent Fenwick, returned to relay the views of this small Moscow group to fellow members of Congress and other Washington officials. A month later, Representative Fenwick introduced legislation calling for the formation of a congressional commission composed of members of Congress and representatives of the executive branch to monitor implementation of the Helsinki Accords. Despite this broad mandate, the intent underlying the formation of such a commission was from the outset to establish a vehicle which could and would use the provisions of the Helsinki Accords to spotlight Soviet violations of human rights. Although the commission, since its formation in May 1976, has on occasion directed the focus of its hearings and papers to the compliance records of non-Soviet countries, the vast majority of its work—judging from the commission's listings of published reports and public hearings—has focused on the Soviet Union and Eastern Europe.[17]

Origins of the Moscow Group

In May 1976, at roughly the same time as the U.S. Congressional Helsinki Commission was being created, Orlov and ten other well-known activists in the long-standing movement for the defense of human rights in the Soviet Union announced the formation of the Moscow Committee to Promote Observance of the Helsinki Accords in the USSR. The Group's name was selected carefully to emphasize its fundamental loyalty to the system and its desire to cooperate with the authorities, if the latter adopted a positive and conscientious attitude toward the Soviet Union's human rights obligations. The Group was formed openly and there were no secrets about the way it operated or its membership. In fact, its formation was announced at a special news conference held at Sakharov's apartment for members of the Western press. The U.S. Congressional Helsinki Commission in a special report summarized the early intentions and activity of the Moscow Group as follows:

> Far from assaulting Soviet rule, the Public Group [i.e., the Moscow Group and similar groups subsequently created in several republics] set out from the beginning only to call it to account. In announcing its formation, the Moscow Group proclaimed that its "aim . . . is to promote observance of the humanitarian provisions of the Final Act" and its "first goal is to inform" signatory heads of state and "the public about cases in direct violation" of Principle VII and the provisions of Basket III on human contacts, information and cooperation in culture and education. The members declared that they "proceed from the conviction that the issues of humanitarianism and free information have a direct relationship to the problem of international security."[18]

The idea to establish a Moscow Helsinki Watch Committee should be credited to Yury Orlov. After years of patiently and respectfully petitioning the authorities for important changes in policy, Orlov grew increasingly convinced of the need to appeal beyond Soviet borders for support in order to influence Soviet behavior toward dissidents—in particular, to international public opinion, Communist parties abroad, international organizations, and foreign governments. Earlier in his conflict with the authorities, Orlov had observed that liberal Western public opinion reacted positively to the dissidents' cause. He recalled, for example, the efforts of Dr. Philip Handler, president of the American Academy of Sciences, whose outspoken defense helped cut short the official attacks on Academician Sakharov.[19] Hence, the Moscow Group was formed because the veteran dissidents needed a new way to legitimize and revive their struggle against the official repression of human rights activists. In particular, they needed a means to spread their message to a wider Soviet audience. They realized that the Soviet public obviously could not be influenced to support their struggle if they did not hear their message. They also were aware of the very limited and often interrupted circulation of most *samizdat* documents. Consequently, the dissidents increasingly turned to the West for support. They realized that, based on past experience, many of the *samizdat* documents smuggled to the West eventually were broadcast back to the Soviet Union by foreign radio stations and, in this way, were made available to a much larger Soviet audience.

Andrei Amalrik, a former Soviet dissident and a close associate of Yury Orlov's, sheds further light on the formation, intentions, and essential character of the Moscow Group:

> In January 1976 I discussed with Yury Orlov and Anatoly Shcharansky whether we would suggest that a Group be formed in each of the countries which had signed the Helsinki Declaration to check how far the rights specified in the Declaration were being enjoyed. We decided that we should take the initiative ourselves and form a Group, then invite people in other countries to do the same thing.
>
> I discussed with Orlov the Declaration which should be issued when the Group was formed, and who should be invited to join the Group. We wanted to include people with different points of view provided that they were generally concerned with encouraging the exercise of human rights in the USSR. With regret I decided that I should not join the Group myself because I had already received permission to leave the USSR.

The main object of the Group was to help the Soviet Government and other signatory countries implement the Declaration by providing information about violations of human rights.[20]

Recruitment of Group Members:
The Company Orlov Kept[21]

Orlov was extremely selective in his choice of candidates for membership in the Moscow Watch Group. Aware that members would be the objects of close scrutiny by the KGB and probable targets of harsh attacks in the official press, he selected veteran dissidents who were steadfast in their convictions and also widely respected in the dissident community. To lead the Group, Orlov chose Andrei Sakharov, referred to by many Soviet dissidents as the father of the contemporary human rights movement in the USSR. Sakharov, however, declined the invitation, offering instead to act as an advisor to the Group.[22] Orlov became the Group's chairman.

Of the Group's remaining ten founding members, three—Alexander Ginzburg, Petro Grigorenko, and Anatoly Marchenko—had been incarcerated on one or more occasions for their dissident activities before joining the Moscow Watch Group; hence, each had a criminal record with the authorities. A brief profile of these individuals is in order because, from the viewpoint of the KGB, they were probably Orlov's most objectionable Group associates.

Ginzburg was imprisoned first in 1960 for two years. The official charge was forgery, but the actual offense was his editorship of the *samizdat* journal *Syntax*.[23] Ginzburg was arrested several more times after his release in 1962. In January 1968 he was tried along with three others and sentenced to five years' imprisonment for compiling the *White Book*, a collection of documents on the trial of dissident writers Sinyavsky and Daniel. In 1974, after the forcible expulsion of Alexander Solzhenitsyn from the USSR, Ginzburg was appointed by Solzhenitsyn to manage the Russian Public Fund for Aid to the Families of Political Prisoners. In this role, Ginzburg distributed money and other material assistance to the families of political prisoners. Solzhenitsyn, incidentally, subsidized the fund through the sale of his writings in the West. Ginzburg's final arrest for "anti-Soviet agitation and propaganda" came in February 1977, shortly before Orlov's.

Prior to becoming an outspoken critic of some of the regime's policies, Major General Petro Grigorenko had received five decorations, including the order of Lenin, and seven medals for his military service in World War II (during which he was twice wounded). In 1960, he criticized Khrushchev's "personality cult" as closely resembling Stalin's and protested official discrimination against Jewish military officers in the awarding of promotions. For this and related activity, Grigorenko was arrested in 1964 by the KGB and eventually diagnosed by the Serbsky Institute for Forensic Medicine as mentally insane and incarcerated in a psychiatric hospital. Subsequently, he was expelled from the Communist Party and demoted to the rank of private. After his release in 1965, Grigorenko continued his human rights activities, speaking out against political and national repression in the USSR, especially on behalf of Crimean Tatars. In early 1969 he was again arrested and sent to a special psychiatric hospital, where he was confined until 1974. In November 1977, he was granted a six-month travel visa to the United States for medical treatment and a visit to his son. While in the United States, Grigorenko was accused of undermining the prestige of the Soviet Union and was stripped of his citizenship by the Supreme Soviet.

Unlike the other founding members of the Moscow Group, Anatoly Marchenko was not free at the time of its formation. In a gesture of symbolic support, Marchenko joined the Group while still serving a sentence of four years' exile in Chuna (Irkutsk *oblast*) in the Soviet Far East, following his 1975 conviction for alleged violation of the rules of administrative surveillance imposed after his release from prison in 1970. Marchenko was first imprisoned from 1960 to 1966 for his dissident activities. In 1968 he was sentenced to two years in camp for "anti-Soviet slander" and alleged passport violations. His 1968 conviction followed the publication in *samizdat* of his book *My Testimony*, the first eyewitness account of political camps and prisons in the post-Stalin period.

Finally, a brief sketch of Group member Anatoly Shcharansky is deserved, given the enormous attention focused on him and his Moscow Group associates by the Western and Soviet news media during 1977 and 1978. Shcharansky was recruited by Orlov to join the Group to add balance to it. A long-time activist in the Jewish emigration movement, he graduated from the Moscow Institute of Applied Physics in 1972. Shortly thereafter, according to an official explanation, he was denied permission to emigrate from the Soviet Union due to his previous access to state secrets.

However, there was another important reason why Orlov recruited Shcharansky. He was fluent in English and, as a result of his advocacy of Jewish emigration, had developed many contacts with foreign journalists and diplomats stationed in Moscow, as well as with visiting foreigners, including U.S. congressmen. The impressions of Shcharansky's foreign dealings, recorded by one foreign journalist, *Time* magazine's Moscow bureau chief (1976-78) Marsh Clark, are interesting. Shcharansky had on several occasions acted as Clark's interlocuter and translator in discussions with Andrei Sakharov. According to Clark: "Shcharansky seemed merely to be busying himself while awaiting emigration to Israel, for which he had repeatedly applied, perhaps believing that by making himself obnoxious to the authorities they would kick him out. How wrong he was."[24] Shcharansky was arrested just after Orlov in 1977 and charged with "anti-Soviet agitation and propaganda" and treason.

Activities of the Moscow Group

As the Group's name suggests, its members dedicated themselves to promoting Soviet compliance with the humanitarian provisions of the Helsinki Final Act. Toward this end, members monitored and documented an extremely broad range of issues and ultimately, prior to Orlov's 1977 arrest, released nineteen reports and supplementary materials. Collectively, they documented cases of maltreatment of political prisoners, unjust trials, persecution of religious believers, separation of families, interference with mail and telephones, and denial of the right to leave the country.[25]

The Group based its reports on information gleaned from letters and phone calls, or from messengers sent from distant parts of the Soviet Union. In this regard, the influence of foreign radio stations was crucial. After hearing about the work of the Moscow Group on foreign radio broadcasts, many ordinary Soviet citizens began sending information to the Group on human rights violations in various parts of the Soviet Union. The Group then checked the accuracy of this information by referring to official documents such as secret instructions to trials or legal decisions. Frequently, the Group would send its members outside of Moscow to remote regions of the USSR to make firsthand evaluations of alleged violations. Writing in 1981 before the Moscow Group disbanded, Alexeyeva summarizes the intensive and painstaking research effort involved with the following caveat.

> The Moscow Helsinki Group documents do not reflect the personal bias of its members, but rather the information which was received. The Group members only registered and examined the accuracy of the reports which they received.
>
> However, the Group does not always have the possibility of directly checking the facts . . . received. Sometimes, Group documents include reports from citizens about violations of their rights based only on their testimony (oral refusals in the OVIR [visa office] or beatings in prison, etc.). The Group has often appealed to CSCE [Conference on Security and Cooperation in Europe] signatories and public opinion to create an international commission to examine the information compiled by the Group about violations of the Final Act by the Soviet authorities.[26]

The carefully researched documents of the Moscow Group focused primarily on the failures of the Soviet regime to observe the Helsinki Accords. This was natural. It was not, of course, the purpose of the Group to spotlight positive developments in Soviet society unrelated to the Final Act nor to dwell unduly on shortcomings of the system. Accordingly, the Group acted judiciously and selected violations which it judged as best representing the regime's unwillingness to observe the Helsinki Act. Despite this measured approach, from a Western point of view, the several hundred documents of the various Soviet Helsinki Watch Committees and their affiliates amounted to a searing indictment of the Soviet system and, in particular, its observance of international standards of human rights.

Domestic Links

Inspired by the Moscow Group, similar Helsinki Watch Groups quickly arose in Ukraine, Lithuania, Armenia, and Georgia. They, in turn, were joined by a number of groups with narrower interests: the Christian and Catholic Committees to Defend the Rights of Believers, the Adventist, Pentecostal, and Baptist Rights Groups, the Working Commission on the Abuse of Psychiatry for Political Purposes, and the Disabled Rights' Group. Although these groups undoubtedly had many sympathizers who shared their general interests and specific grievances, the total open membership was minute. In December 1979, the U.S. Helsinki Commission reported a total membership of sixty-six men and women in the Helsinki Watch Groups and twenty-six persons in the affiliated groups.[27]

The relationship between the Moscow Group, the non-Russian Helsinki Watch Groups, and the other affiliated groups was a mutually supportive one. The Moscow Group served as an "internet" for the human rights community in the Soviet Union as well as abroad. In this capacity, it stimulated communication and coordination between and among the constituent elements of that community and its foreign supporters. In return for information gathered by the other Soviet Helsinki Committees and their affiliated groups, the Moscow Group made available its experience and superior access to Western correspondents and diplomats in Moscow. These assets were made available to repressed persons and groups situated in the distant republican cities and towns, which were virtually inaccessible to foreign reporters and embassy staffers. Despite the obvious special interests of many of the groups associated with the Moscow Committee, they all supported the fundamental intention of the Helsinki Accord. As formulated by Yury Orlov, it is that

> the non-violent struggle for the fundamental rights of the individual, for decency and against cruelty, for toleration and for the free circulation of information offers a more sure and lasting basis for confidence and peace than can be achieved by political efforts alone. The problems of security in today's world are inseparable from humanitarian problems. This is the rationale for the humanitarian provisions of the Final Act. And why all peoples and all governments have a stake in their fulfillment.[28]

East European Connection

The success of the Moscow Group also had an impact outside the Soviet Union. In Czechoslovakia, the initiatives taken by Orlov and his colleagues inspired the formation of a similar committee called Charter '77; in Poland, they helped encourage the formation of KOR, the Workers' Defense Committee. One Western writer summed up the hopeful mood spurred in East Europe by the Helsinki Accords and its supporters as follows:

> The Helsinki Accords became a universal point of reference throughout Eastern Europe. In East Germany, people crowded into government offices clutching copies their own government had printed. In Czechoslovakia, Poland, and Rumania nonconformist writers, students, and workers cited the Accords in appeals to authorities.[29]

It should be noted that all of this occurred against a backdrop of increasing political tension in Eastern Europe. Particularly troublesome was Poland. There workers united and rioted in 1976 to protest sudden increases in food prices. The protests were massive and violent. Indignant workers set fire to the Communist Party headquarters in Radom and tore up railroad tracks outside of Warsaw. Only as a last resort did the Polish government grudgingly rescind increases in food prices in order to restore order. Such a course, predictably, further alienated workers from the authorities and led to the creation of KOR by leading Polish intellectuals.

Increasing discontent also was evident elsewhere in East Europe. In Czechoslovakia intellectuals and ousted leaders of the Dubcek regime challenged the government's authority. On January 1, 1977, they addressed an appeal to officials entitled Charter '77, which emphasized the discrepancy between the international human rights obligations accepted by the government and the behavior of the secret police and the courts. Despite subsequent arrests of leading dissidents, hundreds of other persons signed the appeal. Rumania and East Germany similarly showed signs of intellectual protest and nonconformity. Particularly conspicuous in the latter was the massive drive for emigration.

Beyond Eastern Europe, similar groups were formed in Norway, Holland, Switzerland, the United States, and other countries. In addition to providing the moral impetus for the formation of foreign Watch Committees, the Moscow Group established working relations with some of them. One consequence of this was that the Moscow Committee became the first Soviet unofficial group to issue joint statements with foreign organizations such as KOR and the nongovernmental U.S. Helsinki Watch Committee. Hence, despite the many differences in the worlds of Soviet and East European dissidents and nonconformists, the Helsinki Act provided a common link in their respective struggles for the rule of law. Activists in Eastern Europe and other countries were totally united when, in conformity with Basket Three provisions of the Final Act, they requested their governments to honor their fundamental right to an open exchange of information and to observe other domestic and international laws on human rights.

Domestic Roots

Although stimulated by the spirit of Helsinki, the work of the Soviet Helsinki Groups was a natural outgrowth of the Soviet human rights movement of the mid-1960s.[30] As mentioned earlier, many of the founding members of the Moscow Group were veterans of the conflict between Moscow intellectuals and the KGB which began with scattered protests over the trials of nonconformist writers Sinyavsky and Daniel in 1966 and gathered momentum with the denunciation of the Soviet-led invasion of Czechoslovakia in 1968. These heady years led to the emergence of the "democratic movement," known also as the Soviet human rights movement. During this period, the movement included a diverse mixture of persons, ranging from distinguished members of the scientific and creative intelligentsia to groups of dedicated activists largely recruited from young students and intellectuals. The former typically would confine their activities to signing occasional protest statements, while the latter engaged in illegal public demonstrations, circulated *samizdat* literature and constantly risked arrest and imprisonment. Despite their differences, both of these groups were united by their commitment to greater intellectual freedom and civil rights and the rule of law.

The efforts of Orlov and the regional Helsinki Monitors in the Soviet Union did not depart fundamentally from these goals. In fact, the efforts were a continuation of the tradition embodied in the Soviet human rights movement and a broadening of it in accord with the international commitments made by the Soviet Union under the Helsinki Final Act. Although the efforts of the human rights movement never generated wide public support, they were not inconsequential. The movement managed to break through the "inertia of fear," which immobilized Soviet intellectuals and the public in general.[31] Furthermore, as Andrei Sakharov notes: "It has changed the moral climate and created the spiritual preconditions needed for democratic changes in the USSR and for the formulation of an ideology of human rights throughout the world."[32]

Foreign Dimension

Although the Soviet human rights movement began in the mid-1960s as essentially a domestic conflict between the regime and its intellectual critics, it slowly but steadily assumed a foreign dimension; by 1977 the arrests of Soviet Helsinki Monitors became the focus of a major confrontation between President Carter and Brezhnev. Several factors contributed to this dynamic and unexpected development, including the significantly increased opportunity for contact between foreign correspondents in Moscow and dissidents, a result of detente in Soviet-American relations; the growing boldness of some young dissidents; the enormous growth in the volume and reliability of *samizdat* sources available to foreign diplomats, reporters, and others; and the new and sensational nature of the contemporary dissident movement and of the KGB's repression of such daring personalities as Alexander Solzhenitsyn, Vladimir Bukovsky, and Andrei Sakharov. Within the span of a few years, Western media coverage of the dynamic dissident movement mushroomed. In the late 1960s, for example, newspapers and magazines were avidly reporting the intensified official attacks on Solzhenitsyn: the seizure of all his unpublished manuscripts, the withdrawal of his few published works from official circulation, and his expulsion from the Soviet Writers' Union. The effect of such dramatic reporting was not to sell newspapers and magazines, but to slowly build Western public support for repressed individuals who seemed to share many fundamental Western values. Moreover, in the 1970s it cast increasing doubt on the popular conception of detente as encouraging a relaxation in Soviet attitudes toward Western values.

In the United States, news of the Soviet human rights movement and the Helsinki Final Act produced the spiritual and political preconditions necessary for the creation of, to borrow Andrei Sakharov's phrase, "an ideology of human rights."[33] In the 1960s and early 1970s, conditions were ripening for human rights advocacy to become a more important instrument of U.S. foreign policy. The demoralizing American experience in Vietnam, the intensifying repression of prominent intellectuals, religious believers, and others in the Soviet Union, as well as traditional U.S. support for democratic values and religious freedom created a mood among Americans and their leaders which promoted a greater moral component to U.S. foreign policy—a desire in part to fill the moral and political vacuum left by Vietnam and the Watergate affair.[34] This mood found concrete expression in actions such as the presidential victory of Jimmy Carter and the passage of the Jackson-Vanik amendment to the U.S. Trade Act of 1974. Named after its cosponsors, this amendment was clearly an effort to coerce the Soviet Union and other Warsaw Pact countries into allowing freer emigration of the Jewish population by requiring that nonmarket economies meet set standards of emigration before most-favored-nation (MFN) tariff status would be granted. The reaction of Soviet leaders was not surprising. They refused to accept the concept of MFN treatment, arguing that it constituted an unwarranted interference in Soviet internal affairs—in short, an effort to blackmail and intimidate a world power.

In addition to the signing of the Helsinki Final Act, another development that encouraged the activities of Soviet dissidents and the Helsinki Monitors in particular was the 1976 U.S. presidential election. During the presidential campaign, the incumbent, President Ford, was criticized sharply—even by members of his own party, including Governor Ronald Reagan—for not being more outspoken on human rights violations by the Soviet Union. In particular, Ford was attacked for not receiving Solzhenitsyn (expelled from the USSR in 1974) at the White House. Following Carter's presidential victory, the White House pursued a new style of diplomatic relations that placed the issue of human rights squarely on the U.S. foreign policy agenda.

Carter's interest in including human rights questions as a component of U.S. foreign policy was manifested conspicuously and repeatedly in U.S. relations with the Soviet Union. Shortly after he entered the White House, for example, President Carter received a letter from Sakharov asking him to appeal publicly on behalf of repressed human rights activists and religious believers in the Soviet Union and Eastern Europe. Carter reacted immediately. He quickly sent a personal letter to Sakharov through the diplomatic pouch, an act which infuriated Soviet leaders. Then, a few weeks later, in a special press conference, Carter stressed that he saw no relation between his outspoken criticism of the human rights situation in the Soviet Union and the strategic arms limitation talks. Another act that outraged Soviet leaders was President Carter's White House meeting with exiled Soviet dissident Vladimir Bukovsky, an individual who frequently had been described as a criminal by the Soviet press.

What followed during the remainder of the Carter administration may be described as an escalating war of words about Soviet dissidents between the United States and the Soviet Union, which by the summer of 1978 reached a point probably unprecedented since the height of the Cold War. President Carter's continued support for this repressed group was reinforced by the efforts of the U.S. Congressional Helsinki Commission, the State Department, Radio Liberty, and the Voice of America. The group also found support in the independent and persistent efforts of nongovernmental organizations such as Amnesty International, Keston College, U.S. Helsinki Watch, various emigré groups, and the foreign radio stations of the BBC and Deutsche Welle. The result of these collective efforts was a virtually unprecedented media blitz of the Soviet Union. The intensity of this campaign was heightened by the severe sentences meted out to Helsinki Monitors in 1978.

The arrest and trial of Orlov and other Helsinki Monitors provoked sharp and widespread criticism from several West European governments, the European Economic Community, Norway, Canada, Israel, and the United States. In the United States, President Carter, in addition to strongly criticizing the arrests of Orlov and others, ceased consideration of a visit to Moscow as a reflection of his disapproval of Soviet behavior. In nongovernmental action, prominent U.S. scientists boycotted professional conventions in the USSR, refused to participate in scientific exchange activities, and sent cables to Brezhnev. In Europe, similar actions were taken by individuals and various professional organizations. Significantly, even communist parties in Western Europe, including the French Communist Party, expressed strong disapproval of the arrests and trials of Orlov and the other Helsinki Monitors.[35] Together, these varied reactions focused the spotlight of international attention on the Soviet Union and inadvertently heightened international tensions, particularly in U.S.-Soviet relations.

KGB Repression of the Moscow Group

From May 1976, when the Moscow Group was formed, until his arrest nine months later, Yury Orlov was kept under constant surveillance by the KGB. During these months, the authorities took a decidedly restrained and cautious approach, repeatedly warning rather than arresting Orlov and his close associates. For example, on the day of the Group's formation, cars filled with KGB agents appeared in front of Orlov's home and tried to prevent the Group's creation by warning Orlov that his actions were illegal and anti-Soviet. A few days after the public announcement of the Group's formation, Orlov was taken into custody and formally warned that the Group was illegal and must disband. Failure to comply, according to officials, would lead to his arrest. Despite further official warnings, Orlov and his colleagues continued their efforts. During the time remaining before Orlov's arrest, he and the other Helsinki Monitors and their associates were subjected to increasing repression, including house searches with the confiscation of documents, KGB interrogations, job dismissals, house arrests, harassment of family members, detentions, difficulties with residence permits, and administrative surveillance. Despite the searches, interrogations, and detentions, Orlov and the Moscow Group managed by early 1977 to issue nineteen carefully documented papers on Soviet violations of Basket Three provisions of the Helsinki Final Act.

As the fall 1977 Belgrade follow-up conference to the Helsinki Accords approached, the KGB accelerated its campaign to suppress the Moscow Group and the other Watch Committees in the USSR. In early January 1977, the KGB searched the apartment of Orlov and several other Moscow Group members. A few weeks later, articles appeared in the official press accusing Orlov, Ginzburg, and Shcharansky of anti-Soviet activity. A week later, on February 10, Orlov was arrested while visiting the apartment of fellow Group member Ludmila Alexeyeva and taken to Lefortovo Prison. There he spent the next fifteen months in pretrial detention while the state prepared its case and apparently waited patiently for the Belgrade Review Conference to draw to a close. The arrest of Orlov, Ginzburg, and Shcharansky in early 1977 marked the beginning of a crackdown on Soviet Helsinki Monitors that would culminate in late 1982 with the dissolution of all such groups in the Soviet Union.

Summary of Charges

The state's indictment of Yury Orlov was the product of fifteen months' work (six months more than is routinely permitted by Soviet law) by the KGB Investigation Department and was nearly forty pages long. It charged Orlov with "anti-Soviet agitation and propaganda" (Article 70, Part I, of the RSFSR Criminal Code) and noted that he systematically prepared and distributed documents containing slanderous fabrications discrediting the Soviet state and public order. The indictment emphasized that Orlov called on others to subvert the system's foundations.[36] Orlov's activities as leader of the Moscow Helsinki Group formed the bulk of the indictment.

Orlov's trial finally began on May 15, 1978 in Moscow City Court. Four days later the court passed sentence. He received the maximum penalty for a first offender under Article 70: seven years in a strict-regimen labor camp and five years in exile.

THE HYPOTHESIS

The main thesis of this chapter is that Soviet officials greatly exaggerated the foreign dimension of the conflict with Orlov and the Moscow Group. As a result, they misread the nature of the conflict and greatly magnified the threat posed to the regime by Orlov and his colleagues immediately prior to his 1977 arrest. Influenced by the extreme and stereotypic conceptions of dissidents and of Western psychological warfare that pervade official pronouncements, as well as by the very real contacts between dissidents and foreigners, Soviet authorities viewed the activities of Orlov and his associates as an organic element of a carefully calculated and foreign-inspired campaign to undermine the prestige and security of the Soviet Union, rather than seeing it as an essentially domestic effort by disillusioned but loyal citizens to promote fuller Soviet compliance with the human rights provisions of the Helsinki Final Act.

All of this, of course, does not mean that if the dark screen through which Soviet officials viewed Orlov and his foreign supporters were removed, his activities would be viewed as innocuous and tolerable. Soviet authorities did have cause to be concerned with the actions of Orlov and the Helsinki Monitors. Their *samizdat* activity did challenge the Party's control of information, as well as embarrass the regime and undermine its international prestige. But official images of the nature of the conflict greatly clouded official perception. In particular, the authorities lost sight of the fact that early Soviet policy toward Orlov and various leaders of the Soviet human rights movement greatly affected the course of Orlov's thinking and actions. By pursuing an unresponsive and frequently repressive policy, the authorities slowly but steadily transformed Orlov from a loyal, hard-working citizen and member of the Communist Party, who in the mid-1950s offered constructive criticism through Party channels, into an occasional signer of respectfully worded appeals addressed exclusively to Soviet officials and ultimately into an open and active critic of regime policies, an associate of veteran dissidents and foreign supporters in Moscow and abroad. In this sense, Soviet policy effected a self-fulfilling prophecy.

The rest of this chapter will describe the official images relevant to the 1978 trial of Yury Orlov, analyze any discrepancy between these and accurate images, and draw some conclusions regarding the sources of dominant official images and their consequences for official perception and action.

OFFICIAL IMAGES: GENERAL BACKGROUND

Historical Legacy

Contemporary Soviet images of Yury Orlov and other members of the Soviet scientific and creative intelligentsia participating in the human rights movement were not formed simply in reaction to the dissident activities of Orlov and his associates. They were conditioned by earlier official conceptions of internal and external adversaries. Distant, but nevertheless relevant, are the popular conceptions of the intelligentsia in traditional Russian society, which have filtered down through Soviet history and which now, with the aid of Russian fiction, form part of the collective memory of the people.

The intelligentsia of nineteenth-century Russia was a uniquely Russian phenomenon. Unlike the intellectual community in Europe at the time or today's Soviet intelligentsia (which refers essentially to the white-collar workers of the state), the Russian intelligentsia was a small group of men and women from various classes, given to critical thought and abstract ideas.[37] Tibor Szamuely further defines the composition and thought of this peculiarly Russian group:

> A significant proportion of the intelligentsia consisted of people who were, at best, semi-educated, by either European or Russian standards: failed students, lapsed seminarians, auto-didacts, etc. At the same time a large part, probably the greater and most highly civilized part of the educated class—higher civil servants, university professors, engineers, scientists, many professional people—were never regarded as belonging to the intelligentsia, either by themselves or by others. . . The *intelligent* was, above all, an enemy of Tsarist autocracy and of all its works. His hostility could, and did, take a variety of forms, but it was ever-present, and it was this basic characteristic which set the intelligentsia apart from all other strata of Russian society. . . . The Russian intelligentsia was a social stratum composed of those politically aroused, vociferous and radical members of the educated classes who felt totally estranged from society, who rejected the social and political system of Tsarist autocracy, and who single-mindedly nurtured the idea of the imperative downfall of that system.[38]

Rejected by the public because of their extreme dedication to revolutionary ideas and repressed by the police for their intense and uncompromising hostility toward the state, the members of the intelligentsia grew increasingly alienated, suspicious, and conspiratorial. A particularly significant development was the rise of conspiratorial underground groups that rejected the basic values of Russian society and sought to change the status quo through revolutionary actions. This activity predictably reinforced official hostility toward and distrust of intellectuals and led to increased repression. It promoted the general image of members of the intelligentsia as fanatics, revolutionaries, and enemies—more precisely, as implacable enemies of the state with a fervor for martyrdom, educated but rootless conspirators totally estranged from society and determined to destroy the political and social system, radicals who betray their native traditions due to their radical devotion to socialism.[39] To summarize, the image of the Russian intelligentsia that has been handed down in Soviet history and Russian fiction is of a misguided, alienated, and unrepresentative group in fanatical and violent opposition to authority.

It is against this very general backdrop of traditional images that some Soviet officials probably view the dissident activity of Orlov and other alienated members of the intelligentsia. However, there is another less distant prism through which Soviet officials and the general public view these actions of Orlov and other dissidents, namely, the image of the Soviet Union as the target of an increasingly sophisticated campaign of Western-inspired subversion during an era of peaceful coexistence. Within this context, it is instructive to highlight three Soviet concepts: anti-Sovietism (and, more generally, anticommunism), Western psychological warfare, and human rights as an instrument of subversion.[40]

Anti-Sovietism

Although Soviet officials have been talking about anti-Sovietism and ideological struggle since the Revolution, this fact should not be allowed to obscure important changes in the more recent official discussions of Western-inspired subversion of the USSR and the socialist system in general.

In a book published in 1976, entitled *Contemporary Anti-Communism: Policy and Ideology*, a team of Soviet authors traces the evolution of contemporary anticommunism from the early days of the Soviet state. The authors define the phenomenon as the West's principal ideological and political instrument in its effort to slander the socialist system, misrepresent its policies and aims, and sow domestic dissent.[41] This work leads the reader to the inescapable conclusion that decades after the Revolution, anti-communism remains a vital and increasingly disguised force: a Western weapon for halting the social development of the socialist system and undermining its cohesion.

The "chief trend of anticommunism" is anti-Sovietism.[42] According to an editorial which appeared in the leading political and theoretical journal of the Party at about the time the contemporary dissident movement was forming, anti-Sovietism

consists basically of slander of the socialist system and falsification of the policies and aims of the Communist Parties and of Marxist-Leninist doctrine. Anti-Sovietism is evidence of the West's fear in the face of the growing might of the Soviet Union and the revolutionizing influence of its example upon the working people of the capitalist countries. . . . Today's credo of anti-Sovietism is to carry the war of ideas into the socialist countries, to penetrate the very heart of communist ideology.[43]

Soviet officials writing in the mid-1960s and later typically describe a deepening crisis of anticommunism, a substantial erosion in the influence of ultra-conservatives, those reactionary forces which openly oppose a relaxation in East-West tensions. To cope with this "growing social and political isolation," the West has entrusted the defense of its special interests to "more flexible representatives of anticommunism who have shown better adaptability to the new situation in the world arena."[44] Consequently, strategists such as Zbigniew Brzezinski have had to modify their tactics and adapt them to new conditions. However, they have not renounced their hostile intention. According to *Pravda*:

The essence of such tactics is, without openly opposing peaceful coexistence, to use the easing of tension to harm socialism and the world revolutionary movement.

Anticommunists . . . want to secure various kinds of political and ideological concessions from socialist countries in order to interfere in their internal affairs. While hypocritically appealing to the socialist countries for ideological tolerance, our opponents are at the same time doing all they can to expand and step up their subversive propaganda.[45]

Psychological Warfare: "The Secret War"

The growing power and prestige of the socialist system has forced the West to devise new and different forms of anticommunism.[46] Unable to confront the Soviet Union militarily in a nuclear era, the West has had to resort increasingly to ideological subversion, or psychological warfare as it is commonly termed by Soviet writers. In support of this position, the authors of *Contemporary Anti-Communism* cite a 1967 U.S. Congressional study which, in their view, emphasizes that the struggle between both superpowers will be settled not by military means, but through a war of words or propaganda.[47] The 24th Party Congress summarized the character, scale, and methods of the West's psychological war against the Soviet Union as follows:

> We are living under conditions of unabating ideological struggle, which imperialist propaganda is waging against our country, against the world of socialism, using the most subtle methods and powerful technical means. All the instruments that the bourgeoisie has of influencing minds—the press, cinema and radio—have been mobilized to delude people, to make them believe that under capitalism they are living in a near-paradise, and to slander socialism.[48]

Writing several years later, Semyon Tsvigun, a leading Soviet expert on the subject of ideological subversion, reinforced this image of psychological warfare in a major statement in *Kommunist*.[49] In that article he emphasized the heightened danger of Western subversive actions and described the "secret war" against the Soviet Union:

> A powerful intelligence-subversion apparatus, various punitive organs and numerous official and unofficial anti-Soviet centers and organizations have been set up in the West to wage a secret war against the Soviet Union.
>
> The main types of Western subversive activity aimed at the USSR are espionage, provocations directed at Soviet citizens and establishments abroad, and ideological diversions.
>
> The objective of ideological diversions is to weaken the socio-political fabric of socialism, to undermine the leading role of the communist parties and their influence among the masses, to trigger the "erosion of communist ideology, to promote a bourgeois outlook and, finally, to create havoc in the political and economic life of the socialist countries."
>
> Our class enemy is resorting to ideological diversion, aware that "its effect is manifested secretly and, frequently, is not noticed by the people against whom it is aimed." It is not by chance that ideological diversions are compared to a "cancerous tumor" which steadily spreads throughout the entire body unless removed in time.[50]

According to Tsvigun, Western psychological warfare is a massive and costly effort, judging from its machinery. There are, Tsvigun estimates, more than 400 anti-Soviet centers and organizations in the West that are intensively working to subvert the Soviet Union;

included are various Zionist organizations, the NATO Information Service and the National Labor Alliance (NTS).[51] Within this subversive network, the United States is described as playing a pivotal role:

> The United States holds a leading position in the extensive subversive ideological activities conducted against the socialist countries. Ideological subversions have become an inseparable part of U.S. foreign policy and the American intelligence services consider their participation in them as important as customary espionage.[52]

Human Rights and Psychological Warfare

The Western campaign for human rights, which was so conspicuous during the latter half of the 1970s, was, from the viewpoint of numerous authoritative Soviet spokesmen, above all, one of the more cunning and subtle tactics devised by the United States and its allies in their intensifying effort to subvert the ideological basis of the socialist system. Put simply, it was a cover for Western propaganda. Samuil Zivs summarized the view shared by leading Soviet officials in a book entitled *Human Rights, Continuing the Discussion*:

> The human rights campaign occupies a central place in the strategy and tactics of psychological warfare. Since 1977, it has been elevated in the United States to official government policy [Zivs suggests it was previously a covert operation, principally of the intelligence services].
>
> The human rights campaign serves the strategic goal of anti-Communism—weakening the political systems in socialist countries. It is part of the concept of eroding communist ideology, of plans to "reform" socialism from within, and subvert it by employing people hostile to its ideals.[53]

The Soviet conviction that the human rights issue was largely a weapon of psychological warfare was confirmed when President Reagan assumed office and, in the eyes of Soviet officials, essentially abandoned the human rights tactic for a new campaign—Soviet terrorism.

Finally, it is worth noting the admonition of Georgi Arbatov, who warns foreigners that the U.S. human rights campaign—of the late 1970s—should not be viewed narrowly. According to Arbatov:

It should be seen against the background of certain military efforts, foreign policy maneuvers, and other propaganda campaigns. It would be proper to recall, for instance, that in some key American foreign policy documents, like NSC-68, basic changes in our internal structure were put forward as a sine qua non for peaceful coexistence. Many actions in U.S. foreign policy in recent years reflect those guidelines.[54]

It is against this general backdrop of historical images of internal and external adversaries that attention will now shift to the general and specific images of Yury Orlov and his associates.

OFFICIAL IMAGES OF YURY ORLOV

The trial of Yury Orlov opened on May 15, 1978 in Moscow City Court and ended four days later. From the opening session, the courtroom's atmosphere did not promote an objective trial of the case. The presiding judge was Valentina Lubentsova, an official with a long-standing reputation for open hostility to the Soviet dissident movement. In 1968 she presided over the trial of five prominent dissidents who protested the Soviet intervention in Czechoslovakia, and in 1972 she heard the case of Vladimir Bukovsky.[55] In each instance, the defendants received heavy sentences following proceedings marked by an open presumption of guilt and various expressions of unconcealed hostility from the judge, the prosecutor, the state's witnesses, and the audience.

The prosecutor in the Orlov case was Moscow Deputy Procurator S.A. Emelyanov. Evgeny S. Shalman was the attorney appointed by the state to defend Orlov.

The trial was the culmination of more than fifteen months of detention for the defendant—almost twice the period normally permitted by Soviet law for a pretrial investigation. Soviet officials probably justified the extension by emphasizing the need to formulate an ironclad case against a prominent dissident whose case would certainly attract close international scrutiny. This concern was ultimately reflected in the fifty-eight volumes of evidence amassed by KGB investigators during this period.[56] Such an effort was complex and time-consuming, and included the careful selection and rehearsing of some of the prosecution's witnesses.[57] It was further complicated by the authorities changing the formulation of the indictment several times. According to Orlov, shortly after his arrest investigators even had considered charging him with treason because of his contacts with members of the U.S. Congress.[58] Another important factor delaying the trial of Orlov was the Belgrade Review Conference, which began in the fall of 1977. By postponing the trial until after the conference ended, Soviet officials minimized international criticism of the Orlov case at this forum.

In keeping with Soviet politico-legal tradition, the court proceedings were only nominally open. Orlov's wife, Irina, and his two sons, Alexander and Dimitry, were admitted; but none of their many friends, who had gathered long before the courtroom was officially opened, gained access. As is customary, the audience was screened carefully by the KGB, and only those judged politically reliable— and thus deemed "public representatives"—were admitted. Most of those in attendance were local workers (unskilled), engineers, and staffers from scientific institutes.[59] The result of this selection process was an openly hostile audience which, by means of shouts and rude remarks, continuously disrupted the efforts of Orlov and his attorney to present a serious defense.

The limiting of court attendance to only three of Orlov's relatives or friends, a rather routine practice, was probably motivated by the acute concern of Soviet authorities that the proceedings remain orderly and not degenerate into an anti-Soviet slander session and that they act in accord with the educational role of criminal proceedings prescribed in Article 2 of the Code of Criminal Procedure: "Criminal proceedings must facilitate . . . the education of citizens in the spirit of undeviating execution of Soviet laws and respect for the rules of socialist communal life."[60] In practice, this means that Article 2 often serves as an excuse for gross violations of legal procedure (even in nonpolitical cases). Valery Chalidze, a Soviet legal specialist and former dissident now living in U.S. exile, sheds further light on this important principle, which affects the character of the proceedings and ultimately the fate of the defendant:

> . . . the educational role of the law and the court is an essential element of Soviet legal doctrine. Great importance is attached to it, and in the attitude of Soviet court officials safeguarding the principle of public court procedure one can notice much greater concern for assuring the educational role of a court session than for defending the defendant's right to open trial. A Soviet jurist writes: "To achieve the required educational impact of court proceedings during a homicide trial the

composition of the court audience is important. Of course, it is impossible to prevent the presence in the court of close relatives of the defendant and the victim or limit their number in some way. If the court visitors consist predominantly of these persons, then there is always the danger, first, that they will spread incorrect information about the trial, with the result that other citizens will be misinformed. Secondly, the educational impact of the court procedure is constantly diminished. Therefore, if need be, the judge must take measures to assure the presence of public representatives at the court and, consequently, the correct interpretation of the trial among other citizens.[61]

In accord with the above legal principle, the "representatives of the public" observing the trial of Yury Orlov were individuals chosen to ensure the educational role of the proceedings and not casual observers there by chance.

Outside the courtroom, the atmosphere was emotionally charged. During the four days of the trial, scores of Orlov's friends and sympathizers remained in vigil outside the courtroom, having been denied permission to attend the trial on the pretext that there was no room in the courtroom. An eyewitness account (confirmed by several Western correspondents) of the scene outside the courtroom appears in the *Chronicle of Current Events*:

> As is usual in such cases, the court building was surrounded by police and KGB officials in civilian clothes. In comparison with previous occasions . . . the behavior of the police and state security officials differed only by more demonstrative, indeed, blatant crudeness, insolence and shamelessness. Already before the 15 May session, several people who had been waiting in the court building since early morning . . . were literally thrown from the porch into the street.[62]

The heavy police presence was reinforced by a large civilian crowd intended to represent the "anger of the Soviet people."[63] The behavior of this group was rude and provocative. In addition to rowdy shouts and insulting jokes, these supporters of the KGB engaged in more provocative activity. Some, for example, ridiculed, spat on, and even struck a religious nonconformist who had traveled to Moscow to attend the trial.[64] Before the proceedings ended, several of Orlov's sympathizers, who refused to disband, were arrested for disorderly conduct or "hooliganism."

Foreign observers, and reporters in particular, also were treated contemptuously. They were denied admission to the courtroom and harassed as they waited outside. They were insulted and threatened with shouts of: "We will shoot you, you Zionists, Jews!"[65] Furthermore, in their zeal to prevent leaks of the details of trial proceedings to foreign embassies and news services, the KGB clashed with aggressive foreign correspondents. For example, during a break called a few hours after the opening session of the trial, the KGB forcibly disbanded a group that had gathered to hear and record the trial impressions of Irina Orlova. In the process, police confiscated the cameras and tape recorders being used by foreign reporters.[66]

The suspicions of officials that members of Orlov's family might try to record the proceedings of the trial were confirmed on the first day when authorities confiscated their tape recorders. Subsequently, family members were repeatedly warned not to take notes, to leave the room during the breaks, or even to go near the windows. In addition, they were searched carefully before and after the remaining court sessions. In an apparent effort to break the defiant spirit of Irina Orlova, she was stripped naked and searched in the presence of three male KGB officials.[67] Despite these various official efforts, an official transcript of the proceedings was compiled and sent to the West.[68]

Inside the courtroom, the pervading mood was one of profound hostility and open contempt for the defendant and his associates. An open presumption of guilt by the judge and prosecutor was evident throughout the trial. The judge, for example, assumed from the outset that all the documents alleged by the prosecutor to be slanderous were, in fact, so. Her tone toward the defendant was contemptuous, demeaning, and intolerant. Significantly, whenever Orlov tried to explain his views or describe the activities of the Moscow Group, Judge Lubentsova interrupted him. Frequently, she lost her temper, shouted, and insulted Orlov.

The court's atmosphere and, in particular, its contempt for Orlov, was reflected in the following sample statements:

[Judge, interrupting
Orlov] :   "No one asked you to explain these petitions you submitted to the court! Stand up straight, don't prop yourself up! You're not giving a lecture."[69]

| [Prosecutor, inter- rupting Orlov]: | "The accused Orlov is engaging in political agitation! I ask the court to take notice of this."[70] |

As the proceedings progressed, so did the intensity of Lubent-sova's intolerance of, and hostility toward, the defendant. Efforts by Orlov and his attorney Shalman to detail the defendant's views and present other essential background information were constantly interrupted and ruled irrelevant. These efforts were viewed by the state as an effort to use the courtroom as a forum for the further slander of the Soviet Union—in other words, to obstruct the educational purpose of the trial.

The court's conspicuously negative attitude toward the defendant served only to provoke further an already rowdy audience. Orlov's efforts to present a defense were disrupted repeatedly by angry remarks and shouts from the onlookers. During his final speech, the spectators became particularly unruly.

| [Orlov to the court]: | What will uninformed people think when they hear the word "subversion" applied to me? They will think I am calling for a foreign intervention . . .[71] |
| [Audience members, shouting angrily to Orlov]: | Yes, you are calling for a foreign intervention! . . . Spy![72] |

This exchange was followed by angry shouts from the judge when Orlov attempted to explain the constructive nature of his criticism of the state and the difference between international cooperation and subversion.

| [Judge, inter- rupting Orlov]: | Defendant Orlov, you do not understand how to properly defend yourself! I declare your testimony finished. Begin your closing remarks.[73] |

Before Orlov had completed a few sentences, the patience of the court had visibly reached its limit. The judge and her assistants rose and left the courtroom abruptly. Orlov was then led away by the guards. The following day, he received the maximum sentence for a first offender: seven years' strict regime camp and five years of exile.

Orlov appealed his conviction to a higher court, but the verdict was upheld. In his appeal, he stressed that his case had not been heard in an objective manner and claimed the following major violations of legal procedure: the court did not call the defense witnesses he requested, it rejected his numerous petitions, it did not read or analyze the documents figuring prominently in the indictment, and finally, the official record did not reflect the court proceedings accurately.[74]

It should be noted that Orlov's court-appointed attorney, Evgeny Shalman, presented an aggressive defense throughout the proceedings and attempted to call all the witnesses requested by Orlov. The court, however, rejected virtually all of Shalman's petitions. Recognizing the futility of reasoning with an obviously hostile court, Orlov thanked Shalman for his legal and moral support and dismissed him before making his final plea. Shalman was then removed forcibly from the courtroom by the guards and locked in a nearby room. He was able to return to the courtroom only after he managed to phone the Presidium of the Moscow Bar and receive their support.

During the fifteen-month-long pretrial investigation, Orlov denied official charges that the *samizdat* materials authored and disseminated by him were slanderous and libeled the Soviet state. He also contended that there was absolutely nothing subversive or anti-Soviet about the Moscow Helsinki Group. According to Orlov, they had appealed to foreigners, and the Helsinki signatories in particular, because they were unable to draw the attention of Soviet leaders. They reasoned that by appealing to foreign heads of state, international organizations, and world opinion, they would ultimately attract the attention not only of the KGB, but also of Soviet leaders.

General Images

During the course of the 1978 trial, a number of general images of Orlov and his fellow Helsinki Monitors emerged from statements that were made by the judge, prosecutor, and members of the officially screened audience and recorded in the unofficial transcript. Viewed as a whole, these general images constitute a composite and authoritative picture of Yury Orlov as a renegade or a deserter from Soviet society and the Party; an idler and a parasite; a politically immature person who fell under the influence of anti-Soviet organizations and propaganda centers and subsequently remained a willing pawn in their efforts to subvert the prestige and security of the USSR; a traitor who conspired with foreigners in Moscow; an enemy of detente; a dangerous state criminal and an unrepenting lawbreaker; and an anti-Soviet agitator and propagandist, who fabricated documents alleging gross Soviet violations of human rights and slandering Soviet domestic and foreign policy and who disguised his subversive aims under the cover of twisted and self-serving interpretations of peaceful coexistence, detente, and the Helsinki Final Act.[75]

Pretrial Publicity

Once the decision had been made to arrest and prosecute Orlov and other Helsinki Monitors, the Soviet press began to devote more attention to his case.[76] The purpose of the media campaign was essentially twofold: to discredit Orlov and his domestic and foreign associates and to serve notice to the West that the Soviet Union would not be blackmailed by the unprecedented and escalating international campaign in defense of arrested Soviet Helsinki Monitors, other dissidents, and nonconformists.

One of the most prejudicial attacks appeared in *Literaturnaya gazeta* shortly before Orlov's arrest.[77] It was prepared by Alexander Petrov-Agatov, a one-time member of the Soviet Union of Writers. Angered by recent foreign press and radio reports that appeared to glorify Soviet dissidents as fighters for human rights and as Helsinki observers, Petrov wrote to *Literaturnaya gazeta* to set the record straight. He begins his account by confessing that he himself was a former dissident and convicted criminal and, hence, became closely acquainted with many of the dissidents. Based on Petrov's testimony, a most unflattering general image emerges: the dissidents are "liars and pharisees" and not the lofty moral figures, fearless fighters for human rights, or "models of rectitude and purity" that foreigners so frequently proclaim them to be.[78] More precisely, the dissidents are deluded, "embittered, morally unstable," unemployed, money-grubbing persons who enjoy expensive life styles and engage in shady, illegal money dealings. Orlov and Helsinki Monitors are characterized as uncaring, egotistical, and extremely ambitious. Furthermore, Orlov was, according to Petrov, promiscuous in his relations with women; he married three times, abandoned his children, and left them without material assistance.[79]

On February 12, 1977, just two days after the arrest of Orlov, a major article in *Pravda* provided an official justification for the unfolding crackdown on Helsinki Monitoring Groups.[80] In addition, the article served as a timely and authoritative response to the growing tide of Western criticism over Soviet treatment of dissidents. Entitled "What Is Behind the Furor over 'Human Rights?,'" the lengthy editorial is less strident in tone than the piece by Petrov. But despite this difference in style, there was no fundamental discrepancy in the general images expressed. The article dismissed Soviet dissidents, including Orlov, as a "pitiful handful of characters with anti-Soviet sentiments," guilty of slandering their homeland and people; "an insignificant and tiny group of people who do not represent anyone or anything, are remote from the Soviet people and exist merely because they are supported, paid, and praised by the West."[81] Moreover, the editorial set what it termed the "campaign of slander and provocations" over imaginary violations of human rights in the broader context of the West's periodic allegedly anti-Soviet campaigns, which were depicted as serving to justify massive and increasing military spending.

During the next few months, Soviet authorities stepped up their press campaign to discredit Soviet dissidents and their Western supporters. On March 5, 1977, *Izvestiya*, in an open letter from former dissident Sanya Lipavsky, attempted to "open the eyes of individuals still deceived by Western propaganda" about the persecution of dissidents.[82] Lipavsky's letter reinforces earlier official conceptions of dissidents as renegades and traitors and, notably, highlights the close collaboration between dissidents and foreigners (Moscow diplomats and foreign correspondents) for the alleged purpose of organizing subversive activity against the Soviet Union. After a bitter confession of past wrongdoing, Lipavsky tells why he grew steadily disillusioned with dissidents, including Orlov. He concludes his appraisal by noting:

I . . . became convinced that adventurists and money-grubbers are disguising themselves as defenders of "human rights." The aim of these individuals is to create publicity for themselves and earn steady incomes from abroad by staging provocations and assisting reactionary forces in the West.

I witnessed incessant fighting for leadership and the right to distribute funds. . . . Increasingly, I became convinced that the activities of these toadies would bring nothing but harm to the Soviet people, and this alarmed me. . . . In the future I will devote all of my energy to unmasking the hostile activities of the renegades and traitors to the homeland who sold out to the CIA.[83]

Lipavsky's public confession and warning to the Soviet people was followed by an afterword in *Izvestiya* by correspondents D. Morev and K. Yarilov.[84] The article focuses sharply on the link between dissidents and U.S. intelligence and describes "the path of treason and espionage onto which Lipavsky was pushed by CIA staff members, who used diplomatic passports as a cover for their anti-Soviet activity, and by their anti-Soviet associates, who acted under the cover of 'fighters for human rights.'"[85] To further reinforce this general image of Soviet dissidents as agents of Western-inspired subversion against the USSR, *Izvestiya* carried an interview conducted in early May with Lipavsky entitled "How I Was Recruited by the CIA."[86] This article portrays dissidents as an artificial opposition incited and supported by Western enemies primarily for espionage operations against the Soviet Union. It singles out the activities of Yury Orlov and others for special criticism and describes the Moscow Helsinki Group as a group organized at the suggestion of foreigners. Furthermore, Lipavsky cites other subversive activity, such as the use of U.S. diplomatic channels and foreign correspondents to transmit information to and from prominent dissidents.

The most authoritative summary of general images of dissidents came in *Pravda* on March 22, 1977, shortly after the arrest of Orlov and statements by President Carter and other prominent international personalities in defense of Soviet dissidents. The speaker was President Brezhnev, and his remarks were taken from his address to the 16th Congress of Soviet Trade Unions. In that speech Brezhnev emphasizes that dissident or constructive criticism is permitted in the Soviet Union, but that anti-Soviet activity cannot be tolerated:

In our country it is not forbidden "to think differently" from the majority, to criticize different aspects of public life. We regard citizens who offer well-founded criticism and strive for improvement as well-intentioned critics and we are grateful to them. Those who criticize wrongly, we regard as people who are mistaken.

However, it is a different matter entirely when a few persons, who have alienated themselves from our society, actively oppose the socialist system, pursue the path of anti-Soviet activity, break laws, and, finding no internal support, turn abroad for assistance, to subversive centers—those engaged in propaganda and intelligence. Our citizens demand that these allegedly prominent figures be treated as opponents of socialism, as traitors, and as accomplices, if not agents, of imperialism. Naturally, we take and will continue to take, measures against them under Soviet law.[87]

The cumulative effect of these pretrial attacks on Orlov, other dissidents, and their alleged Western supporters was to present readers with a more complex picture of the conflict between the authorities and dissidents than was supplied by foreign radio and press accounts and, therefore, to cast serious doubt on the characters and intentions of dissidents and their foreign supporters. For Orlov and other arrested Helsinki Monitors, the press attacks served yet another purpose. They introduced the state's brief against the dissidents to Soviet—and foreign—audiences and, in effect, amounted to a preliminary trial in the press.

The general images of Orlov and his associates in Soviet official statements following his conviction corresponded closely to those appearing in the *samizdat* trial transcript and in the pretrial official commentary. For example, an official summary of the court proceedings appeared immediately after Orlov's conviction in *Moskovskaya pravda* under the headline "On a Hostile Wavelength."[88] In it, the author portrays Orlov as an inveterate anti-Soviet, an ill-intentioned falsifier and slanderer of the Motherland, and a traitor who regularly conspired with foreigners to undermine Soviet prestige and security. Particularly noteworthy about this official account is the fact that its general images of Orlov closely mirror those reported in the unofficial trial transcript.

About a month after Orlov's conviction, another detailed official account of the case appeared in *Sovetskaya kultura*, the tri-weekly newspaper of the Party's Central Committee. Prompted, no doubt, by the heavy and sustained Western criticism over the conviction of Orlov, the piece, written by V. Nikolayev, poses the question: "Who Guards the Anti-Soviets, and Why?" The answer is simple, according to the author: detente's opponents.[89] Nikolayev describes Orlov as a renegade, a liar, an anti-Soviet slanderer, a traitor, an enemy of detente, and a paid agent of foreign anti-Soviet centers, who is not an honest person or a Helsinki Monitor as some Westerners argue.[90]

In addition to official press commentary, important official statements appeared in several Soviet books and journals. One of the most detailed and authoritative commentaries appeared in Samuil Zivs' book *Human Rights: Continuing the Discussion*.[91] As mentioned earlier, Zivs is a prominent Soviet legal expert and a leading spokesman for the Soviet Union on questions of human rights and dissidents. His book was apparently intended to serve as a definitive reply to Western critics of the Soviet human rights record. Although published in English and intended largely for a foreign audience, the general images of Orlov and his associates that surface in Zivs' discussion of the case are, nonetheless, significant. They are essentially consistent with the official and unofficial sources surveyed earlier. Specifically, Zivs portrays Orlov as an anti-Soviet slanderer, a lawbreaker, a common criminal, and an agent of Western anti-Soviet centers. Zivs takes pains to emphasize that Orlov was not an innocent victim persecuted for his dedication to human rights, but a wrecker of detente and the spirit of Helsinki.

A concise and authoritative synthesis of earlier Soviet references to the Orlov case and other Helsinki Monitors appears in *The Soviet Viewpoint*, a series of interviews with Georgi Arbatov, director of the Institute of the U.S.A. and Canadian Studies in Moscow.[92] Like Zivs's book, this work was published primarily for a foreign audience. Less hostile in tone than other official spokesmen, Arbatov is still extremely critical of Soviet dissidents and their Western supporters. He describes Orlov and the other Monitors as incorrigible lawbreakers operating under the cover of the Helsinki Final Act; a small group working to create the false impression that widespread political opposition exists in the USSR; persons closely linked to anti-Soviet foreigners and organizations, often paid agents of foreign anti-Soviet centers; and persons typically calling for foreign interference in their country's internal affairs.[93] Arbatov's use of the phrase "foreign agent" is interesting. He defines it loosely and then pointedly asks Americans to consider a hypothetical situation:

whether American dissidents who supply Soviet journalists or diplomats in the United States with information slandering their country and urging foreign interference in U.S. internal affairs might appear to be acting as agents of a foreign power.[94]

Much more hostile in tone, but fundamentally similar in substance, are the general images of Orlov and other dissidents that appear in a book entitled *CIA Target—the USSR*.[95] The work's author is Nikolai Yakovlev, an extreme conservative and perhaps the foremost historian in the USSR. Yakovlev's book is a Soviet bestseller and has been reprinted three times since its release in 1980, a clear indication of top official approval of its contents. As the book's title suggests, Yakovlev stresses the link between dissidents and foreigners. He describes leading dissidents such as Orlov as pawns of the CIA and other anti-Soviet centers; as persons who act largely on cue from their foreign masters; as "an assault force" in the psychological war against the Soviet Union; as dropouts; and as conceited and pretentious idlers who blame their own inferiority complex on society.[96]

Finally, the writings of Semyon Tsvigun, the deceased deputy head of the KGB, deserve mention. He was probably the Soviet Union's leading expert on dissidents and nonconformists. Unlike Yury Andropov, who was essentially a politician by career, Tsvigun had been a professional security officer since 1945.[97] Together with Andropov, he managed the unprecedented dissent and nonconformity that emerged increasingly after the mid-1960s. Among Tsvigun's many articles on Soviet security policies and their implementation, two items published in 1980 and 1981 in the party journal *Kommunist* stand out as major statements.[98] Together, they provide a comprehensive and analytical critique of Soviet dissent and its place within the broader context of contemporary East-West relations. In these writings Tsvigun portrays the Soviet Union as facing an atmosphere of intensified imperialist subversive activity—a reflection of an increasing East-West ideological confrontation. In particular, he criticizes the United States for having organized a provocative campaign in defense of human rights in order to embarrass and undermine the Soviet Union and other socialist countries. Significant are the general images of Soviet Helsinki Monitors—including Orlov—and other dissidents which are found in Tsvigun's 1980 article. According to Tsvigun, the dissidents are agents of imperialist propaganda and intelligence services.

Moreover, they are no more than a "few renegades, individuals who have alienated themselves from Soviet society and taken the path of anti-Soviet activity . . . politically unstable or morally corrupt individuals with a lust for easy profits and money-grubbing."[99]

Character

The official images of the character or personality of Orlov that came out during the 1978 trial agreed fundamentally with those expressed in official sources before and after the trial. According to the unofficial transcript, Orlov was a politically immature person and an inveterate anti-Soviet. Procurator Emelyanov, for example, observed in his prosecuting speech that

> in their efforts to blacken the Soviet system, foreigners rely on politically immature Soviet citizens, various drop-outs of society, and even mentally-ill persons. . . . In 1956, under the pretense of criticizing the cult of personality, Orlov attempted to subvert the policies of our party and, consequently, was expelled from the party. Thereafter, Orlov steadily fell under the influence of foreign anti-Soviet organizations and propaganda centers.[100]

Throughout the trial the prosecution and its witnesses emphasized Orlov's deep hostility toward the Soviet system, his cunning and deceptive nature, and, in particular, his untiring efforts to slander the Soviet system. The procurator and judge both repeatedly stressed that Orlov was an anti-Soviet to the core. As evidence they noted, in addition to the indictment's charges, Orlov's persistent efforts to use the courtroom to slander Soviet authority further and, generally, his obstreperous and unrepentant attitude toward the court. Further proof of Orlov's incorrigible anti-Soviet character reached officials shortly after his conviction. Immediately after arriving at Perm Camp No. 35, Orlov told the camp administrators that he had been sent by the Moscow Helsinki Group as an observer to report on camp conditions, especially on the poor food conditions reported by inmates and the illegal practices of the camp administrators, who were allegedly punishing prisoners for their formal complaints.[101]

The official images of the character of Orlov and his associates that appeared in officially released commentary surrounding the trial were uniformly negative and extremely hostile. Writing in *Literaturnaya gazeta* just several days before Orlov's arrest, Alexander Petrov, a former dissident and alleged close acquaintance of Orlov's, delivered a scathing attack on his character and on Orlov's close associate Alexander Ginzburg. According to Petrov, Orlov and his colleagues were not saints as their Western supporters typically suggested, but egotistical, power- and money-hungry individuals, who were also quite promiscuous.[102] Petrov details their characters, based on alleged firsthand observation:

> Yury Orlov, who himself is bursting to be a leader of the "dissidents," expressed his displeasure more than once with the fact that the West speaks mostly about Sakharov while "Alex and I (that is, Ginzburg and Orlov—A.P.) have to do all the work. I would not include Sakharov in the leadership any longer."
>
> Indeed, the moral qualities of the "dissidents" are by no means all that they and Western propaganda claim. About the character of Alexander Ilyich Ginzburg let me briefly note: Persistently described in the West as a "writer" . . . this "writer" is quite indiscriminate in his relations with women, as incidentally, is Yury Orlov, who has married three times, abandoned his children and left them without material assistance.
>
> No, their designs are not pure. They are possessed by ambition, egotism and pride, the vices to which I was prey until I stood at the precipice. I speak of a spiritual precipice, more frightening than any abyss. . . . I myself became convinced that the activity of Orlov, Ginzburg and the other "dissidents" has nothing in common with humanitarian aid to one's neighbors or with the "defense of human rights." Their group deals in matters which, I am deeply convinced, undermine the interests of our Motherland, its culture and its spiritual well-being and which run counter to the interests of our fellow-countrymen. The "dissidents" gather various embittered, morally unstable persons, all kinds of failures who blame all their troubles on Soviet rule. And outright criminal elements scurry around these individuals.[103]

Perhaps the most hostile attack upon the character of Orlov and his fellow dissidents appeared in *Pravda* just days after his arrest. Cast as an editorial, the article portrayed Orlov and his colleagues as unpatriotic and hypocritical dropouts of Soviet society, individuals whose anti-Soviet character was carefully concealed under the cover of a struggle for human rights. Their true character, *Pravda* charged, was revealed when they left the Soviet Union and then often openly worked for anti-Soviet organizations such as Radio Free Europe and the publication *Kontinent*.

The editors' hostility toward the dissidents, however, did not stop here. As a further reflection, they reprinted selections from one of the many letters reportedly received by *Pravda* in which Soviet citizens "angrily condemn and repudiate the renegades who have sold themselves to the reactionary forces of imperialism." The "typical letter" selected is from G. Zhukov, a veteran of the Great Patriotic War from Gomel. He describes dissidents as

> . . . traitors and enemies of Soviet power. These moral monsters do not like the family of the great Soviet people. . . . They despise the people's power that was won and defended in hard-fought, bloody battles. Thousands of lives were sacrificed before and during the Revolution; hundreds of thousands died in the Civil War, and tens of millions during the fascist invasion. These moral monsters are not pained by these sacrifices, by the thousands upon thousands of invalids and cripples, by the millions of orphans. Without a twinge of conscience, they fight for the "freedom" and "rights" brought by Hitlerite fascism, which drenched Europe in blood. They fight for capitalist freedom, under which millions have no rights, are unemployed and barely able to subsist; a freedom under which thousands languish in prisons and concentration camps.[104]

This description of dissidents as ungrateful and unpatriotic citizens was reinforced during Orlov's trial when three witnesses summoned by the prosecution to describe Orlov's scientific work each described him as a capable, but extremely ambitious, individual, a person who actively associated with foreigners, slandered the Soviet Union, and lacked the basic patriotism required of a scientist.[105]

Finally, it should be noted that Soviet commentaries published following Orlov's conviction did not differ substantially from the earlier official images of his character. Typical was *Moskovskaya pravda*, which portrayed Orlov as a malicious and persistent slanderer, a person with no respect for the law.[106] Although written for foreign audiences, the previously mentioned books by Samuel Zivs and Georgi Arbatov, interestingly, reinforce this view of Orlov's personality. Zivs emphasizes that Orlov was not a noble-hearted champion of peace and human rights and, in particular, a dedicated supporter of the Helsinki Final Act, but an experienced and dedicated anti-Soviet slanderer and a confirmed lawbreaker.[107] Arbatov's comments are similar. He underlines the deceptive and cunning nature of Orlov, noting that he used the Helsinki Act as a cover for his anti-Soviet activity.[108]

To conclude, official images of Orlov's character in *samizdat* and official sources describe a person lacking political maturity and sufficient vigilance against anti-Sovietism. In official eyes, Orlov's weak moral character and his desire for fame led to his increasingly active and subversive collaboration with anti-Soviet citizens and foreigners. His profound anti-Soviet character and his desire to be a martyr led to a stubborn defiance of Soviet law and an unwillingness to repent in the face of overwhelming evidence.

Nature of the Conflict

The conflict between Orlov and his fellow Helsinki Monitors and the authorities, as it appears in the unofficial trial transcript and from officially released statements relevant to the case, has two essential dimensions—a domestic and a foreign one. From the viewpoint of the court, the nature of the case was straightforward. Orlov was guilty of illegal political activity. He had brazenly and persistently violated Soviet laws and norms which define as criminal any deliberate and systematic effort to undermine socialism. One Soviet spokesman termed such disregard for law and societal norms "elitist solipsism" and observed:

> Some dissident "champions of human rights" claim immunity before law, although they systematically commit deliberate acts either punishable by law or balancing between a criminal offense and what is socially opprobrious but not strictly illegal. By openly spurning both law and public opinion, they acquire the syndrome of "elitist solipsism"— a belief that an exceptional individual is free to do anything he wants.[109]

In the opinion of the court, Orlov was such an individual. Despite clear and repeated official warnings, he continued to slander the Soviet Union and even incited others to do so. Eventually official patience ran out, and Orlov was made to realize that he was not above the law. A *Pravda* editorial issued two days after his arrest explains the action as legally prescribed:

> . . . in accordance with Soviet laws, charges may be brought against individuals who engage in anti-Soviet propaganda and agitation aimed at undermining or weakening the social and political system established in our country or who engage in the systematic dissemination of knowingly false fabrications, which defame the Soviet state and social system. Hence, what we are talking about here are penalties for premeditated actions provided for under Articles 70 and 190 of the Russian Republic's Criminal Code, as well as the corresponding articles of the other Union republics' criminal codes.[110]

More fundamental and objectionable, in official eyes, than this domestic breach of Soviet laws and norms was the foreign dimension of the conflict. The authorities viewed the conflict between Orlov and the state principally as a fight for the "freedom of anti-Soviet activity," including the right to export slander, rather than as a struggle for human rights. In general terms, they saw it as a hostile and devious campaign of ideological subversion or psychological warfare against the USSR, directed and supported largely by the United States. Within this broader context, officials viewed the unprecedented foreign campaign in defense of Soviet dissidents (conspicuously supported by President Carter) as much more than the hostile and hypocritical rhetoric of the Soviet Union's chief adversary. Writing shortly after Orlov's conviction, one Soviet correspondent expressed the dominant image as follows:

> The provocative Western campaign in "defense of human rights in the Soviet Union" is an integral part of the "psychological warfare," organized, orchestrated and paid for by the NATO leaders. The real reasons for this campaign are by no means dictated by a desire to defend "human rights." They are dictated by the selfish interests of reactionary military circles, which in order to conceal the arms race, carry out Zaire-type interventions and fan other conflicts, constantly need to fuel and fan various anti-Soviet myths in order to discredit the policy and intentions of the USSR in every possible way and on any pretext.[111]

Writing a few months later, a *Pravda* correspondent, in a typical statement, reinforced this analysis and detailed further the intentions behind this allegedly foreign-inspired conflict:

On the ideological level this Western campaign for "human rights" is based on the so-called "theory of erosion of communism." An official document entitled "Ideology and Foreign Policy" was prepared in the United States on the basis of the recommendations of the authors of this "theory." It is said, in particular, that the task of the United States and its allies is to "create the conditions for the erosion of communist ideology" in the USSR and other socialist countries by taking "special measures" from outside. These included the "encouragement of forces of nationalism," the contrasting of so-called "humane" or "democratic socialism" with Marxism-Leninism, the undermining of the socialist community's unity, the activation of antisocialist forces and even the creation of some kind of opposition. Almost 18 years have passed since the adoption of this document, but it is still the guide for psychological warfare services.[112]

Soviet officials consistently portrayed the conflict between Orlov and the authorities as essentially a struggle against Western-inspired subversion. In official eyes, Orlov was a willing pawn in a new and more refined campaign of psychological warfare; he joined foreign forces that professed to protect the Helsinki Final Act while, in fact, working to undermine it.[113] Without foreign interference, the anti-Soviet activities of Orlov and his associates, and hence the conflict, would have eventually died a natural death, according to authorities. From their point of view, the dissidents lacked any significant social support for their crime of slander. Their only notable support came from hostile anti-Soviet centers in the West.[114]

Activity

Throughout his trial Orlov insisted that his activity, and that of his Helsinki associates, was not criminal, but fully in accord with the international pledges made by the Soviet Union at Helsinki and elsewhere. Quite simply, the defense argued, Orlov was an innocent victim persecuted by the police for his dedication to human rights.

Soviet officials vehemently disagreed with this assessment. They interpreted the actions of Orlov as illegal political activity. Judge Lubentsova's image of the defendant's activity was typical of official statements. She asserted that Orlov was not being tried for his views or beliefs, but for concrete criminal actions which damaged the prestige and security of the Soviet Union. Procurator Emelyanov repeated this view in his prosecuting speech and specifically charged Orlov with carrying on "anti-Soviet agitation and propaganda" in order to undermine Soviet power and with fabricating and disseminating slanderous falsehoods and documents which defamed the Soviet political and social system.[115] A summary of Orlov's objectionable activities appears in *Moskovskaya pravda*; it closely mirrors the description contained in the prosecutor's speech:

> . . . Orlov's anti-Soviet views began to be formed as early as the late 1950s.
> From minor grumbling about Soviet shortcomings and difficulties, he gradually moved on to vigorous anti-Soviet activity. In the past a physicist, Orlov gave up his scientific work to engage himself in the fabrication of slanderous information for the foreign press, radio, foreign anti-Soviet organizations and propaganda centers with the aim of subverting the Soviet system. To give his ideas a factual appearance he called them "appeals" or "documents." There are many of these "appeals" in the criminal case, such as those bearing impudent titles of "Moscow appeal," the "Appeal from Soviet scientists" and others.
> The slanderous information was passed on by Orlov to foreign journalists, or was sent to Western embassies, various international organizations and foreign propaganda centers.
> Orlov would use any method. He would distort facts and even blatantly lie.
> Orlov tried to defame socialism and the USSR's internal and foreign policy, and called for subversion of the existing system in our country and struggle against it. He warned the West of some sort of "danger," by which it is allegedly threatened by the socialist states, and appealed to the Western nations to unite in a struggle against the socialist states and to interfere in the USSR's internal affairs. In his scribblings he sought to prove that the Soviet Union allegedly is not following its international agreements and that democratic freedoms are absent in our country.[116]

In addition to sending objectionable information out of the Soviet Union, Orlov was also guilty of smuggling foreign propaganda into the country, according to official investigators:

During the pretrial investigation and the court proceedings it was proved that Orlov had been receiving anti-Soviet literature, including the official bulletins of "Radio Liberty" and of the coordinating bodies of NATO's psychological war. He was arranging gatherings of anti-Soviet and nationalist-minded people with the participation of foreigners, at which questions about hostile future anti-Soviet activity were discussed.[117]

According to Soviet officials, Orlov was not content with trying to subvert the Soviet system from within or through infrequent contacts with anti-Soviet foreigners. Between 1973 and 1977, he steadily increased his preparation and dissemination of slanderous anti-Soviet materials as well as his contacts with foreigners in Moscow and abroad.[118] Writing in *Izvestiya* shortly after Orlov's arrest, Lipavsky, the repentant former dissident, highlights the alleged active and subversive collaboration between foreign diplomats in Moscow and dissidents such as Orlov. He recalls that embassy staffers

. . . met regularly with "dissidents" to coordinate their anti-Soviet activity. They incited the "dissidents" to hold various "protest demonstrations," to send tendentious and slanderous letters to foreign organizations and to carry out other actions meant to create the impression abroad that there is some kind of "opposition" in the USSR and that civil liberties are lacking in our country.

After the European conference in Helsinki, the Western conductors gave the signal to fabricate information on alleged violations of "human rights" in the USSR. It was at their prompting that Yury Orlov, with the help of V. Rubin, set up the so-called "Group to Monitor Observance of the Helsinki Agreements in the USSR."[119]

Writing more recently, George Arbatov reinforces this view of the activity of Orlov and his associates. In his account, he emphasizes that in Soviet society dissidents such as Orlov are a fringe phenomenon whose survival depends critically on foreign support.

A typical feature of these [dissident] groups . . . has been their close ties with foreign citizens and organizations. They have relied on foreign media, often actually worked for them, and received various kinds of assistance from abroad, including financial aid in some cases.[120]

Orlov's increasing contacts with foreigners—along with the efforts of prominent Western officials, private persons, and international organizations to intervene in his behalf in the face of KGB warnings and threats—outraged Soviet officials. The interventions were viewed by Soviet officials as an effort by foreign anti-Soviets to whitewash or protect their agent, Orlov. Further proof that Orlov was acting as an agent of foreign anti-Soviet interests was found by Soviet officials shortly after his arrest. It came in the form of a "minicampaign" on the right of foreign lawyers to defend dissidents in Soviet courts.[121] This campaign refers to the efforts of distinguished Western lawyers such as John Macdonald from Great Britain and Edward Bennett Williams from the United States to obtain Soviet approval to defend Orlov and other arrested dissidents in Soviet courts of law. Such requests astounded Soviet officials, who interpreted them as yet another act of Western arrogance and interference in the internal affairs of the USSR and, in particular, its legal procedure. Samuil Zivs describes such legal requests as pointless and provocative and offers a view of the official hostility and sense of outrage generated by what was perceived as a heavy-handed effort by prominent anti-Soviets to protect their agents:

> First of all, it is common knowledge that there are no universal instruments of international law providing for the rights of a lawyer to act in a foreign trial, or for any obligation of a court to admit a foreign lawyer as a defense counsel. . . . Soviet legislation clearly states who may defend the accused in court. . . . It follows that there are absolutely no legal grounds for foreign lawyers' demands to be admitted as attorneys in Soviet courts.
>
> While on the subject of such claims by British, French and American lawyers, we might note that in a number of Western countries there even exist restrictions for their own professional lawyers. In the United States, a lawyer admitted to the bar of a State may not have the right to plead in Federal courts. In France, while most attorneys belong to independent orders attached to courts of appeals, there is also the Order of Advocates at the Council of State and the Court of Cassation whose members are admitted to plead in these two bodies. In Great Britain, lawyers are divided into Queen's Counsels and barristers (members of an Inn of Court), on the one hand, and solicitors with no right to speak as advocates in higher law courts, on the other.

The clamor about foreign lawyers seems to have been raised simply for the sake of publicity. Besides, this minicampaign looked very much like an attempt at direct interference in Soviet legal proceedings. . . .

Almost all the foreign lawyers who appointed themselves attorneys in the 1978 cases dealing with dissidents had by that time taken part in noisy anti-Soviet gatherings. . . . Such conduct alone violates professional ethics and makes these lawyers unacceptable.[122]

Orlov, then, was not being tried for his views or beliefs, but for his criminal and subversive activity, according to the authorities; he was being tried for his preparation, dissemination, and transmission to the West of slanderous anti-Soviet materials. In addition, Soviet officials viewed Orlov's frequent contacts with Moscow foreigners with great suspicion and judged them to be a violation of an important societal norm.

Intentions

What, in official eyes, motivated Orlov and his associates to pursue such activities? Throughout his 1978 trial, Orlov attempted to demonstrate that his actions involved no criminal intention. He had compiled and disseminated the Moscow Group documents and related materials for humanitarian purposes and not to subvert the state. His aim, he argued, had been to join with other Soviet citizens to promote the observance of human rights pledges made by the Soviet government at Helsinki. In this pursuit, he had not advocated in any way weakening or overthrowing the system. Moreover, he emphasized that his attitude toward the existing order was a critical, but loyal, one.

Soviet authorities disagreed. During the initial trial and the subsequent appeal, court officials repeatedly asserted that Orlov's preparation and circulation of slanderous documents confirmed that his intention was to undermine and weaken the state. They viewed his frequent contacts with foreigners as further evidence of his criminal and subversive design.

Orlov, on the other hand, insisted that his contacts with foreigners were neither illegal nor subversive. He maintained that he distributed the documents to foreign correspondents and diplomats in Moscow for transmission abroad not to weaken Soviet authority, but to attract the attention of Soviet leaders. After respectfully and patiently petitioning key Soviet officials for reforms for several years, Orlov had concluded that it was futile to appeal directly to Soviet officials. During his final speech, he underlined the unbridgeable communication gap which exists between the Soviet leaders and the dissidents. Drawing on his personal experience, he asked the court:

> What means . . . are available for a citizen to approach his government? (Indignant cries in the courtroom.) We do not have the means by which to address our government. My [1973 Open] appeal to Brezhnev probably got as far as the regional KGB office. Certainly, it went no further than the city office of the KGB.
>
> The crucial question is what means are there for a Soviet citizen to approach his own government, other than indirectly through the governments of other countries. This is why we want the documents of the Helsinki Group to be discussed at the Belgrade Conference.[123]

Throughout the trial, the court paid less attention to the expressed motives of the defendant than to what it perceived to be the harmful consequences of his actions. In official eyes, the fifty-eight volumes of pretrial documentation of the case conclusively established Orlov's criminal intent. His references to the Moscow Group and the Helsinki Final Act were viewed as cunning efforts to conceal his anti-Soviet intentions and to invite foreign interference in Soviet affairs.

The most objectionable aspects of Orlov's intentions concerned the foreign connection. Orlov's fundamental aim, in the words of one Soviet official, was to assist hostile foreigners in their efforts to

> . . . create endless problems for the Soviet authorities, to foster an ersatz opposition inside our country, to create the image of the USSR as a police state, and finally to sow seeds of hostility toward the USSR in the West, so as to wreck attempts at lessening international tensions and curbing the arms race.[124]

Toward this end, the Moscow Helsinki Group served, according to officials, as a deceptively clever cover for the illegal and subversive political activities of dissidents such as Orlov and their foreign supporters. Georgi Arbatov summed up the dominant image of Orlov's Group as follows:

> Their real primary aim is to provide foreign media with materials designed to create an impression in the West that there exists in the USSR a widespread political movement opposing the Soviet state and the Soviet society, to arouse and mislead the Soviet public by rumors and messages transmitted via Western media to the USSR.[125]

In short, the aim of Orlov and his foreign supporters was consistently portrayed by Soviet officials as a persistent desire to sabotage efforts to improve East-West relations and, ultimately, to incite widespread Soviet opposition to the regime.

DISCREPANCIES BETWEEN OFFICIAL IMAGES AND TRUE IMAGES

Was the general image held by Soviet authorities of Yury Orlov— a renegade, a traitor, an anti-Soviet slanderer, a conscious pawn of foreign anti-Soviet and intelligence services, an idler and parasite, an immoral and money-grubbing person—accurate, partially accurate, or false? Before answering this broader question, once again it is necessary first to compare official images of the character of Orlov, the nature of the conflict, and the activity and intentions of Orlov and his dissident colleagues with reasonably accurate images and then to judge them accurate, partially accurate, or false.

Character

Was Orlov an inveterate anti-Soviet, an outcast from the Party and society, a person driven by a profound desire for power, fame, and money? Was he an immoral person, an idler, and a parasite?

The official image of Orlov's character was partially accurate. It did have a partial basis in fact, although on the whole it was a gross caricature. As mentioned earlier, Orlov had openly criticized past Party practices as early as 1956 and his critique, with its accompanying calls for Party reforms, was viewed by Soviet leaders as rare impudence and anti-Soviet activity. Orlov's subsequent expulsion from the Party and his voluntary exile to Armenia left him a marked man—a renegade—in official eyes.[126] Developments after his return to Moscow in the early 1970s reinforced this earlier image. Despite these confrontations with the authorities, Orlov did not develop a profoundly hostile attitude toward the state. He was critical, but loyal.

Was Orlov a power-hungry and fame-seeking individual? Although Orlov eventually became chairman of the Group and gained a position of leadership within the Soviet human rights movement as well, he was not driven in this activity by an insatiable thirst for power or glory. Instead of immediately appointing himself head of the Group, Orlov offered the post to Andrei Sakharov, hoping that this would bestow more respectability on the Group in Soviet and foreign eyes and, thus, improve the Group's chances of attaining its objectives. The formation of the Moscow Group is a telling illustration of Orlov's unselfish conduct.

Was Orlov an immoral, money-grubbing person and an idler? Once again official images did have a partial basis in fact. Regarding Orlov's allegedly immoral lifestyle, several points are worth noting. Orlov, in fact, had been married before meeting Irina, and after 1973 he did associate increasingly with Moscow dissidents, some of whom were previously convicted for dissident (nonviolent) activity and others whose lifestyles have been described by former Western journalists in Moscow as colorful and unconventional.[127] Routinely harassed by the KGB and increasingly isolated from the mainstream of society, many dissidents did gather frequently in the tiny apartments of friends for mutual support. Moreover, there undoubtedly were festive occasions when some drank and loudly discussed pressing philosophical and political questions long into the night, occasionally with foreign visitors. The lifestyle of these dissidents and their friends was probably viewed by the KGB as bohemian or deviant and distasteful.

The official image of Orlov as a promiscuous person and an uncaring father who used the dissident cause to extract influence and money from its domestic and foreign supporters seems unfounded. False, also, is the conception of Orlov as an idler and parasite, frequently implied or stated explicitly during his trial and in officially released statements. Although it is true that Orlov had been professionally unemployed since 1974—a result of his open dissent and subsequent blacklisting by the authorities—he was neither an idler nor a parasite. As Orlov himself attempted to point out during the trial, he was consistently active in scientific research, even during his lengthy pretrial detention; between 1974 and 1977 he wrote and published several scientific articles and did voluntary work at the Erevan Physics Institute. He survived by tutoring students and by accepting only modest contributions from sympathetic scientists and the Russian Social Fund.

In short, Orlov did not have a profoundly hostile disposition toward Soviet authority. Although admittedly critical of specific practices of the Party, Orlov was essentially a loyal and patriotic citizen, as illustrated by his record of military service and Party membership and his considerable efforts to avoid open and active dissent. Until he was fired in the early 1970s for dissident activity, Orlov was a "constructive critic" of the regime, to borrow Brezhnev's phrase. He used Party-approved channels for criticism and addressed his open appeals exclusively to Soviet leaders.

Nature of the Conflict

Was the conflict between Orlov, his fellow Monitors, and the authorities essentially an official struggle against Western-inspired subversion? Did the Moscow Group wage a new and more refined campaign of psychological warfare, using the Helsinki Act as a cover? Or was the conflict principally, as Orlov and his colleagues unsuccessfully contended, a genuine struggle for greater observance of international standards of human rights in the USSR?

The official image of the nature of the conflict was partially accurate. What began in the early 1950s as a growing disillusionment of Soviet intellectuals, unregistered religious believers, and others with the direction of post-Stalin policies gradually and unexpectedly assumed a foreign dimension, until in the late 1970s the foreign element greatly overshadowed the domestic roots of the conflict. The summer of 1978 was especially important. During that period, the international campaign in support of repressed or imprisoned Soviet dissidents reached an unprecedented pitch, marked by a direct confrontation between Presidents Carter and Brezhnev.

Despite the conflict's increasingly prominent foreign dimension, its official image as fundamentally a struggle against Western-inspired, orchestrated, and financed subversion was grossly exaggerated and false. Subversion, in the conventional sense of the word, was never at the crux of the conflict. Orlov and his associates never acted or endorsed actions to overthrow the system. At the same time, however, it must be acknowledged that Western moral support for the dissidents, particularly after the signing of the Helsinki Act, was massive and sustained. In the United States, for example, the president, Congress, and various public groups all actively and openly supported the struggle of Soviet Helsinki Monitors and their associates. In addition, foreign radio stations broadcasting to the Soviet Union, and the foreign media in general, publicized highly virtually any new development in the conflict between early 1977 and fall 1978. The net effect of these and similar efforts, as numerous dissidents have noted, was to provide foreign inspiration for the Soviet human rights movement.

Finally, the official image of Orlov, Ginzburg, and the other Helsinki Monitors as paid agents of foreign propaganda centers and intelligence centers did have a tenuous basis in fact. Welfare organizations, such as AID (to Russian Christians) and Solzhenitsyn's Russian Social Fund, did provide money or other material support to repressed Soviet political prisoners and their families. Hence, there was an element of foreign financial support in the conflict. Moreover, Ginzburg was, strictly speaking, a paid agent of Solzhenitsyn's, whose Russian Social Fund he directed after Solzhenitsyn's 1974 exile from the USSR. In this role, Ginzburg admittedly distributed funds earned from the sale of Solzhenitsyn's writings abroad to needy Soviet dissidents and their families. A close associate of Ginzburg's, Orlov was probably officially viewed in the light of Ginzburg's suspicious Social Fund activities.

The conflict between the Soviet dissidents and the authorities, even at the time of Orlov's arrest, was still fundamentally domestic in nature, although it had acquired an international dimension after the Helsinki agreement.

Activity

Did Yury Orlov, as the indictment charged, engage in "anti-Soviet agitation and propaganda"? Did he systematically prepare and disseminate documents containing slanderous fabrications discrediting the Soviet state and public order? Was the activity of Orlov and his associates criminal, or was it fully in accord with pledges made by the Soviet Union in Helsinki and elsewhere?

The official images of the activities of Orlov and his followers were partially accurate. During the pretrial investigation and the trial proceedings, Orlov himself admitted that he had engaged in many of the activities which the state deemed hostile. He had drafted *samizdat* reports and supplementary materials on topics related to alleged violations of the human rights provisions of the Helsinki Act; he had distributed copies of these documents to foreign journalists and embassy staffers in Moscow, aware that this information, in turn, probably would be disseminated still further to Western sources, including foreign radio stations; he had granted interviews to several foreign journalists, during which he made critical statements about Soviet domestic and foreign policy; he had submitted some of his *samizdat* writings to *Posev,* an emigré publication perceived officially as extremely anti-Soviet; he had met regularly with foreigners visiting Moscow and urged them and others to appeal to foreign leaders and international organizations to support and publicize the cause of Soviet dissidents and nonconformists; and he had made comparisons in his *samizdat* writings between conditions found in contemporary Soviet society and conditions found under slavery, feudalism, and Nazi Germany. Orlov also acknowledged receiving newspaper clippings and transcripts of Radio Liberty reports on Soviet dissent and related issues from foreign journalists.

Although official images of Orlov's activity did have a basis in fact, it should be stressed that, on the whole, they were very misleading. For instance, they failed to register that Orlov and the Moscow Group had always acted openly and not conspiratorially. Members of the Group never concealed their identities or actions and only protected the anonymity of their messengers. Furthermore, while the Group's *samizdat* reports did, in effect, discredit the practices of Soviet leaders, they were not slanderous. As indicated earlier, they were the product of the thorough and painstaking research of many persons. Any errors which occurred were unintended, usually matters of detail rather than substance, and—once detected—readily and openly acknowledged. On this important point, it is useful to note the finding of John Macdonald, the distinguished British barrister. Based on intensive interviews with more than twenty witnesses, most of whom had firsthand knowledge of

Group members and their collective efforts, as well as on careful study of the Moscow Group's documents, he concluded that the Group, and Orlov in particular, took extraordinary pains to verify their reports of alleged Basket Three violations and that the documents were accurate in all their essentials.[128]

The crucial question remains: Was the activity of Orlov and his associates criminal or fully in accord with pledges made by the Soviet Union in Helsinki and elsewhere? The answer is both. By Soviet legal and social norms, Orlov's actions constituted illegal political activity, international slander, and a lack of sufficient political vigilance and civic-mindedness. However, by international standards, Orlov was engaged in legitimate human rights advocacy and the simple pursuit of Helsinki pledges made by his government.

Intentions

Were the actions of Orlov and his fellow Monitors intended to "sow international distrust, national enmity" and "fan anticommunism" as many Soviet officials maintained? Were they designed to erode Soviet prestige, slander the social and political system, and assist the West in its alleged campaign of psychological warfare against the Soviet Union?

Here the official image was clearly false. Key facts about Orlov's background and the history of the Soviet human rights movement were ignored by overzealous KGB investigators preoccupied with a search for facts to confirm their case. Judging from all the available evidence, it is quite clear that Orlov and his colleagues acted out of a genuine concern for Western-styled human rights. It seems that they intended only to discredit certain specific Soviet practices perceived as major violations of international human rights standards and not to launch a sweeping attack to "defame" and "blacken" the Soviet system, as the procurator contended. Orlov underlined this point repeatedly during the proceedings, but to no avail. He admitted that his attitude to the system was a critical one, but added that he favored gradual democratic changes and did not intend in any way to subvert the Soviet system.[129]

Why did Orlov increasingly collaborate with foreigners in Moscow and abroad during the 1970s? Was it to provide sensational stories for the foreign press in order to undermine Soviet prestige and ·security, as one official claimed? Although some sensational stories, in fact, did surface in the flood of Western reporting on Soviet dissent during 1977 and 1978, this was an unintended consequence of the Moscow Group's activity.

Group members were not "conscious pawns" in a Western-inspired ideological campaign against the USSR. They appealed to foreigners, including the press and foreign radio stations, out of a growing sense of desperation in their unsuccessful struggle with the authorities. The Group's aim, as stated by Orlov, was to bridge the existing communication gap: to inform Soviet leaders and world public opinion about alleged human rights violations in the USSR, hoping that world indignation would pressure Soviet leaders to adopt a less repressive stance toward dissidents and nonconformists.

In summary, the intent of Orlov and his associates was not to subvert the Soviet Union in any conventional sense of the word or to act as "shock troops" for foreign ideological subversion. Instead, it was to criticize and discredit specific practices—perceived human rights violations—in the hope of attracting concessions from Soviet leaders. More generally, the Moscow Group's aim was to promote the observance of international standards of human rights in the USSR.

CONCLUSIONS

1. Most of the official images analyzed of Orlov and his fellow Monitors were oversimplified and stereotypic, but there was an element of truth in them. Many of the allegations regarding activity preceding Orlov's arrest (for example, collaboration with members of the U.S. Congress and receipt of foreign writings from Western reporters in Moscow) which, at a glance, seemed totally fabricated, were found to be partly or largely accurate and held with conviction.

2. The trial record shows that there was little that was tentative about official perceptions of Orlov and his dissident associates. Under the influence of longstanding stereotypes (about dissidents and foreigners), KGB investigators and court officials distorted incoming information and slanted the testimony of official witnesses to fit their image of the hostile intentions of Orlov and his Soviet and foreign supporters.

3. The actions of Orlov and his associates were found to be both criminal by Soviet standards and fully in accord with pledges made by the Soviet Union at Helsinki and elsewhere. By Soviet legal and social norms, Orlov's actions constituted illegal political activity and international slander. However, by international standards, Orlov was engaged in legitimate human rights advocacy and simple pursuit of Helsinki pledges made by his government. At the core of this conflict were the fundamentally different and conflicting conceptions of human rights, subversion, and the spirit of Helsinki held by Soviet officials and dissidents such as Orlov.

4. The activities of Orlov and his associates, although greatly exaggerated by official stereotypes about the foreign origins and subversive nature of the conflict, were, by 1976 (formation of the Moscow Group), not innocuous and tolerable. The Monitors' *samizdat* activity did challenge the Party's control of information, embarrass the regime, and undermine its international prestige.

5. Orlov and his fellow Group members were loyal, but critical, Soviet citizens. Their efforts to appeal to local and central officials before turning to foreigners for assistance illustrate this point. It seems, however, that officials were convinced largely by increasing foreign support for Soviet dissidents that the intentions of Orlov and his associates were extremely hostile. Orlov's efforts, in fact, were intended to improve the system's performance (human rights record) rather than to subvert the system.

6. Contrary to expectation, no fundamental differences were found in the official images of Orlov expressed in official releases for foreign and domestic consumption. The only notable differences were in the tone of the statements. With few exceptions, most ranged from extreme to moderate hostility. No evidence was found of any trend toward more perceptive official conceptions of dissidents such as Orlov.

NOTES

1. The following profile of Orlov draws on basic facts found in *CCE*, no. 50, pp. 1-2; *A Chronicle of Human Rights in the USSR* (hereafter *CHR*, no. 25, pp. 85-88; *CHR*, no. 26, pp. 9-11; and Ludmila Alexeyeva, *Delo Orlova* [The Case of Yury Orlov] (New York: Khronika Press, 1980), pp. 8-9.

2. "Yury Orlov, An Autobiographical Note," *CHR*, no. 25, p. 85.

3. Alexeyeva, p. 8.

4. *CHR*, no. 25, p. 86.

5. Ibid.

6. Ibid., p. 87.

7. Valentin Turchin, "In Defense of Yury Orlov," *CHR*, no. 26, p. 9.

8. Robert L. Bernstein, "A Statement in Behalf of Yury Orlov," *International Sakharov Hearings*, September 29, 1979, p. 2.

9. *CHR*, no. 25, pp. 87-88.

10. Ibid., p. 88.

11. See Appendixes G and I for a more detailed breakdown of Orlov's activities during this period.

12. *Arkhiv samizdata* (Radio Liberty's collection of *samizdat* documents, hereafter cited as *AS*), 2425.

13. Joshua Rubenstein, *Soviet Dissidents: Their Struggle for Human Rights* (Boston: Beacon Press, 1980), pp. 217-20.

14. Bernstein, p. 2.

15. Rubenstein, p. 214.

16. Ibid.

17. Lisa L. Helling, "U.S. Human Rights Policy toward the Soviet Union and Eastern Europe During the Carter Administration," *Denver Journal of International Law and Policy* 9 (Winter 1980):93-97.

18. "Soviet Law and the Helsinki Monitors," p. 117.

19. *New York Times*, September 10, 1973.

20. *In Defense of Dr. Yury Orlov* (New York: Amnesty International, USA, 1978), p. 7.

21. The relevance of the following section on the recruitment and background of Moscow Group members needs to be made explicit. During his 1978 trial, Orlov was judged not simply according to his own activity, but also based on the character and actions—distant and recent—of his associates.

22. Sakharov's unwillingness to act as the Group's leader was not in any way a reflection of his lack of support for or confidence in Orlov and the Moscow Group effort. His backing for the Group was unstinting from the start and dramatically symbolized by his calling a press conference for foreign journalists in his Moscow flat to announce—together with several of the Group's founding members—the formation of the Moscow Helsinki Group. Furthermore, the fact that Sakharov's wife, Elena Bonner, was a Group monitor meant that he received constant firsthand reporting on the Group's activities.

23. Brief biographical sketches of Ginzburg, the three Helsinki monitors which follow, and numerous other Soviet dissidents may be found in *Profiles: The Helsinki Monitors*, U.S. Congress, Commission on Security and Cooperation in Europe, December 10, 1979.

24. Marsh Clark, "A Letter from the Publisher," *Time*, July 24, 1978, p. 2.

25. U.S. Congress, Commission on Security and Cooperation in Europe, *Reports of Helsinki-Accord Monitors in the Soviet Union, The Right To Know, The Right To Act*, May 1978, p. 7. For a listing of the nineteen Group documents, see Appendix I.

26. U.S. Congress, Commission on Security and Cooperation in Europe, *A Thematic Survey of the Documents of the Moscow Helsinki Group*, by Ludmila Alexeyeva, May 12, 1981, pp. 2-3, 5.

27. CSCE, "Profiles," p. 2. These figures should not obscure the massive support of unregistered Christians in the USSR for the small group of religious leaders included in this leadership circle. Thousands of religious nonconformists—Pentecostals, Baptists, Jehovah's Witnesses, Adventists, Catholics, Russian Orthodox believers and others—have appealed openly to authorities to respect their rights, including the right to emigrate on the grounds of religious persecution: see, for example, U.S. Congress, Commission on Security and Cooperation in Europe, *On the Right to Emigrate for Religious Reasons: The Case of 10,000 Soviet Evangelical Christians*, May 1979.

28. Bernstein, p. 3.

29. Rubenstein, p. 237.

30. For a chronology of relevant domestic and foreign developments, see Appendix H.

31. The phrase "inertia of fear" is borrowed from the title of a book by exiled Soviet dissident Valentin Turchin, *The Inertia of Fear and the Scientific Worldview* (New York: Columbia University Press, 1981).

32. *Andrei Sakharov from Exile* (New York: International League for Human Rights, 1983), p. 8.

33. Sakharov, p. 8.

34. For a useful discussion of historical developments relevant to the emergence of human rights advocacy under President Carter, see, for example, Arthur Schlesinger, "Human Rights and the American Tradition," *Foreign Affairs* 57, America and the World 1978, pp. 503-26.

35. Elizabeth Sheetz, "Western Reaction to the Orlov Trial," *Radio Liberty Research*, no. 120/78, May 30, 1978.

36. TASS, as reported by UPI, May 15, 1978.

37. L.G. Churchward, *The Soviet Intelligentsia* (London: Routledge & Kegan Paul, 1973), pp. 6-12.

38. Tibor Szamuely, *The Russian Tradition* (New York: McGraw-Hill Book Co., 1974), pp. 144-45.

39. For a more detailed discussion of the critical ideas of leading members of the Russian intelligentsia, see: Tibor Szamuely, pp. 147-79; Vladimir C. Nahirny, "The Russian Intelligentsia: From Men of Ideas to Men of Convictions," *Comparative Studies in Society and History* 4 (July 1962):403-35; and Chs. 2 and 3, respectively, "The Genesis of the Russian Intelligentsia," and "The Formation of a Russian Intelligentsia," in Shatz, pp. 12-13.

40. Although these concepts have roots in the tenets of Soviet Marxism, it is useful to view them more broadly as Soviet concepts: conceptions which are also rooted and reinforced by much of Soviet, and even Russian, historical experience.

41. O. Reinhold and F. Ryzhenko, eds., *Contemporary Anti-Communism: Policy and Ideology* (Moscow: Progress Publishers, 1976), p. 7. Written for an English-speaking audience, this book represents the collective efforts of twenty-one Soviet experts on the subject of contemporary anti-Communism.

Unfortunately, apart from an introductory listing of contributing authors, the essays which follow are unattributed.

42. "Anti-Sovietism: A Major Current in the Ideology of Contemporary Imperialism," (Editorial), *Kommunist*, no. 10, 1965, p. 64.

43. Ibid.

44. Kudinov and V. Pletnikov, "The Easing of Tension and the Maneuvers of Anti-Communism," *Pravda* August 9, 1974, p. 3.

45. Ibid.

46. Reinhold and Ryzhenko, p. 7.

47. Ibid., p. 191.

48. 24th Congress of the CPSU, as quoted by Reinhold and Ryzhenko, pp. 111-12.

49. Semyon Tsvigun, "Subversion as a Weapon of Imperialism," *Kommunist*, no. 4, 1980, pp. 108-19.

50. Ibid., pp. 109, 114, 115.

51. Ibid., p. 116.

52. Ibid., p. 115.

53. Zivs, p. 172.

54. Georgi Arbatov and Willem Oltmans, *The Soviet Viewpoint* (New York: Dodd, Mead & Co., 1983), p. 148.

55. Elizabeth Sheetz, "The Orlov Trial," *Radio Liberty Research*, no. 111/78, May 15, 1978.

56. "The Trial of Yuri Orlov," Document no. 50, *Reports of the Helsinki Accord Monitors in the Soviet Union*, vol. 3, CSCE Staff, November 7, 1978.

57. Regarding the selection, background, and rehearsing of witnesses for the prosecution, see *CCE*, no. 50, pp. 9-12.

58. Ibid., p. 19.

59. "On a Hostile Wavelength," (Editorial), *Moskovskaya pravda*, May 19, 1978, p. 3.

60. Code of Criminal Procedure, RSFSR, as quoted in "Soviet Law and the Helsinki Monitors," p. 130.

61. Ibid. For a perceptive and more detailed discussion of the educational role of the Soviet court, see Harold J. Berman, *Justice in the USSR: An Interpretation of Soviet Law*, rev. ed. (Cambridge: Harvard University Press, 1966), pp. 299-311.

62. *CCE*, no. 50. p. 16.

63. Ibid., p. 17.

64. Ibid.

65. Ibid., p. 16.

66. Ibid.

67. Ibid., p. 3.

68. Unofficial transcripts of the initial and appeal trials of Orlov—fifty-five and six pages in length, respectively—reached Radio Liberty in Munich through *samizdat* channels; they are referenced by Radio Liberty and hereafter referred to as *AS* 3549 and *AS* 3550. The unofficial record of the proceedings was recorded from the memory of Irina Orlova at the end of each session by members of the Moscow Helsinki Group.

69. *AS*, 3549, p. 11.

70. *AS*, 3549, p. 15.

71. *AS*, 3549, p. 51.

72. Ibid.

73. Ibid., p. 54.

74. *CCE*, no. 50, pp. 18-19.

75. *AS*, 3549.

76. For a discussion of this decision and the December 1976 "policy turning-point," see Reddaway, pp. 175-79.

77. Alexander Petrov-Agatov, "Liars and Pharisees," *Literaturnaya gazeta*, February 2, 1977, p. 14.

78. Ibid.

79. Ibid.

80. "What Is Behind the Furor over 'Human Rights?'" (Editorial), *Pravda*, February 2, 1977, p. 4.

81. Ibid.

82. Sanya Lipavsky, "Open Letter to the Presidium of the USSR Supreme Soviet (with copies to the U.S. Congress and the United Nations)," *Izvestiya*, March 5, 1977, p. 3. According to David Shipler (*New York Times*, December 16, 1979), Lipavsky had worked, on various occasions since 1962, as an informer for the KGB regarding currency speculation and other issues. In return for such cooperation, the secret police spared Lipavsky's father from the death penalty following a conviction for stealing.

83. Ibid.

84. D. Morev and K. Yarilov, "The CIA: Spies and 'Human Rights,'" *Izvestiya*, March 5, 1977, p. 6.

85. Ibid.

86. Sanya Lipavsky, "How I Was Recruited by the CIA," *Izvestiya*, May 8, 1977, p. 4.

87. Leonid Brezhnev, "Speech at the 16th Congress of Soviet Trade Unions," *Pravda*, March 22, 1977, p. 3.

88. *Moskovskaya pravda*.

89. V. Nikolayev, "Who Guards the Anti-Soviets, and Why?" *Sovetskaya kultura*, June 20, 1978, p. 7.

90. Ibid.

91. Zivs, pp. 101-2.

92. Arbatov, pp. 161-62.

93. Ibid.

94. Ibid., p. 163.

95. Nikolai Yakovlev, *CIA Target—the USSR*, 3rd ed. (Moscow: Progress Publishers, 1982).

96. Ibid., p. 145.

97. Malcolm Haslett, "General Tsvigun: Defender of Soviet Morality," *BBC Current Affairs Talk*, no. 10/82, January 21, 1982.

98. Tsvigun, "Subversion as a Weapon of Imperialism"; and Semyon Tsvigun, "The Intrigues of Foreign Intelligence Agencies," *Kommunist*, no. 14, 1981, pp. 88-89.

99. Tsvigun, "Subversion as a Weapon of Imperialism," p. 112.

100. *AS*, 3549, p. 45.

101. *CCE*, no. 50, p. 19.

102. Petrov, p. 14.

103. Ibid.

104. Ibid.

105. *AS*, 3549, pp. 22-26.

106. *Moskovskaya pravda*.

107. Zivs, pp. 101-2.

108. Arbatov, pp. 161-62.

109. Zivs, p. 104.

110. *Pravda*, "What Is Behind the Furor over 'Human Rights?'"

111. Nikolayev, p. 7.

112. V. Bolshakov, "'Human Rights' in the Strategy of Psychological Warfare," *Pravda*, August 12, 1978, p. 4.

113. Zivs, p. 102.

114. Nikolayev, p. 7.

115. *AS*, 3549, p. 46.

116. *Moskovskaya pravda*.

117. Ibid.

118. Zivs, pp. 101-2.

119. Lipavsky.

120. Arbatov, p. 161.

121. Zivs, p. 109.

122. Ibid., pp. 111-13.

123. *AS*, 3549, pp. 53-54.

124. Arbatov, p. 165.

125. Ibid.

126. For an insight into the permanent stigma attached to individuals who openly criticize the Soviet state, see Lev Kopelev's memoir, *To Be Preserved Forever* (New York: J.B. Lippincott Co., 1977).

127. See, for example, George Feifer, "No Protest: The Case of the Passive Minority," pp. 418-37.

128. Bernstein, p. 4. For a summary of some of the statements made by witnesses to John Macdonald, see "The Orlov Tribunal," *Index on Censorship* 6 (November-December 1977):52-57.

129. *AS*, 3549, p. 11.

7

Conclusions

And in this matter [the arrest and trials of so-called "dissidents"]
let no one take offense: to protect the rights, freedom, and security
of the 260 million Soviet people from the activities of such renegades
is not only our right but also our sacred duty. It is our duty to those
individuals who 60 years ago, under the guidance of Lenin's Party,
embarked on the road of building socialism and communism. It is
our duty to the people who in defense of their socialist Motherland
and their right to live the way they want, sacrificed 20 million lives
in the Great Patriotic War against fascist aggressors. It is precisely
for the rights and freedom of these individuals that we will never
depart from that road!

Leonid Brezhnev[1]

What is unusual in one culture is the rule in another, what one culture
considers abnormal another considers normal, what is cast out and
despised by one group as unnatural and psychopathological is the
very trait that another group nurtures as a desirable foundation for
its whole social pattern.

Abraham Maslow[2]

This concluding chapter will summarize the principal findings
of the preceding chapters and evaluate some important case study
findings from the perspective provided by this work's conceptual

framework and its review of the literature on dissent. More precisely, this chapter will draw some tentative conclusions regarding vital components of the official belief system and related subjects, raise some unresolved questions and issues, suggest several possible avenues for future research on official perceptions of the dissent conflict, and, finally, offer a few considerations regarding the future direction of the conflict.

The principal findings of Chapters 2-4 may be summarized briefly. Chapter 2 found that Western study of Soviet dissent has not gone far enough: the study of Soviet official perceptions of dissidents, nonconformists, and related issues remains greatly underdeveloped; its theoretical content is inadequate; and its analysis for the most part lacks rigor. Chapter 3 made a modest effort to redress this situation. It introduced the concept of the image to the study of the conflict between Soviet authorities and dissidents and advanced a loose and tentative framework to facilitate the description and interpretation of how Soviet officials see dissidents, nonconformists, and the context of the conflict. Chapter 4 examined the principal data and methodological problems surrounding research into Soviet perceptions of the conflict and developed a strategy to permit a preliminary assessment of this important, but neglected, dimension of the conflict.

Chapters 5 and 6 presented two case studies, one of religious nonconformity and the other of intellectual dissent, in order to illustrate this study's central hypothesis, namely, that Soviet official perceptions of dissidents and religious nonconformists during the Brezhnev era have been influenced by highly negative and stereotypic images of dissidents rather than by accurate images. Although the two case studies, not surprisingly, proved inadequate to support a systematic discussion of official images of dissidents and nonconformists during the Brezhnev era, they did permit detailed observations to be made on a few vital components of the official belief system—official images of internal and external adversaries and of the nature of the conflict—and on some important related issues.

TENTATIVE CONCLUSIONS

Intensive study of the cases of Vladimir Shelkov and Yury Orlov elaborated this work's principal hypothesis about the stereotypic images of dissidents and nonconformists prevalent among Soviet officials. The case studies also revealed an almost obsessive Soviet preoccupation with the motives and behavior of foreign supporters of dissidents and nonconformists. The resulting tendency to link perceived internal and external enemies in a conspiracy to undermine the system was found to lead to a greatly exaggerated assessment of the actual challenge posed by individuals such as Shelkov and Orlov, an assessment that was used to justify extremely coercive policies. These and other findings will now be discussed in greater detail.

Images of Adversaries and Self

Official images of Shelkov as a religious extremist and fanatic and Orlov as a renegade dissident—as well as the more specific images of each individual—were found to be greatly distorted, stereotypic, tending to caricature, but nevertheless, held with a measure of conviction by Soviet officials. A major finding of the case studies is that there is a higher correlation between official stereotypes of dissidents, nonconformists, and foreigners and accurate images than is commonly acknowledged by Western analysts, particularly with regard to the smuggling of censored materials and unauthorized contacts with foreigners. Although most of the general and specific official images of Shelkov, Orlov, their respective associates, and foreign supporters did have a partial basis in fact—what social scientists sometimes refer to as the "kernel of truth" present in stereotypes which makes them so misleading— official images were found to be ultimately oversimplified, misleading, and outdated.

This element of truth, and the emotionally charged and rigid nature of official stereotypes reflected in the court proceedings, provided Soviet officials with something clearly recognizable and therefore objectionable in the behavior of dissidents. Consequently, the "kernel of truth" probably permitted them to articulate official stereotypes with a larger measure of conviction than might otherwise have been the case.

Closely linked with official images of internal and external opponents are official self-images: Soviet authoritative statements relevant to the cases and period investigated reveal a polarized, black-and-white contrast of Soviet officials and foreigners. The latter, particularly those from the United States, are repeatedly depicted as devious and diabolical enemies who are determined at all costs to subvert the Soviet system ideologically. Soviet officials, on the other hand, see themselves as politically vigilant, mature, and obedient agents of Soviet law and order, pursuing a defensive policy and motivated by values of loyalty, duty, and discipline.

Nature of Conflict

The intensive studies of the Shelkov and Orlov cases, as well as the extensive survey of the more general official writings relevant to the dissent conflict, cast considerable doubt on the conventional Western view that Soviet officials accurately perceive the nature of the conflict and the challenge posed to the system by dissidents. This evidence suggests that Soviet officials grossly distort the foreign dimension of the conflict, in particular any linkage between dissidents and foreigners, and greatly exaggerate the challenge ultimately posed to the regime by individuals such as Orlov and Shelkov. The authorities were predisposed in this direction not only by what many Western analysts describe as the traditional intolerance Russian and Soviet leaders exhibit toward any unauthorized public expressions of dissent, but also, importantly, by the extreme and stereotypic conceptions of Western psychological warfare, anti-communism, and contemporary dissidents and nonconformists which pervade official pronouncements and which are reinforced by the very real contacts between dissidents and foreigners. Thus, the actions of Orlov and Shelkov and their foreign supporters were interpreted as fresh evidence for a conspiratorial theory of Western ideological subversion. Officials, for example, interpreted the actions of Orlov and his associates as an organic element in a carefully calculated, foreign-inspired and supported campaign to undermine the international prestige and the internal security of the Soviet Union, rather than as a domestic effort by disillusioned, but system-supporting, citizens to promote fuller Soviet compliance with international standards of human rights, in particular, the human rights provisions of the Helsinki Final Act. In official eyes, then, the conflict was a foreign-backed effort to legitimize the "right to anti-Soviet activity" and not simply human rights advocacy.

USSR Minister of Justice Vladimir Terebilov summarized the official image of the nature of the conflict aptly and authoritatively. Shortly after the trials of Orlov and Shelkov, he observed:

> I think that the "dissident" problem has been artificially created to step up anti-communism. Of course, it does have its sources. These will not be found in the Soviet legislative system, but in the imperialist centers which work out the strategy for attacks against socialism.[3]

Blind Spots

What are the important blind spots in official perceptions of dissidents and foreigners that contribute to this exaggerated threat appraisal? Drawing once again on this volume's case studies and on the more general official writings reviewed, it is possible to identify four kinds of facts frequently denied or ignored by Soviet officials: the defendants' ethical rather than subversive motives; the individual's repeated efforts to cooperate with authorities in redressing a perceived injustice (for example, Shelkov's efforts to offer constructive comments on the 1977 Draft Constitution to officials when they were solicited formally and Orlov's efforts to act as a constructive critic, first through Party channels and later by submitting appeals exclusively to key Soviet officials before turning to open dissent); collaboration of defendants with foreigners and veteran dissidents out of a sense of desperation rather than from a desire to subvert the system; and the fact that foreign support for dissidents, generally speaking, is a reaction to heightened official repression of an individual or group and not an effort to develop widespread political opposition to the system (as Samuil Zivs contended). Significantly, in the cases of Shelkov and Orlov, officials with rigid and emotionally charged images of the defendants denied or lost sight of these and other crucial facts: facts which, if properly acknowledged, could have challenged the stereotypic images of motives and intentions and possibly mitigated the extreme sentences imposed on both individuals.

Self-fulfilling Prophecy

Closely related to the subject of selective inattention or blind spots in perception is the notion of a self-fulfilling prophecy. This work's case studies provide some empirical support for Robert Dahl's hypothesis, which explains the intolerance of hegemonic regimes toward even seemingly mild dissent by the concept of a self-fulfilling prophecy. In the case of Orlov, by pursuing an un-responsive and frequently repressive policy toward early Soviet dissidents (during the 1960s) as well as Orlov, the authorities slowly but steadily effected a self-fulfilling prophecy. They transformed Orlov from a loyal, hard-working citizen and member of the Com-munist Party, who in the mid-1950s offered constructive criticism through Party channels, into an occasional signer of respectfully worded appeals addressed exclusively to Soviet officials, and finally into an open and active critic of regime policies, an associate of veteran dissidents and foreign supporters in Moscow and abroad. A similar process was at work in the case of Shelkov. A review of the history of the conflict between Soviet authorities and the Seventh-Day Adventists indicates that officials greatly exaggerated any challenge or potential threat posed to the regime by the True and Free Adventists in the late 1920s and grossly magnified any foreign connections with sect members (this finding reinforces the point made earlier by Bohdan Bociurkiw and other Western analysts regarding the extreme security consciousness of Soviet authorities). Officials subsequently reacted with extreme and often erratic re-pression. In time, they set in motion a self-fulfilling prophecy, by progressively alienating and politicizing individuals such as Shelkov and his codefendants and forcing them to act illegally and "con-spiratorially," thereby confirming official suspicions.

Belief System in Action

The *samizdat* transcript of the trials of Shelkov and Orlov pro-vide a candid glimpse (not for foreign or Soviet public eyes) of the official belief system in action. They confirm the existence of negative and emotionally charged stereotypes of dissidents, non-conformists, and foreigners at the operational level of the conflict and clearly demonstrate the presence of an affective, rather than an analytical, official orientation to the conflict. The trial records indicate that there was little that was tentative about official perceptions of the defendants, who were viewed in accord with the prevailing general images of dissidents and nonconformist Adventist leaders as enemies of the system and as agents of foreign interests. Under the influence of long-standing stereotypes, prejudices, and, undoubtedly, political pressures, officials of the court and the KGB distorted incoming information to fit their images of the hostile intentions of subversive internal opponents linked with a devious external enemy. At the core of these images was a profound contempt for the perceived values and actions of the defendants and their respective groups, which meant a total lack of empathy for the defendants. Court officials seem to have been motivated by what Stanley Milgram terms an "administrative outlook": they acted as obedient and unquestioning agents of authority, as "thoughtless agents of action."[4]

The unofficial transcripts also suggest that the stereotypic images articulated in the courtroom serve more than the political or propaganda function typically highlighted by Western analysts. The behavior of court officials and the carefully screened audience suggests that official images also serve important sociological and psychological functions.[5] During the trials of Shelkov and Orlov, for instance, official images of the defendants as enemies of the state served the sociological function of enhancing group solidarity and the psychological function of focusing and releasing official and audience hostility. In short, the *samizdat* transcripts suggest that the intensity of the emotional commitment of officials to these stereotypes may be far greater than commonly assumed by Western analysts.

UNRESOLVED QUESTIONS AND ISSUES

The close study of Soviet official images of dissidents and related issues can shed light on certain aspects of the official belief system, but it also leaves many questions and issues unresolved. A few of these will now be highlighted.

First, there is much that we simply do not know and are unlikely to learn in the foreseeable future about the view from the Kremlin. How informed are and were Soviet leaders and members of the ruling elite, both today and during the period we have discussed, about key actors and issues relevant to the dissent conflict? How nuanced is their picture of the conflict? Is their information as timely and accurate as some Western analysts assume? Or is it greatly distorted as a result of the biases and political interests of the many layers of the KGB and other large bureaucracies through which it is filtered? Do Politburo members such as Brezhnev purposefully tone down their publicly articulated images of dissidents, as one student of Soviet dissent has speculated, or are the extremely hostile images of dissidents and foreigners generated by KGB information gatherers and policy influencers perhaps simplified and slightly toned down as a result of filtering through official think tanks and Central Committee departments? And are the resulting stereotypes held by high-level officials the consequence of deception, self-deception, or both?[6] Answers to many of these questions are difficult to formulate in view of our present lack of knowledge. Nevertheless, it is reasonable to assume, based on statements by Brezhnev and other Politburo members, on this volume's case studies, and on our general knowledge of large bureaucracies, that the images of Soviet leaders are probably no more accurate than the images of their information gatherers within the KGB, who screen relevant information and events through dominant and stereotypic images before transmitting them to the political elite.

Second, the court proceedings as reflected in the *samizdat* transcripts raise an important question regarding the development of socialist legality. Contrary to expectations and Soviet politico-legal tradition, the attorneys appointed by the court to defend Shelkov and Orlov both presented aggressive legal defenses. Shelkov and Orlov were both convinced of the genuineness of their respective lawyers' efforts to defend them vigorously and expressed their gratitude openly.

Particularly noteworthy were the efforts of Orlov's attorney, Evgeny Shalman, who attempted to call all the witnesses requested by Orlov. Although virtually all of Shalman's petitions were rejected by the court, the fact that he was permitted to continue in this line is unusual and significant. Interestingly, Shalman survived the trial to defend yet another dissident shortly thereafter.[7] To date, only a few similar developments have been reported during Soviet political trials. Such developments are significant and deserve closer attention. They may be indicative of more perceptive views of dissidents within the legal bureaucracy and even a measure of empathy for them.

Finally, it is appropriate to note that the two *samizdat* transcripts provided an important check on stereotypes expressed in the official press, revealing virtually identical conceptions. Furthermore, the hostile tone evident in the press closely mirrored that present in the courtroom. Reporting in the official press presented the Soviet public and foreign readers with a highly accurate reflection of the prejudices and stereotypes expressed by the authorities during the two trials. The close correspondence between official images expressed in official press accounts and in *samizdat* reports of the trials suggests that official press coverage of political trials provides an accurate indicator of official biases and prejudices toward dissidents and related issues.

FUTURE RESEARCH

This study has provided a preliminary assessment of an important, but neglected, dimension in Western study of Soviet dissent, that is, official perceptions of dissidents and related issues. Although the data could not support a systematic discussion of official images of dissidents and nonconformists in the Brezhnev era, they did illustrate the central hypothesis and allow detailed observations to be made on important aspects of the problem. What directions might future research on the perceptual dimension of the conflict take?

1. An important and rather obvious next step is to extend the study of official images to include more intensive case studies of different types of dissent. Adequate data (in the form of extensive official writings and detailed *samizdat* trial transcripts) are now available to permit intensive study of important cases of national dissent and workers' protest.[8] With regard to disabled rights activism, no trials have yet taken place; hence there are no unofficial trial records. However, some official commentary is available, and an imaginative, although rough, analysis of official perceptions of this form of dissent should be possible. In addition, extensive, but only partially exploited, data exist on some important early cases of intellectual dissent, including those of Joseph Brodsky and of Sinyavsky and Daniel. Intensive study of these and other early cases may

not only permit a longitudinal analysis of official perceptions of intellectual dissent, but may also provide more reliable descriptions of the contemporary roots of official images of dissidents such as Orlov.

A greater number of case studies of different dimensions of dissent and nonconformity would permit us to extend our limited knowledge of Soviet perceptions of various aspects of the dissent conflict: to determine, for example, whether official images of different types of dissent accurately reflect the substantial differences in types of dissent, or whether these differences are blurred by officials. The research questions formulated in this work (Chapter 5, Introduction) can serve as a starting point toward this effort. For instance, researchers could investigate whether official reaction to nationalist and workers' dissent and disabled rights activism has had the effect of a self-fulfilling prophecy, or whether perceptions of foreign enemies result in greatly exaggerated official estimates of the threat posed by these types of dissent.

2. Future research should also attempt to broaden our conceptualization of Soviet dissent. There is a conspicuous need to match the depth of current research into the behavior and thought of dissidents and Soviet policy toward them with greater breadth: to approach the study of Soviet dissent as a political and social conflict with important domestic and international dimensions. This work's case studies underline the need to devote more serious analytic attention to the study of foreigners as key political actors in the conflict. Not only is an objective analysis of the intentions and activities of foreign governments, groups (especially emigré groups), individuals, radio stations (which broadcast to the USSR), and others required, but also an analysis of how these perceptions influence official attitudes, threat assessment, and policy. Currently, Soviet perceptions of foreigners, though prominent in official writings related to the conflict, have, with few exceptions, escaped the attention of Western analyses of Soviet threat perceptions. In addition, more serious attention should be directed to the influence of authoritative contemporary Soviet formulations of concepts such as psychological warfare, ideological subversion, anticommunism, slander, anti-Soviet activity, and human rights.

3. In addition to expanding the scope of Western study of Soviet dissent, there is a need to develop more rigorous analytic techniques, which may permit a more systematic and objective

analysis of the perceptual dimension of the conflict. Traditional image study is a starting point, an empirical and tentative approach which, over time, could provide a less speculative basis for discussions of Soviet perception and motivation. However, other techniques exist. Imaginative scholars, with experience in traditional and quantitative content analysis, may find that the voluminous official and *samizdat* writings provide a rich vein of data for the rigorous study of the expression of political hostilities associated with the conflict, as well as for numerous other subjects. In this regard the writings of Ole Holsti and Alexander George (see Bibliography) pertaining to content analysis techniques, propaganda analysis, and the study of official belief systems should prove suggestive.

4. Future research into the Soviet dissent conflict requires a greater multidisciplinary effort. This conflict is extremely complex, multifaceted, and, in an important sense, cross-cultural. Many Soviet dissidents and nonconformists may be viewed legitimately as contributing to an antiofficial counterculture; and the cultural, political, and historical differences which separate foreign supporters of dissidents from Soviet official culture are obvious. The result, as illustrated by this work's case studies, is a collision of very different cultural conceptions (for example, permitted dissent and human rights) separated by their basis in fundamentally different ways of perceiving the world.

To bridge this gulf and to advance Western understanding of Soviet dissent requires the efforts not only of political scientists, but also of legal scholars, political and social psychologists, sociologists, historians, and scholars from other disciplines. A useful strategy to bring the diverse perspectives and skills of scholars to bear on a common problem is collaborative research. For instance, a legal scholar may find it fruitful to team up with a political or social psychologist to design a framework and method to exploit the wealth of *samizdat* trial transcripts for insights into the official belief system and, in particular, the development of socialist legal consciousness with respect to political trials. The possibilities for collaborative research are many and quite stimulating.

5. There is a need to develop more culturally specific questions concerning the problem-solving capabilities of Soviet leaders with regard to the dissent conflict. It is not enough for researchers to be more specific about the relationship among the numerous factors they view as contributing to the conflict and influencing official

views and policy toward dissidents. There is also a need for our research questions to be sensitive to Soviet culture and perceptions. The two case studies illustrate that what may be viewed in one society as normal and acceptable can, as Abraham Maslow suggests, be seen as deviant, immature, regressive, and even pathological behavior in another society. Viewed in this light, the crucial question is not whether any new political elite emerging in the post-Stalin era will permit modest, but unauthorized, human rights advocacy within its system. Rather, the salient question is whether members of this political elite will support activities which during the past two decades have consistently and authoritatively been defined as criminal and as anti-Soviet. Only after answers to these types of questions are generated will we be in a position to make informed and specific judgments about the learning capacity and problem-solving capabilities of the Soviet regime.

FINAL CONSIDERATIONS

What are the prospects of a new political elite, a generation raised in the post-Stalin era, emerging to adopt a fundamentally less coercive orientation toward individuals such as Shelkov and Orlov? The obstacles to such a development are formidable and take many forms. Only a few will be highlighted here.

One of the most formidable is the conceptual barrier which separates members of the political elite from dissidents: the wall of extremely hostile, stereotypic images of contemporary dissidents and foreigners and the more general official conceptions of foreign subversion and anticommunism. All of these images and conceptions are rooted in historic memories of foreign invasions and Marxist-Leninist assumptions about socialism's implacable enemies and have recently been reinforced not only by steady official rhetoric about internal and external enemies of the Soviet state, but also by the more than twenty-year-old post-Stalin tradition of aggressively suppressing all activity defined as "anti-Soviet" and subversive. Will members of the new political elite, steeped in this contemporary political tradition, be able to see beyond this wall? More important, will they have the political will and courage (or from the Soviet perspective, the political immaturity and insufficient vigilance) needed to not only reexamine but also break down the stereotypic and extremely hostile images of contemporary dissidents and foreigners that have pervaded Soviet society since the 1960s, as well as the older and more general images?

This is a tall order, indeed. The political risks inherent in such a course to a career-climbing elite are immense, and the returns, arguably, marginal. This volume's case studies and related data offer no hope for a fundamentally less repressive official orientation toward dissidents in the foreseeable future. Quite to the contrary, the ability of Soviet authorities (mid- and high-level) to relate more to caricatures than to flesh-and-blood individuals was vividly illustrated in the cases of Yury Orlov and Vladimir Shelkov. Early official images of Shelkov's Reformist sect as Nazi collaborators, for example, have become an authoritative legend which is firmly embedded in Soviet political culture and tenaciously held, it seems, even by officials who had direct contact with Shelkov and his associates. Despite dramatic changes in the political leadership (during Shelkov's long-running conflict with the state) and a lessening of its antireligious policy (during the past three decades), official conceptions of the Reformist Adventists have remained essentially unaltered and emerged during the Brezhnev era to justify Shelkov's extreme sentence.

Another formidable barrier to a basic change in official orientation toward dissidents (one often neglected in the relevant Western literature) is legal-institutional in nature. During the more than twenty-year, post-Stalin history of the suppression of open dissent and nonconformity, an important network of laws has been carefully erected by Soviet leaders to provide the KGB with important weapons in its effort to ensure internal security and suppress open dissent. The legal network is also designed to close what many Soviet dissidents have described as the large discrepancy between Soviet constitutional guarantees of human rights and the legal and extra-legal practices of the KGB against dissidents.[9] Significantly, these laws have also institutionalized or enshrined official biases and stereotypic images of dissidents in various laws about "anti-Soviet activity." Hence, in addition to challenging traditional conceptions, any Soviet officials who advocate a fundamentally less coercive orientation face an important legal obstacle. They run the serious risk of appearing to obstruct socialist legality.

This leads to a third important consideration, the KGB. Assigned with managing the dissent conflict on a day-to-day basis and serving as the main information link between dissidents and the ruling political elite, the KGB bureaucracy has a vested, professional interest in promoting and even exaggerating (as the pretrial evidence in the Shelkov and Orlov cases illustrates) official stereotypes of dissidents. Thus, while extreme coercion may prove counterproductive for the political elite—in that it can breed alienation, more open dissent, and international tensions—official stereotypes are extremely useful for the KGB. They reinforce its important position in society by greatly exaggerating the challenge posed by dissidents and foreigners and by conveying this message to the leadership (for example, Tsvigun's open writings). Any members of a new political elite advocating a less coercive orientation toward moderate dissidents, consequently, will likely find themselves in a direct confrontation with the KGB. The prospect of such a conflict is another important disincentive for members of the political elite to break down official stereotypes.

Finally, it should be stressed that official images are a vital indicator of any fundamental change in official orientation. Any basic change in official policy toward dissidents will necessarily be preceded by a fundamental change in official images. Any such sign of a reorientation has yet to be seen.

SUMMARY

This work has attempted to draw attention to the important, but neglected, perceptual dimension of the Soviet dissent conflict. The two case studies undertaken represent a first attempt to closely investigate those vital components of the official belief system which determine perceptions and help shape policy. Together they illustrate the central hypothesis that Soviet official perceptions of dissidents and religious nonconformists have been influenced by highly negative and stereotypic, rather than accurate, images of these internal opponents and that officials have tended to blur important differences between dissidents and religious nonconformists. The case studies also revealed an almost obsessive Soviet preoccupation with the motives and behavior of foreign supporters of dissidents and nonconformists. This tendency to link perceived internal and external enemies as elements of a conspiracy to undermine the system was found to cause Soviet officials to greatly exaggerate the actual challenge posed by individuals such as Shelkov and Orlov. The case studies and related data presented here offer no hope for a fundamentally less coercive official orientation toward dissidents in the foreseeable future.

In addition to exaggerated perceptions of threat, the official belief system was found to be marked by cognitive rigidity (stereotypic images and responses), by important blind spots in official perceptions of the intentions and actions of dissidents and their foreign supporters, and by a total lack of empathy for dissidents. Official policy enacted a self-fulfilling prophecy: official perceptions of high hostility from dissidents and foreigners became self-confirming, while perceptions of low hostility were self-liquidating. Filtered through stereotypic and extremely hostile images and culture-bound conceptions in the official belief system, the efforts of dissidents and their supporters were viewed not as a struggle for basic human rights, but as a foreign-inspired and supported drive to legitimize the "right to anti-Soviet activity" and ultimately to develop a broadly based political opposition to the state.

Another important finding is that the facts behind the conflict between the authorities and Orlov and Shelkov prove much more complex than commonly assumed by Western analysts, and hence, more vulnerable to misinterpretation by Soviet officials. After careful examination, nuances appeared instead of the black-and-white, good-and-evil categories expressed by officials and many Western writers. Significantly, many of the allegations regarding the activities of Shelkov, Orlov, and their respective associates which, at a glance, seemed implausible and totally fabricated to many Western analysts were found to have at least a partial basis in fact and, consequently, to be held with conviction even by officials who had close contact with the defendants. A speculative conclusion is that many high-level officials, whose main link with the dissent conflict is the KGB, probably also find official stereotypes of dissidents, and especially their foreign supporters, plausible.

Finally, it is hoped that the descriptive groundwork laid here, in the form of two intensive case studies and the tentative conceptual framework and method advanced, will leave students of Soviet dissent in a better position to undertake the research necessary for a fuller understanding of official perceptions of the conflict. Image study is a starting point, an empirical and tentative approach which could over time provide a less speculative basis for discussions about Soviet perception and motivation. It should continue as an ongoing audit of an important indicator of fundamental change in official views of, and policy toward, dissidents.

NOTES

1. Brezhnev, *Pravda*, March 22, 1977, p. 3.
2. Abraham H. Maslow, "Personality and Patterns of Culture," in *Psychology of Personality*, ed. Ross Stagner (New York: McGraw-Hill, 1937), p. 416.
3. Vladimir Terebilov, "In Defense of Human Rights" (An Interview), *World Marxist Review*, July 1979, p. 65.
4. Stanley Milgram, *Obedience to Authority: An Experimental View* (New York: Harper & Row, 1974), pp. 176-86.
5. On the various functions official images of enemies can serve, see Alexander Dallin and George Breslauer, *Political Terror in Communist Systems* (Stanford, Calif.: Stanford University Press, 1970), pp. 244-45.
6. Reddaway, p. 159.
7. On August 15, 1978, Shalman defended Alexander Podrabinek, a dissident active in the campaign against psychiatric repression. For a brief summary of Shalman's defense, see *CCE*, no. 50, pp. 82-84.
8. Readers interested in pursuing such research should, as a starting point, consult this volume's discussion of data reliability in Chap. 4 and the detailed listing of *samizdat* trials in Appendix B.
9. For useful background information on these laws, see Reddaway, pp. 174-75.

Appendixes

The Study of
Soviet Perception of Dissidents
and Nonconformists

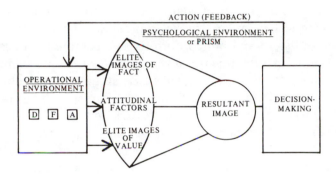

Operational Environment

Key Actors:
Dissidents and noncon-
formists
  Intellectuals
  Nationalists
  Workers
  Disabled rights activists
  Religious noncon-
    formists et al.

Authorities
  Central officials
  Local officials
  Vigilante groups

Foreigners
  Officials
  Journalists
  Private citizens
  Soviet emigres
  Foreign radio stations

Communications

Soviet official media
Direct observation
Samizdat
Western media

Psychological Environment

Elite images
Attitudinal factors:
  Historical legacy
  Ideology
  Personality predispositions

B

List of Political
Trials and Documentation

The following is a selective list of political trials in the USSR since the mid-1960s; the cutoff date for new information is summer 1984. Alphabetical in order, the list represents all major aspects of contemporary dissent and nonconformity and is intended to serve as a starting point for subsequent studies of official images of internal adversaries (included are this volume's case studies). Cases described in sufficient detail were selected following a survey of relevant data in the *Chronicle of Current Events* (*CCE*), indisputably the most comprehensive and important *samizdat* journal; numbers after names refer to specific issues of *CCE* where image-related data may be found. Additional *samizdat* reporting may be found in other issues of *CCE*—each citation is cross-referenced—and in the numerous other *samizdat* periodicals (see Appendix C); detailed biographical information on many of the following individuals may be found in Ludmilla Alexeyeva's *Soviet Dissent*; S.P. de Boer's et al. *Biographical Dictionary of Dissidents in the Soviet Union, 1957-1975;* and Cronid Lubarsky's (ed.) *List of Political Prisoners* (see selected bibliography for full citations). Finally, numbers 1-11 of *CCE* appeared, with annotations, in Peter Reddaway's *Uncensored Russia: The Human Rights Movement in the Soviet Union* (New York: American Heritage Press, 1972), hereafter cited as *UR*.

Abramkin, V.	58*	Amalrik, A.	17
Airikyan, P.	34	Babitsky, K.	*UR*
Akimov, D.	31	Bakhmin, V.	58
Alexeyeva, V.	Keston†	Balakirev, V.	30
Altunyan, G.	62	Barladyanu, V.	46

---

*CCE issue numbers
†Keston College Archives

Bebko, V.	53		Kurnosov, V.	62
Begun, J.	50		Ladyzhensky, L.	34
Bogoraz, L.	*UR*		Landa, M.	46
Bolonkin, A.	51		Lapienis, V.	47
Borisov, V.	11		Lavut, A.	60
Brodsky, J.	Kucherov[1]		Lepshin, I.	53
Bukovsky, V.	23		Lisovoi, V.	30
Buzinnikov, E.	51		Litvinov, P.	*UR*
Chornovil, V.	45		Lukyanenko, L.	50
Dandaron, B.D.	28		Mackevicius, A.	32
Daniel, Y.	*UR*		Malkin, A.	37
Delone, V.	*UR*		Maramzin, V.	35
Dremlyuga, V.	*UR*		Marchenko, A.	*UR*
Dyadkin, I.	58		Maresin, V.	40
Dzhemilev, M.	40		Marinovich, M.	49
Fainberg, V.	*UR*		Markosyan, R.	58
Fedotov, I.	36		Mattik, K.	38
Furlet, S.P.	53		Matulionis, J.	47
Gabai, I.	35		Matusevich, M.	49
Gajauskas, B.	49		Morozov, M.	53
Galanskov, Y.	*UR*		Moroz, V.	17
Gamsakhurdia, Z.	50		Myasnikov, A.	61
Ginzburg, A.	50		Naboka, S.	62
Goldshtein, G.	49		Nazaryan, R.	51
Gorbachev, S.	58		Nekipelov, V.	32
Iesmantas, G.	60		Nikitin, N.	54
Igrunov, V.	40		Niklus, M.	61
Ivanov, A.	48		Nudel, I.	50
Jaugelis, V.	34		Orlov, Y.	50
Kapitanchuk, V.	58		Osipov, V.	37
Kheifets, M.	34		Osipova, T.	62
Kiirend, M.	38		Ovsienko, V.	52
Konovalikhin, V.	51		Patrubavicius, A.	34
Koryagin, A.	62		Peceliunas, P.	60
Kostava, M.	50		Petkus, V.	50
Kovalyov, S.	38		Petronis, P.	34
Krasin, V.	30		Pirogov, S.	32
Krivoi, Y.	Keston		Plumpa, P.	34
Kuleshov, E.	53		Podrabinek, A.	50
Kukk, J.	61		Podrabinek, K.	49

Poresh, V.	57	Skvirsky, V.	53
Povilonis, V.	32	Slepak, M.	50
Pranckunaite, O.	47	Slepak, V.	50
Pronyuk, E.	30	Sokirko, V.	58
Pype, A.	45	Soldatov, S.	38
Rozhdestov, V.	47	Solovyova, S.	Keston
Rudaitis, I.	32	Spalin, A.	53
Rudenko, M.	46	Stasaitis, J.	34
Sadunaite, N.	37	Stus, V.	58
Sakalauskas, A.	32	Terleckas, A.	58
Sasnauskas, J.	58	Tikhy, A.	46
Semanyuk, I.	30	Tsurkov, A.	53
Sergei, M.	53	Tverdokhlebov, A.	40
Shcharansky, A.	50	Varato, A.	38
Serebrov, F.	47	Velikanova, T.	58
Shatalov, N.P.	51	Vins, G.	35
Shelkov, V.	53	Volokhonsky, L.	53
Shevchenko, A.	60	Yakir, P.	30
Shevchenko, N.	Keston	Yakunin, Father G.	58
Skobov, A.	53	Yuskevich, A.	38
Shtern, M.	34	Zdebskis, Father J.	23
Sichko, V.	61	Zinchenko, A.	61
Sinyavsky, A.	*UR*	Zisels, I.	53
Skripnikova, A.	Keston	Zukauskas, S.	32
Skuodis, V.	60		

NOTE

1. A transcript of the trial may be found in Samuel Kucherov, *The Organs of Soviet Administration of Justice: Their History and Operation* (Leyden: E.J. Brill, 1970), pp. 212-34.

C

List of
Samizdat Periodicals

The following is a list of the titles of major *samizdat* periodicals which have appeared since at least the early 1960s. The list is intended chiefly to reflect the broad scope of *samizdat* reporting and, thus, to place this volume's *samizdat* sources in perspective. Essential background information on these and other *samizdat* publications may be found in: Peter Reddaway, "Can the Dissidents Survive?" *Index on Censorship* 9 (August 1980):30-32; F.J.M. Feldbrugge, *Samizdat and Political Dissent in the Soviet Union* (Leyden: A.W. Sijthoff, 1975), pp. 49-54; "Religious and National Dissent in Lithuania," *Hearings before the Commission on Security and Cooperation in Europe, Ninety-Seventh Congress* (Washington, D.C.: Government Printing Office, 1981), pp. 75-76. More recent information on these as well as on new periodicals may be found in the latest issues of *CCE* in a feature section entitled "Samizdat Publications."

GENERAL PERIODICALS AND JOURNALS

CCE
Documents from Helsinki Groups
Political Diary
Kolokol
Problems of Society
The Democrat
Veche
Crime and Punishment

JOURNALS ON SOCIOECONOMIC, POLITICAL, AND CULTURAL THEMES

Searches
Strength in Temperance
Memory
In Defense of Economic Freedoms
Concerning the Draft Constitution
Archive
37
The Watch
Women and Russia
Perspective
Summary
Bulletin of the Action Group To Defend the Rights of the Disabled
    in the Soviet Union

JEWISH JOURNALS

Jews in the USSR
Culture
Modern Hebrew
Exodus
Herald of the Exodus
Iton
White Book of the Exodus

RELIGIOUS PERIODICALS

CLCC (focuses on Catholic nationalism)
The Future
The Path of Truth
The Sorrowing Christ
God and Country
The Fraternal Leaflet
The Bulletin of the Council of Baptist Prisoners' Relatives
Herald of Truth
Community

In the Light of the Transfiguration
Newsletters of Soviet Adventists
Newsletters of the Christian Committee for the Defense of Believers' Rights
Chronicle of the Catholic Church in the Ukraine

NATIONALIST PERIODICALS

CLCC
Perspectives
The Dawn
The National Path
The Bell
The Knight
Alma Mater
Liberty and Fatherland
Ukrainian Herald
Estonian Democrat
Saturday Newspaper
Supplements to the Free Dissemination of Opinion and News in Estonia
The Golden Fleece
The Georgian Herald
Re Patria
In the Name of the Motherland
Crimean Tatar Information Bulletin

D

Chronological History
Of Soviet Adventism

1886   Introduction of Adventism to Russia

1886-1905   Tsarist persecution of Adventists

1905   Declaration of loyalty to Tsar Nicholar II; reforms make Adventists a legal institution

1905-17   Growing debate in Adventist communities over the issue of loyalty to the new regime

1917-27   Persecution of Orthodox Church; freedom for other Christian churches

1924   Fifth All-Union Congress of Seventh-Day Adventists leads to a split between those who support the Bolshevik government and those who refuse state control of religious activities; formation of breakaway faction called Adventists of the Free Remnant (or Reformist Adventists)

1929   Law on Religious Associations (also known as Law on Cults)

1932-45   Period of decline and obscurity for Soviet Adventists and other sects; mass arrests of Reformist Adventists as mass members of an "anti-Soviet organization"

1945-53   War recovery; Soviet Adventists and other sects enjoy a period of relative freedom

1953   Death of Stalin is followed by a further relaxation in official persecution of religion

1959-64	Full-scale attack by Khrushchev on all organized religion; many congregations are driven underground
1965	Relaxation in official church policy follows Khrushchev's ouster
1966-84	Selective, but often extreme, repression of nonconforming believers with vigorous press campaigns
1977	New constitution; Law on Religious Associations is reaffirmed
1977-78	Vigorous campaign against True and Free Adventists; arrests of key leaders

E

Chronological Biography Of Vladimir Shelkov

1886	Adventism is introduced in Russia by a German
1895	Birth of Shelkov to Baptists in Ukraine
1903	Adventist leaders forbid members to read revolutionary literature
1917	Russian Revolution
1923	Shelkov converts and becomes a Bible worker in the Seventh-Day Adventist Church
1924, 1928	Schism among Soviet Adventists at the fifth and sixth All-Union Adventist Congresses; True Remnant sect formed under the leadership of G. Ostwald, a German
1927	Shelkov is ordained a preacher
1928	Law on Religious Associations (or Cults)
1929-31	Shelkov campaigns against state registration among Adventists in Tyumen (Ural Mt. region)
1931	First arrest of Shelkov; sentenced to three years' exile with forced labor
1931-34	Exile in Berezovo (Ural Mt. region)
1934	Release of Shelkov

1934-45	Shelkov remains in hiding to avoid persecution and rearrest for religious activity; interwar years spent in residence in German-occupied Pyatigorsk
1945	Soviet reoccupation of Pyatigorsk and rearrest of Shelkov and others for inciting dissatisfaction with the Soviet system and collaborating with the enemy
1946	Shelkov is found guilty and sentenced to death; sentence is commuted to 10 years in a special regime labor camp
1946-54	Sentence is served in Karaganda (the largest forced labor complex of the Stalin era); Shelkov continues his missionary work in camp
1949	Shelkov is elected chairman of the True Remnant Church while still in confinement
1954	Release of Shelkov six months early due to illness
1954-57	Shelkov resumes his struggle for the Church's independence; supports pacifism of young Adventists and efforts of parents to raise children in the Adventist faith
1957	Arrested in Dzambul (Kaz. SSR); given a "repeat sentence" of ten years for anti-Soviet agitation
1957-59	Serves in Eastern Siberian camps
1959-67	Serves in Mordovian camps and there meets many dissidents (future contacts)
1965	Split among official Adventists; breakaway group merges with and expands Shelkov's True and Free Adventist Church
1967	Release from camp; founding of unofficial "True Witness" Adventist press

1969
Shelkov is rearrested and detained; narrowly escapes a new trial by going into hiding

1969-78
Shelkov exists illegally, underground; moves from one "safe house" to another to avoid arrest

1974
First reports on the persecution of the True Adventists are passed from the groups to the main unofficial human rights journal,   *Chronicle of Current Events*

1976
Closer links are forged between Shelkov's sect and dissidents

1977-78
Shelkov sends letters appealing for support to President Carter, West German Adventist leaders, and signatories of the Helsinki Accords meeting in Belgrade

1978
Shelkov is arrested following an intensive KGB search and a violent raid on his daughter's home

1979
Trial of Shelkov and codefendants; the former is sentenced to five years' strict regimen in a labor camp

1980
Death of Shelkov at 84 in a Siberian labor camp near Tabaga. Leonid Murkin replaces Shelkov as president of the All-Union Church of True and Free Adventists; secret police launches an All-Union search for Murkin

1983
Vigorous but sporadic attacks on Shelkov and the True and Free Adventists continue in the official press; apparent reconciliation between the official Adventist Church and group which broke away in 1965 and joined Shelkov

F

Sample Testimony of True And Free Adventists on The Extreme Persecution Of Religious Believers

1. *Nina Bezdushnaya, S. Bochkovtsy, Chernovtsyobl*: "Teacher V.B. Burshei told the pupils to tie a Pioneer scarf round my son Vitaly's neck by force and, nicknaming him 'the angel,' asked the pupils to ridicule him. Headmaster N.P. Baiko said more than once, 'You eat our bread, breathe Soviet air, but you're worse than all drunkards and chain-smokers.' Often words turned into actions: my children received blows on the face and back from teachers."

2. *Alexander Gorchenko, S. Shilovtsy, Chernovtsy obl.*: "On 22 January 1977, a group of KGB men under the command of KGB Captain Okhotnik broke into the home of believer Karp Galicharsky, who lives in the neighboring village of Klishkovtsy, where I and other believers were gathered at the time. Capt. Okhotnik began to carry out a search, though he had no right to do so. He began to shout at us: 'What sort of meeting is this? No one is to leave! Everyone back in their places!' Then he started to accuse us of breaking the Law on Religious Cults and not submitting to Soviet power, after which he demanded the names of those present. Seeing the illegal actions of these state officials, I refused to give my name. 'Never mind, you'll tell us in another place,' said Okhotnik. Twisting my arms and hitting me on the head and back, they dragged me to the car and took me to the local police station. On the way, they beat me on the head and stomach saying, 'Well, how do you like Soviet power now?' "

3. *Vasily Annenko, Stavropol Krai, Essentuki, s/z Kislovodsk*: "In 1966, because I was a religious believer and lived according to my conscience, I was grabbed, tied up and sent to a psychiatric hospital. They gave me injections . . . beat me, shouted at me, gave me medicines which made me lose consciousness. When I came to, I asked them, 'Why are you killing me? I'm not ill, I'm a believer.' "

NOTE

1.   This selected testimony was submitted in the form of collected letters to the Madrid Review Conference of the Helsinki Accords held in 1980. Copies of the full testimony are on file in London, Washington, and Munich, respectively at Keston College, the Congressional Committee on Security and Cooperation in Europe, and at Radio Liberty.

G

Chronological Biography
Of Yury Orlov

1924   Birth of Orlov to working-class Russian parents in Smolensk *oblast*

1941-44   Works as a lathe operator and has first doubts about Soviet authority

1944   Drafted, attends military school and becomes a candidate member of the Communist Party

1945-46   Continues post-war military service and participates in political discussions with liberal army officers

1946   Recruited to be a Soviet spy but refuses; demobilized

1948-56   Orlov is a full member of the Party

1953-56   Graduates from Moscow University and works at the Moscow Institute of Theoretical and Experimental Physics

1955   Participates in an international conference on nuclear physics in Geneva, Switzerland

1956   20th Party Congress and Khrushchev's de-Stalinization speech; Orlov completes thesis and publishes first professional article; at a party meeting calls for democratic changes; subsequently dismissed from his job, the Party, blacklisted in Moscow and forbidden to defend his thesis; eventually finds work in the Armenian SSR

1963-68   Orlov's outstanding work on high-energy accelerators leads to a doctoral degree; Khrushchev pardons and reinstates "mistaken critics of the regime" in Armenia; Orlov is elected a corresponding member of the Armenian Academy of Sciences

1972   Returns to Moscow and obtains work at the Academy of Science's Institute of Earth Magnetism; Orlov is increasingly drawn to the Soviet human rights movement; placed under house arrest during President Nixon's visit to the USSR

1973   Orlov writes an open letter to Brezhnev which defends Andrei Sakharov and discusses the question of intellectual freedom; becomes a founding member of the Soviet section of Amnesty International

1974

Jan. 1   Dismissed from work for defense of Sakharov and related activity; denied professional work until his 1977 arrest

Feb. 13   Signs appeal in defense of Solzhenitsyn

Mar.   Publishes "Autobiographical Sketch" in *samizdat*

June   Placed under house arrest to prevent participation in an international scientific seminar organized by physicist A. Voronel

June 18   Writes statement in defense of Voronel

July 11   Writes "Statement to the Press" protesting dismissal from his job and KGB persecution

Sept. 1   Signs statement in defense of Yu. Gastev

Nov. 20   Coauthors letter with Khodorovich to Amnesty International requesting support for recently convicted Airikyan

Nov. 29   Signs appeal protesting the arrest of V.N. Osipov

Dec. 16   Signs statement to the press demanding that officials respond to the request of Zhitnikova (Plyushch's wife) for news about her husband

Dec. 20   Appeals in a letter to the International Committee for Human Rights to appoint a lawyer for Zhitnikova in order to help free her husband

1975

Jan. 26   Signs a statement to President Podgorny protesting recent KGB actions against human rights activists

Feb. 24   Together with Khodorovich writes a statement in defense of Plyushch

Apr. 20   Signs letter of the Moscow section of Amnesty International protesting the arrest of S. Kovalev and A. Tverdokhlebov

Apr. 21   Together with Turchin and Khodorovich writes an appeal to public opinion in Western countries arguing that the struggle for human rights in the USSR is of vital interest for the West

July 1   Signs an open letter to KGB Chairman Andropov in defense of Crimean Tatar M. Dzhemilev

July 9   Signs another appeal in defense of Dzhemilev

Aug. 11   Together with M. Landa and G. Podyapolsky sends an appeal to U.S. congressmen in defense of the rights of political prisoners in the USSR

Aug. 16   Signs a petition to the Presidium of the Supreme Soviet for a general political amnesty

Sept. 26   Signs a statement protesting the harsh sentence imposed on V. Osipov

Oct. 3   Signs a letter to Rev. M. Bourdeaux (in London) in defense of Ukrainian Orthodox priest V. Romanyuk

Oct. 10   Writes an appeal with Landa in defense of Airikyan

Oct. 21   Together with Velikanova and A. Lavut writes a letter to Amnesty International and other international human rights organizations defending the right of Kovalev and Tverdokhlebov to free choice of lawyer

Oct. 31   Signs statement of nine Moscow intellectuals on the occasion of Political Prisoners' Day

Nov.   Together with Bogoraz and Alexeyeva writes an appeal in defense of Romanyuk

Dec. 9   Orlov is detained in Vilnius while trying to attend the trial of Kovalev

Dec. 15   Publishes "Is Socialism Without Totalitarianism Possible?" in *samizdat*; argues it is, given decentralization of the economy and private political initiative

1976-77   Orlov meets with members of the U.S. Congress and other foreigners visiting the USSR; forms and acts as chairman of the Moscow Helsinki Watch Group; continues Group's activities, despite repeated warnings from KGB to cease illegal activity: release of nineteen Moscow Group documents (see Appendix I) and much supplementary material prior to arrest; expands contacts and exchange of information with foreign journalists, diplomats, and visitors in Moscow; arrest of Orlov

1978   Trial, conviction and unsuccessful appeal of Orlov; sentenced to seven years in a strict regime labor camp and five years' internal exile

1982   Moscow Helsinki Group disbands

NOTES

1. In addition to sources cited in this volume's discussion of Orlov's background, this chronology draws on information contained in S.P. de Boer, E.J. Driessen, H.L. Verhaar, eds., *Biographical Dictionary of Dissidents in the Soviet Union, 1956-1975* (Boston: Martinus Nijhoff Publishers, 1982), pp. 405-6.

H

Chronology of Relevant Domestic and Foreign Developments

1964   Downfall of Khrushchev; Soviet Union is the object of numerous charges of anti-Semitism from internal and foreign critics

1965   Period of political drift; unprecedented debate between *Pravda* and *Izvestiya* over the degree of freedom Soviet writers should have in expressing their ideas

1966   Brezhnev calls for keener ideological vigilance at the 23rd Party Congress, tempers statement with a warning against administrative interference in cultural affairs; trial of nonconformist writers Andrei Sinyavsky and Yury Daniel for allegedly subversive works contributing to anti-Soviet propaganda results in stiff sentences and provokes indignation among some of the Soviet intelligentsia as well as among members of various non-Soviet Communist parties

1967   Solzhenitsyn's letter to the 4th Congress of Soviet Writers severely indicts the regime's handling of literature; calls for abolition of censorship and protection of persecuted writers

1968   Brezhnev halts the ideological relaxation and launches a campaign of "ideological rectification," denouncing the leading heresies of nationalism and "revisionism"; A. Ginzburg, Y. Galanskov and other dissidents receive harsh sentences; officials accuse Solzhenitsyn of providing misinformation to Western propaganda services; Soviets intervene militarily in Czechoslovakia

1969   Soviet official campaign for ideological conformity continues, targets include Solzhenitsyn, Krasin, Grigorenko and Tvardovsky; Brezhnev insists that peaceful coexistence does not extend to the struggle of ideologies

1970   Official criticism of intellectual dissent remains firm; attack on Solzhenitsyn after award of Nobel Prize; arrest and conviction of Amalrik for predicting the collapse of the Soviet system and its destruction by China

1971   5th Congress of Soviet Writers dismisses dissidents as a handful of idlers and parasites and reflects the ascendance of conformist views in literature. Andrei Sakharov sets up the unofficial Soviet Committee for Human Rights

1972   KGB launches an intensifying crackdown on dissidents in various Soviet republics; advocates of national and cultural rights are particularly hard-hit; arrested include V. Bukovsky, V. Krasin, L. Plyushch, K. Lubarsky

1973   KGB activity draws international attention to the cases of Sakharov, Solzhenitsyn, Yakir, and Krasin; Ukrainian dissidents receive stiff prison sentences; brief respite in repression before and during Brezhnev's visit to the U.S.

1974   Authorities heighten campaign against dissidents, some leading spokesmen are permitted to emigrate or are exiled: Solzhenitsyn, V. Maksimov, P. Litvinov, M. Rostropovich, P. Grigorenko; Soviet leaders refuse to increase Jewish emigration in return for most-favored-nation trading status from the U.S.; *samizdat* resurges

1975   Conference on Security and Cooperation in Europe concludes the Helsinki Accords; Sakharov awarded 1975 Nobel Peace Prize for his human rights efforts and consequently draws world attention to the situation of Soviet dissidents; Amnesty International draws global attention to Soviet dissidents with its publication of a comprehensive report on the Soviet prison system

1976-77   Formation of U.S. congressional and other (govern-
            mental and nongovernmental) Western Helsinki Watch
            Groups results in unprecedented media attention to
            the situation of Soviet dissidents; President Carter's
            human rights campaign focuses on Soviet violations;
            in unprecedented actions, President Carter sends a letter
            of support to a Soviet dissident (Sakharov) and invites
            an exiled dissident (Bukovsky) to visit the White House;
            Soviet authorities react to Western pressures and media
            attention by arresting leading dissidents; Conference to
            Review Implementation of the Helsinki Accords meets
            in Belgrade

1978-79   Western criticism (U.S. congressional hearings, efforts
            by concerned Western scientists and other groups)
            mounts over the trial and conviction of Orlov, Shcharan-
            sky and other leading Soviet dissidents

I

Documents of the Moscow Helsinki Group

1. The Case of Mustafa Dzhemilev, Defender of Crimean Tatars

2. Telephone and Postal Communications

3. On the Conditions of Confinement of Prisoners of Conscience

4. On Separated Families: List of Separated Families Seeking Reunification

5. Repression against Religious Families

6. On the Situation of Former Political Prisoners in the USSR

7. New Arrests on Charges of Religious or Propaganda Activity

8. On the Abuse of Psychiatric Hospitals

9. The Village of Ilinka: Family Reunification

10. On the Flagrant Violations of the Right of National Minorities to Equality before the Law

11. On the Right to Emigrate for Religious Reasons

12. On Ukrainian Refugees

13. The Necessity of Emigration for Economic-political Reasons

14. Emiliya Ilina's Struggle for the Right to Free Emigration

211

15.   On the Expulsion of Seven Students from Venoulis High School (Vilnius)

16.   On House Searches of Helsinki Watchers

17.   About Prisoners of Conscience Who Need Quick Release Due to the State of their Health

18.   On the Situation of the Meskhetians

19.   The Soviet Authorities Break Up the International Symposium of Jewish Culture

NOTE

1. The above is a list of the nineteen Moscow Helsinki Group documents issued before the February 1977 arrest of Yury Orlov. Distributed to Soviet officials as well as to foreigners, these documents served as partial evidence leading to the arrest and conviction of Orlov and other Helsinki Monitors. These reports may also be usefully grouped under the following subject headings related to the Human Rights Basket (Principle VII) of the Helsinki Final Act: Political Freedoms, Minority Rights, Religious Freedoms, Emigration, Family Reunification Information. The list was compiled from the holdings of the U.S. Helsinki Commission in Washington, D.C.

Bibliography

The following bibliography lists the most important Western and Soviet sources used in the preparation of this book. It also enumerates other titles that either provided background information but were not cited in the preceding pages or else may be of potential interest to readers who wish to pursue the subject of this volume beyond the treatment accorded here.

NON-SOVIET SOURCES

Dissent-related Books and Articles

Alexeyeva, Ludmilla. *Delo Orlova* [The Case of Yury Orlov]. New York: Khronika Press, 1980.

_____ . *Soviet Dissent: Contemporary Movements for National, Religious, and Human Rights*. Middletown, Conn.: Wesleyan University Press, 1985.

_____ . *A Thematic Survey of the Documents of the Moscow Helsinki Group*. Washington, D.C.: U.S. Commission on Security and Cooperation in Europe, May 12, 1981.

_____ . Amnesty International. *In Defense of Dr. Yury Orlov*. New York: Amnesty International USA, 1978.

_____ . *Prisoners of Conscience in the USSR: Their Treatment and Conditions*. London: Amnesty International, 1975.

Antic, Oxana. "Church-State Relations during the Brezhnev Era." *Radio Liberty* 451/82, November 12, 1982.

_____ . "The Portrayal of 'Religious Extremists' in the Soviet Press." *Radio Liberty* 10/84, January 3, 1984.

_____ . "Religion in the USSR during Andropov's First Year." *Radio Liberty* 409/83, October 31, 1983.

_____ . "Unregistered Adventists under Fire." *Radio Liberty* 423/84, November 8, 1984.

_____ . "Veiled Lies About the Adventists." *Radio Liberty* 270/83, July 19, 1983.

_____ . "Young People and Atheist Propaganda." *Radio Liberty* 250/83, June 29, 1983.

Avrich, Paul. *Russian Rebels, 1600-1800*. New York: W.W. Norton & Co., 1972.

Azrael, Jeremy. "Is Coercion Withering Away?" *Problems of Communism* 11 (November-December 1962):9-17.

_____ . "The 'Nationality Problem' in the USSR: Domestic Pressures and Foreign Policy Constraints." In *The Domestic Context of Soviet Foreign Policy*, edited by Seweryn Bialer, pp. 139-53. Boulder, Colo.: Westview Press, 1981.

Barghoorn, Frederick C. *Detente and the Democratic Movement in the USSR*. New York: Free Press, 1976.

_____ . *Review of Dissent in the USSR*, edited by Rudolf L. Tőkés (and eleven other works on Soviet dissent). *Studies in Comparative Communism* 16 (Spring/Summer 1983): 99-119.

_____ . *The Soviet Image of the United States: A Study in Distortion*. New York: Harcourt, Brace, 1950.

_____ . *Soviet Russian Nationalism*. New York: Oxford University Press, 1956.

Beck, Carl, et al. *Comparative Communist Political Leadership*. New York: David McKay Co., 1973.

Beeson, Trevor. *Discretion and Valor: Religious Conditions in Russia and Eastern Europe*. London: Collins, 1974.

Berman, Harold J. *Justice in the USSR: An Interpretation of Soviet Law*. Rev. ed. Cambridge: Harvard University Press, 1966.

Bernstein, Robert L. "A Statement in Behalf of Yury Orlov." *International Sakharov Hearings*, September 29, 1979.

Bialer, Seweryn, ed. *The Domestic Context of Soviet Foreign Policy*. Boulder, Colo. Westview Press, 1981.

Bailer, Seweryn, and Gustafson, Thane. *Russia at the Crossroads: The 26th Congress of the CPSU*. London: George Allen & Unwin, 1982.

Bociurkiw, Bohdan R. "Lenin and Religion." In *Lenin: The Man, the Theorist, the Leader. A Reappraisal*. Edited by Leonard Schapiro and Peter Reddiaway. pp. 107-34. London: Pall Mall Press, 1967.

_____ . "Political Dissent in the Soviet Union." *Studies in Comparative Communism* 3 (April 1970): 74-105.

_____ . "The Shaping of Soviet Religious Policy." *Problems of Communism* 22 (May-June 1973): 37-51.

Bociurkiw, Bohdan R., and Strong, John W., eds. *Religion and Atheism in the USSR and Eastern Europe*. London: Macmillan Press, 1975.

de Boer, S.P.; Dreissen, E.J.; and Verhaar, H.L., eds. *Biographical Dictionary of Dissidents in the Soviet Union, 1957-1975*. Boston: Martinus Nijhoff Publishers, 1982.

Boiter, Albert. *Religion in the Soviet Union* (Washington Papers, No. 78). Beverly Hills: Sage Publications, 1980.

Bonavia, David. *Fat Sasha and the Urban Guerrilla: Protest and Conformism in the Soviet Union*. New York: Atheneum, 1973.

Bourdeaux, Michael. "Adventists through the Eyes of Soviet Atheism." *Radio Liberty* 327/76, June 28, 1976.

_____ . "Law as an Instrument of Soviet Communist Party Policy." In *Religious Minorities in the Soviet Union*. Rev. ed., edited by M. Bourdeaux et al., pp. 6-11. London: Minority Rights Group, 1977.

_____ . *Opium of the People: The Christian Religion in the USSR*. Rev. ed. London: Mowbrays, 1977.

Bozeman, Adda B. "Understating the Communist Threat." In *Human Rights and World Order*, edited by Abdul Azia Said, pp. 143-53. New Brunswick: Transaction Books, 1978.

Breslauer, George. *Khrushchev and Brezhnev as Leaders: Building Authority in Soviet Politics*. London: Allen and Unwin, 1982.

Brown, Archie, and Gray, Jack. *Political Culture and Political Change in Communist States*. London: Macmillan Press, 1977.

Brown, Archie, and Kaser, Michael, eds. *The Soviet Union Since the Fall of Khrushchev*. New York: Free Press, 1975.

Brumberg, Abraham. *Review of Dissent in the USSR*, edited by Rudolf L. Tőkés. Survey 22 (Summer/Autumn 1976): 321-25.

Buergenthal, Thomas. *Human Rights, International Law, and the Helsinki Accord*. Montclair, N.J.: Allanheid, Osmun, 1977.

Chalidze, Valery. *To Defend These Rights: Human Rights and the Soviet Union*. New York: Random House, 1974.

Churchward, L.G. *The Soviet Intelligentsia: An Essay on the Social Structure and Roles of Soviet Intellectuals during the 1960s*. Boston: Routledge & Kegan Paul, 1973.

Clark, Marsh. "A Letter from the Publisher." *Time*, July 24, 1978, p. 2.

Claude, Richard P., ed. *Comparative Human Rights*. Baltimore: Johns Hopkins University Press, 1976.

Cocks, Paul; Daniels, Robert V.; and Heer, Nancy Whittier. *The Dynamics of Soviet Politics*. Cambridge: Harvard University Press, 1976.

Colton, Timothy J. *The Dilemma of Reform in the Soviet Union*. New York: Council on Foreign Relations, Inc., 1984.

Connor, Walter C. "Dissent in a Complex Society: The Soviet Case." *Problems of Communism* 22 (March-April 1973): 40-52.

_____. "Mass Expectation and Regime Performance." In *The Domestic Context of Soviet Foreign Policy*, edited by Seweryn Bialer, pp. 155-73. Boulder, Colo.: Westview Press, 1981.

Conquest, Robert. *Power and Policy in the USSR*. New York: Harper & Row, 1967.

_____. *Religion in the USSR*. London: Bodley Head, 1968.

_____. ed. *Justice and the Legal System in the USSR*. London: Bodley Head, 1968.

Crankshaw, Edward. *Review of Dissent in the USSR*, edited by Rudolf L. Tőkés. *Soviet Jewish Affairs* 7 (1977): 69-73.

Dahl, Robert A., ed. *Regimes and Oppositions*. New Haven: Yale University Press, 1973.

Dallin, Alexander, and Breslauer, George W. *Political Terror in Communist Systems*. Stanford: Stanford University Press, 1970.

Dalton, Margaret. *Andrei Siniavskii and Julii Daniel: Two Soviet Heretical Writers*. Wurzburg, Germany: Jal-Verlag, 1973.

Daniels, Robert. *Russia: The Roots of Confrontation*. Cambridge, Mass.: Harvard University Press, 1985.

Deutscher, Isaac. *Heretics and Renegades*. New York: Bobbs-Merrill Co., 1969.

Donaldson, Robert H. "Soviet Conceptions of 'Security.'" In *Toward Nuclear Disarmament and Global Security*, edited by Burns H. Weston, pp. 290-301. Boulder, Colo.: Westview Press, 1984.

Dornberg, John. *The New Tsars: Russia under Stalin's Heirs*. New York: Doubleday & Co., 1972.

Farer, Tom J. "Exaggerating the Communist Menace." In *Human Rights and World Order*, edited by Abdul Aziz Said, pp. 136-43. New Brunswick: Transaction Books, 1978.

Farrell, R. Barry, ed. *Political Leadership in Eastern Europe and the Soviet Union*. Chicago: Aldine Publishing Co., 1970.

Feldbrugge, Ferdinand J.M. "Law and Political Dissent in the Soviet Union." In *Contemporary Soviet Law: Essays in Honor of John N. Hazard*, edited by Donald D. Barry, William E. Butler, and George Ginzburgs, pp. 55-68. The Hague: Martinus Nijhoff, 1974.

_____ . *Samizdat and Political Dissent in the Soviet Union*. Leyden: A.W. Sijthoff, 1975.

Feldbrugge, Ferdinand J.M.; van den Berg, G.P.; and Simons, W.B. *Encyclopedia of Soviet Law*. 2d ed. Boston: Martinus Nijhoff Publishers, 1985.

Feldbrugge, Ferdinand J.M., and Simons, W.B. *Perspectives on Soviet Law for the 1980s*. Boston: Martinus Nijhoff Publishers, 1982.

Forsythe, David P. *Human Rights and World Politics*. Lincoln: University of Nebraska Press, 1983.

Garthoff, Raymond L. *Detente and Confrontation: American-Soviet Relations from Nixon to Reagan*. Washington, D.C.: Brookings Institution, 1985.

Gati, Charles, and Gati, Toby Trister. *The Debate over Detente* (Headline Series No. 234). New York: Foreign Policy Association, 1977.

Gerstenmaier, Cornelia. *The Voices of the Silent*. Translated from the German by Susan Hecker. New York: Hart Publishing Co., 1972.

Glazov, Yuri. *The Russian Mind Since Stalin's Death*. Boston: Martinus Nijhoff Publishers, 1985.

Greenfield, Richard. "The Human Rights Literature of the Soviet Union." *Human Rights Quarterly* 4 (Spring 1982): 124-36.

Griffith, William E., ed. *The Soviet Empire: Expansion and Detente*. New York: Charles Scribner's Sons, 1976.

Hammer, Darrell. *USSR: The Politics of Oligarchy*. Hinsdale, Ill.: Dryden Press, 1974.

Haslett, Malcolm. "General Tsvigun: Defender of Soviet Morality." *BBC Current Affairs Talk* 10/82, January 21, 1982.

Hayward, Max, ed. *On Trial: The Soviet State Versus "Abram Tertz" and "Nikolai Arzhak."* New York: Harper & Row, 1966.

Hayward, Max, and Fletcher, William C., eds. *Religion and the Soviet State: A Dilemma of Power*. New York: Praeger, 1969.

Hazard, John N. *Managing Change in the USSR: The Politico-Legal Role of the Soviet Jurist*. London: Cambridge University Press, 1983.

Helling, Lisa L. "U.S. Human Rights Policy Toward the Soviet Union and Eastern Europe during the Carter Administration." *Denver Journal of International Law* 9 (Winter 1980): 85-118.

Hill, Ronald J., and Frank, Peter. *The Soviet Communist Party*. 2nd ed. London: George Allen & Unwin, 1983.

Hopkins, Mark. *Russia's Underground Press: The Chronicle of Current Events*. New York: Praeger, 1983.

Hough, Jerry F. *Soviet Leadership in Transition*. Washington, D.C.: Brookings Institution, 1980.

_____ . "Thinking about Thinking about Dissent." *Studies in Comparative Communism* 12 (Summer/Autumn 1979): 269-72.

International League for Human Rights. *Andrei Sakharov from Exile*. New York: International League for Human Rights, 1983.

Ioffe, Olimpiad S. *Soviet Law and Soviet Reality*. Boston: Martinus Nijhoff Publishers, 1985.

Johnson, Chalmers, ed. *Change in Communist Systems*. Stanford: Stanford University Press, 1970.

Kaiser, Robert G. *Russia: The People and the Power*. New York: Pocket Books, 1976.

Kamenetsky, Ihor, ed. *Nationalism and Human Rights*. Littleton, Colo.: Libraries Unlimited, 1977.

Kaminskaya, Dina. *Final Judgment: My Life as a Soviet Defense Attorney*. New York: Simon & Schuster, 1983.

Kennan, George F. "Two Views of the Soviet Problem." In *Toward Nuclear Disarmament and Global Security*, edited by Burns H. Weston, pp. 283-90. Boulder, Colo.: Westview Press, 1984.

Kirk, Grayson, and Wessel, Nils H., eds. *The Soviet Threat: Myths and Realities*. Montpelier, Vt.: Capital City Press, 1978.

Klose, Kevin. *Russia and the Russians: Inside the Closed Society*. New York: W.W. Norton & Co., 1984.

Knight, Amy. "The Sixty-fifth Anniversary of the Cheka." *Radio Liberty* 501/82, December 15, 1982.

Kopelev, Lev. *To Be Preserved Forever*. New York: J.B. Lippincott Co., 1977.

Korey, William. *Human Rights and the Helsinki Accord: Focus on U.S. Policy* (Headline Series No. 264). New York: Foreign Policy Association, 1983.

Kowalewski, David. "A Comparison of Religious and Nonreligious Protest in the Soviet Union." *Conflict* 3 (1982): 267-82.

_____ . "Religious Belief in the Brezhnev Era." *Journal for the Scientific Study of Religion* 19 (1980): 280-92.

_____ . *Symbols and Protesters in the Soviet Union*. Ph.D. dissertation, Kansas State University, 1978.

Kruzhin, Peter. "The KGB: Andropov Now Has Two First Deputies." *Radio Liberty* 168/82, April 2, 1982.

Kucherov, Samuel. *The Organs of Soviet Administration of Justice: Their History and Operation*. Leyden: E.J. Brill, 1970.

Labedz, Leopold, ed. *On Trial: The Case of Sinyavsky and Daniel*. London: Collins & Harvill Press, 1967.

Lane, Christel. *Christian Religion in the Soviet Union*. London: George Allen & Unwin, 1978.

Larson, Thomas P. *Soviet-American Rivalry*. W.W. Norton & Co., 1978.

Little, D. Richard, ed. *Liberalization in the USSR: Facade or Reality?* Lexington, Mass.: D.C. Heath & Co., 1968.

Litvinov, Pavel. *Trial of the Four*. Edited by Peter Reddaway. Translated by Janis Sapiets, Hilary Sternberg, and Daniel Weissbort. New York: Viking, 1972.

Loeber, Dietrich A. "The Legal Position of the Church in the Soviet Union." *Studies on the Soviet Union* 2 (1969): 16-39.

Lubarsky, Cronid, ed. *List of Political Prisoners in the USSR*. Munich: USSR News Brief, 1984.

McDougal, Myres S.; Laswell, Harold D.; and Chen, Lung-chu. *Human Rights and World Public Order*. New Haven: Yale University Press, 1980.

McLennan, Barbara N., ed. *Political Opposition and Dissent*. New York: Dunellen Publishing Co., 1973.

Medvedev, Roy. "The Future of Soviet Dissent." *Index on Censorship* 8 (March-April 1979): 25-31.

_____. *On Socialist Democracy*. New York: Alfred Knopf, 1975.

Meerson-Aksenov, Michael, and Shragin, Boris, eds. *The Political, Social and Religious Thought of Russian 'Samizdat'–An Anthology*. Translated by Nicholas Lupinin. Belmont, Mass.: Nordland Publishing Co., 1977.

Morton, Henry W., and Tőkés, Rudolf L., eds. *Soviet Politics and Society in the 1970s*. New York: Free Press, 1974.

Murray, Katherine. "Soviet Seventh-Day Adventists." *Religion in Communist Lands* 5 (Summer 1977): 88-93.

Nahirny, Vladimir C. "The Russian Intelligentsia: From Men of Ideas to Men of Convictions." *Comparative Studies in Society and History* 4 (July 1962): 403-35.

Nanda, Ved P.; Scarritt, James R.; and Shepherd, George W., Jr., eds. *Global Human Rights: Public Policies, Comparative Measures, and NGO Strategies*. Boulder, Colo.: Westview Press, 1981.

Observer [George Feifer] *Message from Moscow*. 2nd ed. New York: Vintage Books, 1971.

Oleszczuk, Thomas. "Soviet Repression: An Empirical Examination–Some Preliminary Findings on Political Trials in Lithuania." Paper presented to The American Association for the Advancement of Slavic Studies, Washinton, D.C., October 16, 1982.

Osnos, Peter. "Soviet Dissidents and the American Press." *Columbia Journalism Review* 16 (November-December 1977): 32-37.

Peace Education Division of the American Friends Service Committee. *Anatomy of Anti-Communism*. New York: Hill and Wang, 1969.

Rahr, Alexander G. "Chebrikov Replaces Fedorchuk as Head of the KGB." *Radio Liberty* 25/83, January 12, 1983.

Reddaway, Peter. "Dissent in the Soviet Union." *Problems of Communism* 32 (November-December 1983): 1-15.

_____. "Freedom of Worship and the Law." In *In Quest of Justice: Protest and Dissent in the Soviet Union Today*, edited by Abraham Brumberg, pp. 62-75. New York: Praeger, 1970.

_____. ed. *Uncensored Russia: Protest and Dissent in the Soviet Union*. New York: American Heritage Press, 1972.

Remeikis, Thomas. *Opposition to Soviet Rule in Lithuania*. Chicago: Institute of Lithuanian Studies Press, 1980.

Reshetar, John S., Jr. *The Soviet Polity*. New York: Dodd, Mead, 1974.

Rigby, T.H.; Brown, Archie; and Reddaway, Peter, eds. *Authority, Power and Policy in the USSR*. 2nd ed. London: Macmillan Press, 1972.

Rothberg, Abraham. *The Heirs of Stalin: Dissidence and the Soviet Regime 1953-1970*. Ithaca, N.Y.: Cornell University Press, 1972.

Rubenstein, Joshua. *Soviet Dissidents: Their Struggle for Human Rights*. Boston: Beacon Press, 1980.

Said, Abdul Aziz, ed. *Human Rights and World Order*. New Brunswick, N.J.: Transaction Books, 1978.

Sakharov, Andrei. *Alarm and Hope*. Edited by Efrem Yankelevich and Alfred Friendly, Jr. New York: Knopf, 1978.

_____. *My Country and the World*. New York: Vintage Books, 1975.

_____. *Progress, Coexistence and Intellectual Freedom*. New York: Norton, 1970.

Sapiets, Marite. "One Hundred Years of Adventism in Russia and the Soviet Union." *Religion in Communist Lands* 12 (Winter 1984): 256-73.

_____. "V.A. Shelkov and the True and Free Seventh-Day Adventists of the USSR." *Religion in Communist Lands* 8 (Autumn 1980): 201-17.

Schapiro, Leonard. *The Origins of Communist Autocracy: Political Opposition in the Soviet State, First Phase, 1917-1922*. Cambridge: Harvard University Press, 1955.

_____ . ed. *Political Opposition in One-Party States*. London: Macmillan Press, 1972.

Schultz, Richard., and Godson, Roy. *Dezinformatsia: Active Measures in Soviet Strategy*. 2nd ed. New York: Pergamon Press, Inc., 1984.

Schwartz, Morton. *The Foreign Policy of the USSR: Domestic Factors*. Encino, Calif.: Dickenson Publishing Co., 1975.

Seton-Watson, Hugh. "The Russian Intellectuals." *Encounter*, September 1955, pp. 43-50.

Sharlet, Robert. *The New Soviet Constitution of 1977: Analysis and Text*. Brunswick: O. Kings Court Communications, 1978.

Shatz, Marshall S. *Soviet Dissent in Historical Perspective*. Cambridge: Cambridge University Press, 1980.

Sheetz, Elizabeth. "The Orlov Trial." *Radio Liberty* 111/78, May 15, 1978.

_____ . "Western Reaction to the Orlov Trial." *Radio Liberty* 120/78, May 30, 1978.

Shelkov, Vladimir. "Complaint to the Central Committee of the Uzbek SSR Communist Party." In *Materials on the Persecution of Soviet Adventists Submitted by the True and Free Adventists to the Madrid Conference*, Keston College Archives, November 1980.

Shipler, David K. *Russia: Broken Idols, Solemn Dreams*. New York: New York Times Book Co., 1983.

Shragin, Boris. *The Challenge of the Spirit*. Translated by P.S. Falla et al. New York: Knopf, 1978.

Shub, Anatole. *An Empire Loses Hope: The Return of Stalin's Ghost*. New York: W.W. Norton & Co., 1970.

Simes, Dimitri K. *Detente and Conflict: Soviet Foreign Policy, 1972-1977*. Beverly Hills, Calif.: Sage Publications, 1977.

_____ . "Human Rights and Detente." In *The Soviet Threat: Myths and Realities*, edited by Grayson Kirk and Nils H. Wessel, pp. 135-47. Montpelier, Vt.: Capital City Press, 1978.

Simon, Gerhard. *Church, State and Opposition in the USSR*. London: Hurst, 1974.

Sinyavsky, Andrei. Testimony on V.A. Shelkov. *International Sakharov Hearings*. Washington, D.C., September 25, 1979.

Smith, Hedrick. *The Russians*. New York: Quadrangle, 1976.

Solchanyk, Roman. "Ideological Secretary in Western Ukraine Calls for Increased Political Vigilance." *Radio Liberty* 344/84, September 13, 1984.

Solzhenitsyn, Alexander. *Detente: Prospects for Democracy and Dictatorship*. New Brunswick, N.J.: Transaction Books, 1976.

_____. "Letter to the Leaders." *London Sunday Times*, March 3, 1974.

_____ . *The Oak and the Calf: Sketches of Literary Life in the Soviet Union*. Translated by Harry Willetts. New York: Harper & Row, 1979.

Solzhenitsyn, Alexander; Agursky, Mikhail; et al. *From under the Rubble*. Translated by A.M. Brock, Milada Haigh, et al. Boston: Little Brown, 1975.

Spechler, Dina R. *Permitted Dissent in the USSR: Novy mir and the Soviet Regime*. New York: Praeger, 1982.

Strong, John W. *The Soviet Union under Brezhnev and Kosygin*. New York: D. Van Nostrand, 1971.

Szamuely, Tibor. *The Russian Tradition*. New York: McGraw-Hill, 1974.

Szymanski, Albert. *Human Rights in the Soviet Union*. London: Zed Books, 1984.

Tőkés, Rudolf L., ed. *Dissent in the USSR: Politics, Ideology and People*. Baltimore: Johns Hopkins University Press, 1975.

Tolz, Vladimir. "Foremost Soviet Historian Nikolai Yakovlev: A Doughty Opponent of the CIA, Dissidents, and Masons." *Radio Liberty* 386/83, October 17, 1983.

Tucker, Robert C. *The Soviet Political Mind: Stalinism and Post-Stalin Change*. New York: W.W. Norton & Co., 1971.

Turchin, Valentin. *The Inertia of Fear and the Scientific Worldview*. New York: Columbia University Press, 1981.

Turner, John E. "Artists in Adversity: The Sinyavsky-Daniel Case." In *Political Trials*, edited by Theodore L. Becker, pp. 107-33. New York: Bobbs Merrill Co., 1971.

Tutle, James C., ed. *International Human Rights Law and Practice*. Philadelphia: American Bar Association, 1978.

Ulam, Adam B. *Dangerous Relations: The Soviet Union in World Politics, 1970-1982*. New York: Oxford University Press, 1983.

_____. *The Rivals: America and Russia Since World War II*. New York: Viking Press, 1971.

U.S., Congress, House. Commission on Security and Cooperation in Europe. *Implementation of the Final Act of the Congress on Security and Cooperation in Europe: Findings and Recommendations Five Years after Helsinki*. Washington, D.C.: Government Printing Office, 1980.

U.S., Congress, House. Commission on Security and Cooperation in Europe. *Implementation of the Helsinki Accords: Repercussions of the Trials of the Helsinki Monitors in the USSR*. 95th Cong., 2d sess. Washington, D.C.: Government Printing Office, 1978.

U.S., Congress, House. Commission on Security and Cooperation in Europe. *Implementation of the Helsinki Accords, Soviet Law and the Helsinki Monitors*. 95th Cong., 2d sess. Washington, D.C.: Government Printing Office, 1978.

U.S., Congress, House. Commission on Security and Cooperation in Europe. *On the Right to Emigrate for Religious Reasons: The Case of 10,000 Soviet Evangelical Christians*. Washington, D.C.: Government Printing Office, 1979.

U.S., Congress, House. Commission on Security and Cooperation in Europe. *Profiles: The Helsinki Monitors*. Washington, D.C.: Government Printing Office, 1979.

U.S., Congress, House. Commission on Security and Cooperation in Europe. *Reports of Helsinki Accord Monitors in the Soviet Union, The Right to Know, the Right to Act*. Washington, D.C.: Government Printing Office, 1978.

U.S., Department of State. *Religion in the USSR: Laws, Policy, and Propaganda.* Foreign Affairs Note. Washington, D.C.: Government Printing Office, 1982.

Vladimirov, Leonid. "Glavlit: How the Soviet Censor Works." *Index on Censorship* 1 (Autumn-Winter 1972): 38-39.

Vogelgesang, Sandra. *American Dream, Global Nightmare: The Dilemma of U.S. Human Rights Policy.* New York: W.W. Norton & Co., 1980.

Voronitsyn, Sergei. "Counterpropaganda: A 'New Weapon' of Soviet Ideologists." *Radio Liberty* 124/85, April 18, 1985.

Walters, Philip. "Christian Samizdat." *Index on Censorship* 9 (August 1980): 46-50.

Weston, Burns H., Ed. *Toward Nuclear Disarmament and Global Security.* Boulder, Colo.: Westview Press, 1984.

White, Stephen; Gardner, John; and Schopflin, George. *Communist Political Systems: An Introduction.* London: Macmillan Press, 1982.

Wishnevsky, Julia. "Dissidence under Andropov: A Return to Stalinist Methods." *Radio Liberty* 411/83, October 28, 1983.

_____. "The Fall of Khrushchev and the Birth of the Human Rights Movement in the Soviet Union." *Radio Liberty* 382/84, October 8, 1984.

_____. "The Right to a Defense in Soviet Political Trials." *Radio Liberty* 434/83, November 17, 1983.

Wolfe, Alan. *The Rise and Fall of the 'Soviet Threat': Domestic Sources of Cold War Consensus.* Washington, D.C.: Institute for Policy Studies, 1979.

Woll, Josephine, and Treml, Vladimir G. *Soviet Dissident Literature: A Critical Guide.* Boston: G.K. Hall & Co., 1983.

Yurenen, Sergei. "Journal Politics: Andropov to Chernenko." *Radio Liberty* 299/84, August 7, 1984.

Image-related Books, Dissertations, and Articles

Almond, Gabriel, and Verba, Sidney. *The Civic Culture*. Princeton: Princeton University Press, 1963.

Axelrod, Robert, ed. *Structure of Decision: The Cognitive Maps of Political Elites*. Princeton: Princeton University Press, 1976.

Axelrod, Robert, and Zimmerman, William. "The Soviet Press on Soviet Foreign Policy: A Usually Reliable Source." *British Journal of Political Science* 11 (April 1981): 183-200.

Berger, Peter. *The Social Construction of Reality*. 2nd ed. New York: Irvington, 1980.

Bialer, Seweryn. "The Psychology of U.S.-Soviet Relations." *Political Psychology* 6 (June 1985): 263-73.

Bociurkiw, Bohdan R. "The Changing Soviet Image of Islam." Paper presented at a UNESCO seminar on Islam held in Paris, December 4-6, 1980.

Boulding, Kenneth E. *The Image*. Ann Arbor: University of Michigan Press, 1956.

Brecher, Michael, ed. *Studies in Crisis Behavior*. New Brunswick, N.J.: Transaction Books, 1978.

Brecher, Michael; Steinberg, Blema; and Stein, Janice. "A Framework for Research on Foreign Policy Behavior." *Journal of Conflict Resolution* 13 (March 1969): 75-101.

Breslauer, George. *Five Images of the Soviet Future: A Critical Review and Synthesis*. Berkeley: Institute of International Studies, University of California/Berkeley, 1978.

Brigham, John C. "Ethnic Stereotypes." *Psychological Bulletin* 76 (1971): 15-38.

Cockburn, Andrew. *The Threat: Inside the Soviet Military Machine*. New York: Random House, 1983.

Cutler, Robert W. "The Formation of Soviet Foreign Policy: Organizational and Cognitive Perspectives." *World Politics* 34 (April 1982): 418-36.

Dallin, Alexander. "The United States in the Soviet Perspective." *Adelphi Papers* 151 (1979): 13-21.

Dawisha, Karen. "The Soviet Union and Czechoslovakia, 1968." In *Studies in Crisis Behavior*, edited by Michael Brecher, pp. 143-71. New Brunswick, N.J.: Transaction Books, 1978.

Deutsch, Morton. "Producing Change in an Adversary." In *International Conflict and Behavioral Science*, edited by R. Fisher, pp. 145-60. New York: Basic Books, 1965.

_____ . *The Resolution of Conflict*. New Haven: Yale University Press, 1973.

Dewhirst, Martin, and Farrell, Robert. *The Soviet Censorship*. Metuchen, N.J.: Scarecrow Press, 1973.

Dobson, Richard B. "Soviet Elite Attitudes and Perceptions: Domestic Affairs." R-25-84. Report prepared for the Office of Research, U.S. Information Agency, Washington, D.C., November 1984.

_____ . "Soviet Elite Attitudes and Perceptions: Foreign Affairs." R-4-85. Report prepared for the Office of Research, U.S. Information Agency, Washington, D.C., February 1985.

Donnelly, Jack. "Cultural Relativism and Universal Human Rights." *Human Rights Quarterly* 6 (November 1984): 400-19.

Dzirkals, Lilita; Gustafson, Thane; and Johnson, A. Ross. *The Media and Intra-Elite Communication in the USSR*. R-2869. Santa Monica, Calif.: The Rand Corporation, 1982.

Ellul, Jacques. *Propaganda: The Formation of Men's Attitudes*. New York: Vintage Books, 1973.

Falkowski, L.S., ed. *Psychological Models in International Politics*. Boulder, Colo.: Westview Press, 1979.

Farrell, John C., and Smith, Asa P., eds. *Image and Reality in World Politics*. New York: Columbia University Press, 1967.

Farrell, R. Barry. "The Open-Closed Policy Dichotomy." In *Approaches to Comparative and International Politics*, edited by R.B. Farrell. Evanston: Northwestern University Press, 1966.

Festinger, Leon. *A Theory of Cognitive Dissonance*. Stanford: Stanford University Press, 1957.

Gelman, Harry. *The Politburo's Management of Its America Problem*. R-2707-NA. Santa Monica, Calif.: The Rand Corporation, 1981.

George, Alexander. "The Casual Nexus Between Cognitive Beliefs and Decision-Making Behavior: The 'Operational Code' Belief System." In *Psychological Models in International Politics*, edited by L.S. Falkowski, pp. 95-124. Boulder, Colo.: Westview Press, 1979.

_____ . "The 'Operational Code': A Neglected Approach to the Study of Political Leaders and Decision-Making." *International Studies Quarterly* 13 (June 1969): 190-222.

_____ . *Propaganda Analysis: A Study of Inferences Made from Nazi Propaganda in World War II*. Evanston: Row, Peterson, 1959.

_____ . "Quantitative and Qualitative Approaches to Content Analysis." In *Trends in Content Analysis*, edited by Ithiel de Sola Pool, pp. 7-32. Urbana: University of Illinois Press, 1959.

Gibert, Stephen P. et al. *Soviet Images of America*. New York: Crane, Russak, 1977.

Griffiths, Franklyn. "Ideological Development and Foreign Policy." In *The Domestic Context of Soviet Foreign Policy*, edited by Seweryn Bialer, pp. 19-48. Boulder, Colo.: Westview Press, 1981.

_____ . "Images, Politics, and Learning in Soviet Behavior Toward the United States." Ph.D. dissertation, Columbia University, 1972.

Guroff, Gregory, and Grant, Steven. "Soviet Elites: World View and Perceptions of the U.S." R-18-81. Report prepared for the Office of Research, U.S. International Communication Agency, Washington, D.C., September 29, 1981.

Halper, Thomas. *Foreign Policy Crises: Appearance and Reality in Decision-Marking*. Columbus: Charles E. Merrill Publishing Co., 1971.

Hansen, Robert Williams. *Soviet Images of American Foreign Policy: 1960-1972*. Ph.D. dissertation, Princeton University, 1974.

Harriman, Philip. *Handbook of Psychological Terms*. Totowa, N.J.: Littlefield, Adams. 1968.

Harris, Nigel. *Beliefs in Society: The Problem of Ideology*. Baltimore: Pelican Books, 1971.

Hazan, Baruch. *Soviet Impregnational Propaganda*. Ann Arbor, Mich.: Ardis, 1982.

Helmreich, William B. *The Things They Say Behind Your Back: Stereotypes and the Myths Behind Them*. New Brunswick, N.J.: Transaction Books, 1984.

Henshel, Richard L., and Silverman, Robert A., eds. *Perception in Criminology*. New York: Columbia University Press, 1975.

van den Heuvel, and Cornelis, Christaan. *Soviet Perceptions of East-West Relationships*. Washington, D.C.: American Bar Association, 1977.

Hoffman, Erik, and Fleron, Frederic J., Jr. *The Conduct of Soviet Foreign Policy*. New York: Aldine-Atherton, 1971.

Hollander, Gayle Durham. *Soviet Political Indoctrination: Developments in Mass Media since Stalin*. New York: Praeger, 1972.

Holsti, Ole R. "The Belief System and National Images: John Foster Dulles and the Soviet Union." Ph.D. dissertation, Stanford University, 1962.

_____ . "Cognitive Dynamics and Images of the Enemy." In *Enemies in Politics*, edited by David J. Finlay, Ole R. Holsti, and Richard R. Fagen, pp. 25-96. Chicago: Rand McNally, 1967.

_____ . "Cognitive Dynamics and Images of the Enemy." In *Image and Reality in World Politics*, edited by John Farrell and Asa Smith, pp. 16-39. New York: Columbia University Press, 1967.

_____ . *Content Analysis for the Social Sciences and Humanities*. Reading, Mass.: Addison-Wesley, 1969.

_____ . "Foreign Policy Decision-Makers Viewed Psychologically: 'Cognitive Process' Approaches." In *In Search of Global Patterns*, edited by James Rosenau, pp. 120-43. New York: Free Press, 1976.

_____ . "The 'Operational Code" Approach to the Study of Political Leaders: John Foster Dulles's Philosophical and Instrumental Beliefs." *Canadian Journal of Political Science* 3 (1970): 123-57.

Hopkins, Mark W. *Mass Media in the Soviet Union*. New York: Pegasus, 1970.

Hoppmann, P. Terrence. "The Effects of International Conflict and Detente on Cohesion in the Communist System." In *The Behavioral Revolution and Communist Studies*, edited by Roger Kanet, pp. 301-38. New York: Free Press, 1971.

Horelick, Arnold L.; Johnson, A. Ross; and Steinbrunner, John D. *The Study of Soviet Foreign Policy: A Review of Decision-Theory-Related Approaches*. R-1334. Santa Monica, Calif.: The Rand Corporation, 1973.

Hough, Jerry F. "Russian Politics: What We Fail to See." *Washington Post*, February 10, 1979, p. 21.

_____ . *The Soviet Union and Social Science Theory*. Cambridge, Mass.: Harvard University Press, 1977.

Hveem, Helge. *International Relations and World Images: A Study of Norwegian Foreign Policy Elite*. Oslo: Unieversitetsforlaget, 1972.

Hyland, William. "The Soviet Union in the American Perspective: Perceptions and Realities." *Adelphi Papers* 174 (1982): 52-59.

Hyman, Herbert. *Political Socialization*. Glencoe, Ill.: Free Press, 1959.

Janis, Irving L. *Victims of Groupthink: A Psychological Study of Foreign Policy Decisions and Fiascoes*. Boston: Houghton Mifflin Co., 1972.

Janis, Irving L., and Mann, Leon. *Decision-Making: A Psychological Analysis of Conflict, Choice, and Commitment*. New York: Free Press, 1977.

Jervis, Robert. "Hypotheses on Misperception." *World Politics* 20 (April 1968): 454-79.

_____ . *The Logic of Images in International Relations*. Princeton: Princeton University Press, 1970.

_____ . *Perception and Misperception in International Politics*. Princeton: Princeton University Press, 1976.

Kanet, Roger E., ed. *The Behavioral Revolution and Communist Studies*. New York: Free Press, 1971.

Kaplowitz, Noel: "Psychopolitical Dimensions of International Relations: The Reciprocal Effects of Conflict Strategies." *International Studies Quarterly* 28 (December 1984): 373-406.

Katz, Zev. *The Communications System in the USSR*. Cambridge, Mass: MIT Center for International Studies, 1977.

Kelly, Rita, and Fleron, Frederick J., Jr. "Motivation, Methodology, and Communist Ideology." In *The Behavioral Revolution and Communist Studies*, edited by Roger Kanet, pp. 53-57. New York: Free Press, 1971.

Kelman, Herbert C., ed. *International Behavior: A Social-Psychological Analysis*. New York: Holt, Rinehart, & Winston, 1965.

_____ . "Social-Psychological Approaches to the Study of International Relations: Definition of Scope." In *International Behavior: A Social-Psychological Analysis*, edited by Herbert C. Kelman, pp. 3-39. New York: Holt, Rinehart, & Winston, 1965.

Klineberg, Otto. *The Human Dimension in International Relations*. New York: Holt, Rinehart, & Winston, 1964.

Knutson, Jeanne N., ed. *Handbook of Political Psychology*. San Francisco: Jossey-Bass, 1973.

Kruglak, Theodore E. *The Two Faces of TASS*. Minneapolis: University of Minnesota Press, 1962.

Lakoff, George, and Johnson, Mark. *Metaphors We Live By*. Chicago: University of Chicago Press, 1980.

Laqueur, Walter. "What We Know About the Soviet Union." *Commentary*, February 1983, pp. 13-21.

Leites, Nathan. *The Operational Code of the Politburo*. New York: McGraw-Hill, 1951.

_____. *A Study of Bolshevism*. Glencoe, Ill.: Free Press, 1953.

Lenczowski, John. *Soviet Perceptions of U.S. Foreign Policy: A Study of Ideology, Power, and Consensus*. Ithaca: Cornell University Press, 1982.

Lengyel, Peter, ed. "Political Dimensions of Psychology." *International Social Science Journal* 35 (1983): 221-335.

Lerner, Daniel, ed. *Propaganda in War and Crisis*. New York: George W. Stewart, 1951.

Lippmann, Walter. *Public Opinion*. New York: Harcourt, Brace, 1922.

McLellan, David. "The 'Operational Code' Approach to the Study of Political Leaders: Dean Acheson's Philosophical and Instrumental Beliefs." *Canadian Journal of Political Science* 4 (1971): 51-75.

Marvick, Elizabeth W., ed. *Psychopolitical Analysis: Selected Writings of Nathan Leites*. New York: Halsted Press, 1977.

Mayer, Richard E. *The Promise of Cognitive Psychology*. San Francisco: W.H. Freeman & Co., 1981.

Maslow, Abraham H. "Personality and Patterns of Culture." In *Psychology and Personality*, edited by Ross Stagner, pp. 408-28. New York: McGraw-Hill, 1937.

Mead, Margaret. *Soviet Attitudes Toward Authority*. London: Tavistock Publications, 1955.

Milgram, Stanley. *Obedience to Authority: An Experimental View*. New York: Harper & Row, 1974.

Neisser, Ulric. *Cognition and Reality: Principles and Implications of Cognitive Psychology*. San Francisco: W.H. Freeman & Co., 1976.

van Oudenaren, John. *U.S. Leadership Perceptions of the Soviet Problem Since 1945*. R-2843-NA. Santa Monica, Calif.: The Rand Corporation, 1982.

234 / *Soviet Images of Dissidents & Nonconformists*

Parchomenko, Walter. *Soviet Official Images of Dissidents and Nonconformists*. Ph.D. dissertation, Georgetown University, 1984.

Pocock, Douglas, and Hudson, Ray. *Images of the Urban Environment*. New York: Columbia University Press, 1978.

Powell, David E. *Antireligious Propaganda in the Soviet Union*. Cambridge: MIT Press, 1975.

_____ . "Rearing the New Soviet Man: Anti-Religious Propaganda and Political Socialization in the USSR." In *Religion and Atheism in the USSR and Eastern Europe*, edited by Bohdan R. Bociurkiw and John W. Strong, pp. 151-70. London: Macmillan Press, 1975.

Qualter, Terence H. *Propaganda and Psychological Warfare*. New York: Random House, 1962.

de Rivera, Joseph. *The Psychological Dimension of Foreign Policy*. Columbus, Ohio: Merrill, 1968.

Rokeach, Milton. *The Open and Closed Mind*. New York: Basic Books, 1960.

Schwartz, Morton. *Soviet Perceptions of the United States*. Berkeley: University of California Press, 1978.

Seth, S.P. "Soviet Image or Japan." *Pacific Community* 8 (April 1977): 490-513.

Simon, Herbert A. "The Behavioral and Social Sciences." *Science*, July 1980, pp. 72-78.

_____ . *Models of Man: Social and Rational*. New York: Wiley, 1957.

Stoessinger, John G. *Nations in Darkness*. New York: Random House, 1971.

Szalay, Lorand B. "Soviet Domestic Propaganda and Liberalization." *Orbis* 11 (Spring 1967): 210-18.

Szalay, Lorand B., and Deese, James. *Subjective Meaning and Culture: An Assessment through Word Associations*. Hillsdale, N.J.: Lawrence Erlbaum Associated, 1978.

Szalay, Lorand; Kelly, Rita; and Moon, Won. "Ideology: Its Meaning and Measurement." *Comparative Political Studies* 5 (July 1975): 151-73.

Tajfel, Henri. *The Social Psychology of Minorities*. Minority Rights Group Report No. 38. London: Minority Rights Group, 1978.

Triska, Jan, and Finley, David. *Soviet Foreign Policy*. Toronto: Collier-Macmillan, 1968.

U.S., Congress, Senate. Committee on Foreign Relations. *Perceptions: Relations Between the United States and the Soviet Union*. Washington, D.C.: Government Printing Office, 1979.

White, Ralph K. "Empathizing with the Rulers of the USSR." *Political Psychology* 4 (March 1981): 121-37.

_____ . *Fearful Warriors: A Psychological Profile of U.S.-Soviet Relations*. New York: Free Press, 1984.

_____ . "Propaganda: Morally Questionable and Morally Unquestionable Techniques." *Annals of the American Academy of Political and Social Science* 398 (November 1971): 26-35.

_____ . "Soviet Perceptions of the U.S. and the USSR." In *International Behavior: A Social-Psychological Analysis*, edited by Herbert C. Kelman, pp. 238-76. New York: Holt, Rinehart & Winston, 1965.

White, Stephen. *Political Culture and Soviet Politics*. London: Macmillan Press, 1979.

Zimmerman, William. "Distinguishing Advocacy and Policy in the Soviet Media: A Research Note." Discussion Paper No. 136, Institute of Public Policy Studies. Ann Arbor: University of Michigan, 1979.

_____ . *Soviet Perspectives on International Relations 1956-1967*. Princeton: Princeton University Press, 1969.

Newspapers and Periodicals

American Political Science Review
Annals of the American Academy of Political and Social Science
Arkhiv Samizdata (Radio Liberty Research)

BBC Current Affairs Talks
British Journal of Political Science
Canadian Journal of Political Science
Christian Science Monitor
Chronicle of Current Events
Chronicle of Human Rights
Current Digest of the Soviet Press
Dissent
Foreign Affairs
Foreign Broadcast Information Service
Government and Opposition
Human Rights Quarterly
Index on Censorship
International Studies Quarterly
Journal of Conflict Resolution
JPRS USSR Report
Keston (College) *News Service*
Kontinent
Nationalities Papers
New York Times
Political Psychology
Posev
Problems of Communism
Radio Liberty Research Papers
Religion in Communist Dominated Areas
Religion in Communist Lands
Right to Believe (Keston College)
Russian Review
Russkaya Mysl
Samizdat Bulletin (San Mateo, Calif.)
Slavic Review
Soviet Review
Soviet Studies
Soviet Union/Union Sovietique
Studies in Comparative Communism
Survey
Time (Magazine)
The Times (London)
UPI
USSR News Brief
Wall Street Journal
Washington Post
World Politics

SOVIET SOURCES

Books and Articles

Aleksandrov, I. "O svobodakh podlinnykh i mnimykh" [Concerning Real and Imaginary Freedoms]. *Pravda* February 20, 1976, pp. 4-5.

Altayev, Yuri, and Vasilyyev, Andrei. "The CIA's Trade Union Cover." *New Times* No. 12 (March 1981): 27-30.

Andropov, Yury. *Speeches and Writings*. New York: Pergamon Press, 1983.

Angarov, Victor. "Madrid: Lost Opportunities." *New Times* No. 14 (April 1982): 5-6.

Arbatov, George. "Relations Between the United States and the Soviet Union— Accuracy of U.S. Perceptions." In *Toward Nuclear Disarmament and Global Security*, edited by Burns H. Weston, pp. 278-83. Boulder, Colo.: Westview Press, 1984.

_____ . *The War of Ideas in Contemporary International Relations: The Imperialist Doctrine, Methods and Organization of Foreign Political Propaganda*. Moscow: Progress Publishers, 1973.

Arbatov, George, and Oltmans, Willem. *The Soviet Viewpoint*. New York: Dodd, Mead & Co., 1983.

Bamnov, B. "Mekhanizm diversiy" [The Sabotage Mechamism]. *Literaturnaya gazeta* April 9, 1980, p. 14.

Belov, Alexander. *Adventisty* [The Adventists]. Moscow: Izdatelstvo "Nauka," 1964.

_____ . *Adventizm* [Adventism]. Moscow: Izdatelstvo Politicheskoy Literatury, 1968.

_____ . "V plenu nesbytochnykh nadezhd" [Captives of Unattainable Hopes]. *Nauka i religiya* No. 3 (March 1978): 30-33.

Blishchenko, I., and Shavrov, V. "U.S. Hypocritical Human Rights Policies." *International Affairs* No. 4 (April 1981): 56-67.

Bogatov, Sergei. "The Balance Sheet of Detente" (two-part article). *New Times* No. 3 (January 1981): 5-7; No. 4 (January 1981): 5-7.

Bogdanov, R.G. *SShA: Voyennaya mashina i politika* [United States: Military Machine and Policy]. Moscow: Nauka, 1983.

Bolshakov, V. "'Prava cheloveka' v strategii psikhologicheskoy voyny" ['Human Rights' in the Strategy of Psychological Warfare]. *Pravda*, August 12, 1978, p. 4.

Bonovsky, Phillip. "Human Rights in America: Past and Present." *International Affairs* No. 5 (May 1978): 96-107.

Borisov, Mikhail. "The American Threat to Peace." *New Times* No. 3 (January 1982): 18-20.

Brezhnev, L.I. *The CPSU in the Struggle for Unity of All Revolutionary and Peace Forces*. Moscow: Progress Publishers, 1975.

_____ . *Socialism, Democracy and Human Rights*. New York: Pergamon Press, 1980.

Burmistrov, V. *Soviet Law and the Citizen's Rights*. Moscow: Novosti, 1974.

Chekhonin, Boris. "Komu sluzhat 'zhivye khristy." [Whom Do the 'Living Christs' Serve]? (two-part article). *Komsomolskaya pravda* October 4, 1984, p. 4; October 5, 1984, p. 4.

Chernenko, Konstantin. *Human Rights in Soviet Society*. New York: International Publishers, 1981.

Chernyavsky, V. "Radio Subversion." *New Times* No. 46 (November 1980): 26-27.

Chkhikvadze, Victor. "A Charter of Social Justice." *New Times* No. 40 (October 1981): 18-19.

_____ . "Human Rights and Noninterference in the Interference in the International Affairs of States." *International Affairs* No. 12 (December 1978): 22-30.

_____ . "The Soviet Political System: Genuine Democracy." *International Affairs* No. 2 (February 1985): 37-45, 61.

_____ . *The State, Democracy and Legality in the USSR: Lenin's Ideas Today*. Moscow: Progress Publishers, 1973.

Derimov, Mikhail. "V pautine TsRU" [In the CIA's Web]. *Pravda Ukrainy*, August 2, 1983, p. 3.

_____ . "Lzheproroki" [False Prophets] (two-part article). *Pravda Ukrainy*, January 31, 1982, p. 4; February 2, 1982, p. 3.

Feofanov, O. "S ideologicheskogo fronta: ugol ataki-prava cheloveka" [From the Ideological Front: The Angle of Attack Is Human Rights]. *Pravda*. April 9, 1985, p. 4.

Filimonov, E. "Krizis very i religioznyy ekstremizm" [The Crisis of Faith and Religious Extremism] *Nauka i religiya* No. 2 (February 1980): 26-28.

Golyakov, S. "Propaganda or Psychological War?" *New Times* No. 39 (September 1981): 26-27.

Grigorev, A. "Osuzhdeniye" [Judgment]. *Pravda Vostoka*, August 7, 1983, p. 4.

Gudkov, Yuri. "What is Behind the Rhetoric?" *New Times* No. 49 (December 1981): 7-9.

Illarionov, Vladimir. "Izuver v roli apostola" [A Fanatic in the Role of an 'Apostle'] *Pravda Vostoka*, May 27, 1979, p. 4.

Inozemstev, N. *Contemporary Capitalism: New Developments and Contradictions*. Moscow: Progress Publishers, 1974.

Kartashkin, Vladimir. "International Relations and Human Rights." *International Affairs* No. 8 (August 1977): 29-38.

_____ . "The Soviet Constitution and Human Rights." *International Affairs*. No. 2 (February 1978): 13-20.

Kassis, V., and Mikhaylov, M. "Chto tvorilos v bunkere 'apostola'" [What Was Going on in the 'Apostle's' Bunker]? *Izvestiya*, May 13, 1979, p. 5.

Klochkov, V.V. *Zakon i religiya: ot gosudarstvennoy religii v Rossii k svobode sovesti v SSSR* [The Law and Religion: From State Religion in Russia to Freedom of Conscience in the USSR]. Moscow: Politizdat, 1982.

Kovalyov, E. "Foreign-Policy Propaganda: Ideological Struggle or 'War of Ideas'?" *International Affairs* No. 2 (February 1982): 94-101.

Kozlov, B. "Freedom of Conscience and Distorting Mirrors." *New Times* No. 5 (January 1985): 23-24.

Krutogolov, Mikhail A. *Talks on Soviet Democracy*. Moscow: Progress Publishers, 1980.

Kudinov, V., and Pletnikov, V. "Razryadka napryazhennosti i manevry anticommunizma" [The Easing of Tension and the Maneuvers of Anticommunism]. *Pravda*, August 9, 1974, pp. 3-4.

Kulikov, A. "Na vrazhdebnoy volne" [On a Hostile Wavelength]. *Moskovskaya pravda*, May 19, 1978, p. 3.

Kuroyedov, Vladimir A. *Church and Religion in the USSR*. Moscow: Novosti Press, 1977.

_____ . *Sovetskoye gosudarstvo i tserkov* [The Soviet State and the Church]. Moscow: Izdatelstvo Politicheskoy Literatury, 1976.

Lenin, V.I. *On Religion*. 3rd ed. Moscow: Progress Publishers, 1969.

Lentin, V.N. *Adventisty sedmogo dnya* [The Seventh-Day Adventists]. Moscow: Izdatelstvo "Znaniye," 1966.

Lipavsky, S.L. "Kak menya verbovalo TsRU" [How I Was Recruited by the CIA]. *Izvestiya*, May 8, 1977, p. 4.

_____ . "Otkrytoe pismo" [Open Letter—to the Presidium of the USSR Supreme Soviet]. *Izvestiya*, March 5, 1977, p. 3.

Luparev, G. "Pravosoznaniye i religiya" [Religion and Recognition of the Law]. *Kazakhstanskaya pravda*, April 3, 1980, p. 2.

Marushkin, Boris. "Chasing the Chimera of 'Moral Leadership.'" *New Times* No. 37 (September 1978): 4-6.

Mayveyev, V. "Ideology and Diplomacy under Detente." *International Affairs* No. 7 (July 1977): 108-17.

Mirsky, Zinovy. "The West's Psychological Aggression." *New Times* No. 29 (July 1980): 18-20.

Mokrishchev, N. "Otluchenyye ot detstva" [Excommunicated since Childhood]. *Trud*, September 21, 1983, p. 2.

Morev, D., and Yarilov, K. "TsRU: shpiony i 'prava cheloveka'" [The CIA: Spies and 'Human Rights']. *Izvestiya*, March 5, 1977, p. 6.

Natalin, Timofei. "Misinformation as Policy." *New Times* No. 13 (March 1982): 22-23.

Nikitin, E. "Zagovor obrechennykh" [Plot of the Doomed]. *Krasnaya zvezda*, December 11, 1984, p. 3.

Pecbenev, Vadim A. *The Socialist Ideal and Real Socialism*. Moscow: Politizdat, 1984.

Perfilev, Marat N. *Soviet Democracy and Bourgeois Sovietology*. Moscow: Progress Publishers, 1970.

Petrov (Agatov), Alexander. "Lzhetsy i farisei" [Liars and Pharisees]. *Literaturnaya gazeta*, February 2, 1977, p. 14.

Pogorzhelsky, D. "Bremen Subversives." *New Times* No. 5 (January 1982): 16-17.

Pribytkov, Victor, ed. *Soviet-U.S. Relations: The Selected Writings and Speeches of Konstantin U. Chernenko*. New York: Praeger, 1984.

Reinhold, O., and Ryzhenko, F., eds. *Contemporary Anti-Communism: Policy and Ideology*. Moscow: Progress Publishers, 1976.

Rusakov, E. "Tropoyu 'psikhologicheskoy voyny'" [On the 'Psychological Warpath']. *Pravda*, April 18, 1980, p. 4.

Rusakova, O. "Human and International Relations." *International Affairs* No. 2 (February 1980): 84-89.

Sergeyev, F.M. *Yesli sorvat masky. . .* [If We Tear Off the Mask . . .]. Moscow: Politizdat, 1983.

Shalamova, N. "Pravda bez maski" [The Truth Unveiled]. *Pravda Vostoka*, July 1, 1983, p. 2.

Shevtsov, V.S. *National Sovereignty and the Soviet State*. Moscow: Progress Publishers, 1969.

Sivachev, Nikolai V., and Yakovlev, Nikolai N. *Russia and the United States: U.S.-Soviet relations from the Soviet point of view*. Chicago: University of Chicago Press, 1979.

Sovetov, A. "The Human Rights Myth and Anti-Communism." *International Affairs* No. 6 (June 1978): 12-21.

Sukharev, Alexander. "Human Rights in the Soviet Union—Putting the Record Straight." *New Times* No. 1 (January 1976): 18-22.

Svetov, B., and Valentinov, V. "CIA-NTS Offshoot." *New Times* No. 43 (October 1981): 28-30.

Terebilov, Vladimir. "In Defense of Human Rights." *World Marxist Review* 22 (July 1979): 64-68.

_____. *The Soviet Court*. Moscow: Progress Publishers, 1973.

Trofimenko, Henry. *SShA: politika, voina, idelogiya* (U.S.A.: Policy, War, Ideology). Moscow: Izdatelstvo "Mysyl," 1976.

Tsvigun, S. "O proiskakh imperialistcheskikh razvedok" [The Intrigues of Foreign Intelligence Agencies], *Kommunist* No. 14 (1981): 88-99.

_____. "Podryvnyye aktsii—oruzhiye imperializma" [Subversion as a Weapon of Imperialism] *Kommunist* No. 4 (1980): 108-19.

Vasilev, V., and Pavlov, P. "Delo partii, delo naroda" [Work of the Party, Work of the People] *Kommunist* No. 5 (1980): 119-28.

Volkogonov, Dmitri. *Mythical "Threat" and the Real Danger to Peace*. Moscow: Novosti, 1982.

Yakovlev, Nikolai. "Anatomy of Americanism" (two-part article). *New Times* No. 49 (December 1981): 18-21; No. 50 (December 1981): 18-20.

_____. *CIA Target—The USSR*. 3rd ed. Moscow: Progress Publishers, 1982.

Yulin, Yu. "Mrakobesy" [Obscurants] . *Turkmenskaya Iskra*, November 1, 1979, p. 3.

Zaritsky, Boris. "Double Standard." *New Times* No. 14 (April 1982): 23-26.

Zivs, Samuil. *Human Rights: Continuing the Discussion*. Moscow: Progress Publishers, 1980.

Zivs, Samuil, and Lokshin, Grigory. "Peace and Human Rights." *New Times* No. 31 (August 1980): 25-26.

Zorin, Valerian. "Human Rights—Realistic Approach." *New Times* No. 15 (April 1977): 18-20.

Newspapers and Periodicals

International Affairs (Moscow)
Izvestiya
Kazakhstanskaya pravda
Kommunist
Komsomolskaya pravda
Kraznaya zvezda
Krokodil
Literaturnaya gazeta
Molodyozh Moldavii
Moskovskaya pravda
Nauka i religiya
New Times
Pravda Ukrainy
Pravda Vostoka
Sotsialisticheskaya zakonnost
Sovetskaya kultura
Sovetskoye gosudarstvo i pravo
TASS
Turkmenskaya Iskra
Trud
World Marxist Review

Index

About the Author

WALTER PARCHOMENKO is a Washington-based writer whose articles on Soviet and East European affairs and international relations in general have appeared in the *New York Times*, the *Wall Street Journal*, the *Christian Science Monitor*, and numerous other publications. He received his Ph.D. in Soviet Politics and International Relations from Georgetown University; during 1985 he was a visiting scholar at Columbia University's W. Averell Harriman Institute for Advanced Study of the Soviet Union, where he completed the research for this book. In an effort to extend this preliminary assessment of Soviet images of dissidents and nonconformists, Dr. Parchomenko is presently preparing a second volume which will develop further this work's methodology and examine other key dimensions of Soviet dissent, such as workers' and nationalist dissent and disabled rights activism. Readers with comments and suggestions about this book or Dr. Parchomenko's general research focus are requested to contact the author directly by writing to:

Walter Parchomenko
7631 Webbwood Ct.
Springfield, VA 22151
U.S.A.

DATE DUE